The
CURTIS
Caper

By JOSEPH C. GOULDEN

G. P. PUTNAM'S SONS
NEW YORK

MANUFACTURED IN THE UNITED STATES OF AMERICA

VAN REES PRESS • NEW YORK

For Jody, who cared for a book, a son and a
husband simultaneously, and with good cheer.

Prologue

CLOSELY pursued by a *Saturday Evening Post* editor, the football bounced into the lap of a *Ladies' Home Journal* writer. With an exasperated flurry of skirts and petticoats she booted the ball back across the room, where it clumped into Clay Blair, Jr.'s, whisky glass. The editor-in-chief of Curtis Publishing Company said something unprintable about the mess made of his manuscripts, and the nightly game ended. The joint staff resumed production of two distinguished American magazines with a combined age of more than three centuries.

On Madison Avenue, a shout disrupted the chatter in an admen's bistro. "Joe Culligan's had it," the man repeated, wresting a $100 bill from his wallet and brandishing it in the air with unsuppressed arrogance. "Curtis Publishing Company out the window in six months! Here's a hundred. Who wants it? Any takers?"

There weren't, only a few guffaws and mutters about "sucker bet." One man who heard and didn't respond to the crack about Matthew Joseph Culligan, the Curtis president, was a Curtis advertising executive who quietly finished his drink, got his topcoat and slipped away to the station for the train ride home. That weekend he started mailing résumés to agencies, stressing his availability.

The Curtis Publishing Company runaway was at full gallop, and all the publishing world knew it. Once the "Gray Lady of Independence Square," the epitome of Philadelphia dignity and correctness, Curtis' public conduct was now that of a Times Square hoyden. Tabloid headlines and sophisticated cocktail party banter alike made Curtis the butt of jokes.

Today, after four years of intensive treatment by assorted corporate doctors—some good, others quacks—Curtis still shows signs of the severe financial, management and editorial pains that have racked its body. To many, the expression on Curtis' face is that of *facies Hippocratica,* the term physicians use to describe a man marked by death. Curtis is struggling gamely, but as late as the spring of 1965 its management was not willing to predict when it would return to profitable operations. Symptoms of the Curtis torment are legion:

Red ink that is gradually engulfing the 12-story Curtis Building in Philadelphia. Losses from 1961 through the end of 1964 total a staggering $40 million. Were it not for piecemeal sale of assets, the figure would be millions of dollars higher. The marble-columned Curtis Building, which founder Cyrus H. K. Curtis built as a publishing showcase, is a sparsely occupied shell, part of which is leased to the City of Philadelphia as storage space for voting machines.

Departure of the editorial brains that made national leaders in their fields of the *Saturday Evening Post, Ladies' Home Journal* and *Holiday,* and their replacement with staffs of constantly changing direction. Many former Curtis editors now won't read the magazines to which they once devoted their talents and their professional lives.

Widespread firings on all levels, from file clerk to board chairman, carried out "with executioner brutality," in the words of a former editor who heard the whisk and thump of the headman's ax himself.

Some of the nastiest executive suite infighting ever to blacken any corporation, compounded many times over by the fact that much of it spilled onto the front pages of the nation's press.

Wariness of ad agencies in scheduling advertising months ahead of time in magazines they fear won't be around to publish it. Curtis' protestations that "our basic business is magazines" draw mixed reaction. The credibility of these statements is weakened by the company's recent history of turmoil.

Finally, the prolonged inability of Curtis management, under erstwhile president Joe Culligan, to halt the aimless, mutiny-marked drifting of the company.

Additionally, history looms over Curtis like a watching vulture—the remembrance of *Collier's*, which went through much the same type of decline and internal upheaval before vanishing from the publishing world in 1957. For a while *View from the Fortieth Floor*, Theodore H. White's novel about the *Collier's* collapse, was popular surreptitious reading fare at Curtis.

The sense of drama at Curtis is heightened by several factors, each of which has added to the public attention it has attracted. From the standpoint of the layman, Curtis is a gripping situation because it involves magazines which, at one time or another, have crossed virtually every threshold in the nation. In the not-too-distant past the American trinity of God, Mother and Country could have rightfully been extended to include the *Saturday Evening Post*. Not every *Post* reader cares about corporate fighting; the majority of them probably were only dimly aware of the fact that such a thing existed. But when "his" magazine is affected by it to the extent that a reader angrily cancels a subscription, or lets it lapse, it becomes an important matter to Curtis Publishing Company.

From the standpoint of the professional, Curtis offers fascinating "how not to do it" case studies in advertising, management, communications and finance. Executives watching the explosive eruptions in Curtis can shudder and say introspectively, "There, but for the sake of a few right decisions, go I." The struggle also has aroused professional sadism, the inward voice that yells "Jump" to the magazine on the ledge. In this instance, Is Curtis going to be around tomorrow, and in what form? Who will be the next editor or executive to be fired, or to stomp out of the Curtis offices with a freshet of invective against those below, above and on a level with him?

For all this, Curtis has evoked sympathy and empathy among

many persons. Decades of goodwill are in the company's vaults, even if in non-negotiable form. Few advertisers or readers are happy about abandoning a magazine friend of a generation's standing. In the case of the *Post,* divorce is particularly wrenching because the *Post* has been more than a magazine. The *Post* brought Tugboat Annie and Alexander Botts' Earthworm Tractor Company into the living room, but it also brought a style, a political orientation, that molded the mores and fashions of middle-class America—far more so than the avant-garde which delighted in ridiculing the *Post* and its content for decades.

Additionally, the Curtis drama was enacted by volatile, highly articulate principals, persons with artistic temperaments accustomed to shouting their rages and their problems to the world. A *Post* fiction editor would have pondered hours whether to test a reader's credulity with such a diverse cast, in one short story, as:

—Dashing Joe Culligan, whose reaction to the Curtis problem was "sell, sell—and sell some more"; a man who came into Curtis like a gush of warm spring air, eyepatch at a jaunty angle, and was carried out two years later on his own shield, victim of a palace uprising.

—Clay D. Blair, Jr., an endomorphic young-man-on-the-run who, in 18 months, completely changed an editorial image which George Horace Lorimer and Ben Hibbs spent 60 years building.

—Serge Semenenko, who is what might be called a one-man triumvirate, a Russian-born jet-set banker from the Brahmin Boston financial district, whose infusions of fresh cash saved Curtis at least three times in two years.

—Marvin D. Kantor, product of the Wall Street financial world, where a dollar is a man's best friend, next to control of an ailing corporation, who first worked with, then against, Joe Culligan.

The Curtis Caper is not a formal history, nor an authorized one, of the Curtis Publishing Company. Nor does it purport

Brought back to life are the days of World War II when the *Post* raised combat reporting to a new high and captured the hearts of America with its Norman Rockwell covers. Yet even then dry rot was spreading and the postwar years saw Curtis moving toward deep financial difficulties with ever-accelerating speed. Some of the reasons dated back many years but others—the failure to diversify holdings after one unsuccessful attempt in the thirties, unwillingness to meet the competition in a circulation war, and its desertion by the Madison Avenue advertising agencies — graphically reveal the many factors that can influence a company's destiny. Although the financial world had long been aware of what was happening at Curtis, the general public was alerted only when sweeping changes of personnel brought Curtis front-page notoriety in million-dollar libel suits and an executive conflict of unparalleled publicity. THE CURTIS CAPER reaches its climax with this internal power struggle of 1964 and lays bare the kind of savage infighting that may be typical of the world of industry but that has never before had such an exact chronicler as Joseph C. Goulden, the author of this book.

In commenting on the writing of THE CURTIS CAPER, Goulden says, "Curtis was a tough story because it involved gun-shy people whose lives had been disrupted, even ruined, by the turmoil. My task was to convince these people I was an objective outsider whose sole interest was the truth. Several times I talked with sources for hours without getting a line of useful information, only to have them suddenly warm up and produce an old letter or photostat containing vital material."

G. P. PUTNAM'S SONS
Publishers Since 1838
200 Madison Avenue
New York 16, New York

PRINTED IN U.S.A.

to be a complete story. "The real history is going to have to be written by a psychiatrist," Cary W. Bok, grandson of founder Cyrus Curtis, remarked one day. Rather, *The Curtis Caper* is a reporter's attempt to analyze, through the words of the principals who were willing to talk, the reasons Curtis Publishing Company got into the situation it did in the late 1950's and early 1960's, and what happened thereafter. As such, it is replete with hindsight and second-guessing, and abounds with Curtis' faults rather than Curtis' virtues. Curtis writes its own history weekly and monthly with its magazines. This story is about the men and women who edited the magazines, sold advertising space in them, and printed them, and the effect their actions and non-actions had upon the company that owned them.

THE CURTIS CAPER

Chapter One

IN the gloomy autumn days of 1964, when there wasn't much else to cheer about, Curtis Publishing Company press agents pointedly stressed there was more to their firm than the magazines by which it is best known publicly. They ticked off long lists of physical assets: the paper mills in Pennsylvania that devour entire forests annually; the sprawling printing plant in Sharon Hill, a Philadelphia suburb, that churns out every copy of every Curtis magazine; a circulation company and a host of kindred affiliates and subsidiaries; 122,000 acres of Canadian timberland beneath which lie rich deposits of copper and silver —possibly worth $400 million.

Curtis' implication was plain: A company owning so many spruce and fir trees and brick-and-stone buildings was sturdy enough to survive occasional foibles by the men charged with managing it.

All this, of course, was irrelevant to the main Curtis problem. Curtis both in appearance and in fact is magazines; without them the other facilities would be of minimal day-to-day value to the company as a whole, unless Curtis became a commercial printer or a commercial papermaker. As go the magazines—and particularly the *Saturday Evening Post,* the big revenue producer—so goes Curtis. And magazines are a transitory ware; nothing is more worthless than last week's issue.

Further, the Curtis magazines were—or had been, at any rate, before 1962—*editors'* magazines, publications reflecting the knowledge, skills and tastes of the men Curtis management considered competent enough to put in positions of authority. A Curtis editor went through life with the unquestioned autonomy of an archbishop, a federal judge or a small-town sheriff; that a business office or advertisting executive would question his judgment or try to influence it was so remote a prospect that it was never even discussed.

The magazines were built by three men, aided by a wife's whim and a distress sale. One of the men was the Man from Maine, Cyrus Herman Kotzschmar Curtis, more merchant than editor; the others were editors Edward W. Bok of the *Ladies' Home Journal* and George Horace Lorimer of the *Saturday Evening Post.*

Curtis made no pretense at editorial genius; indeed, his publishing career met indifferent success until he hired Bok in 1889 to edit the *Journal.* His business acumen, however, and his ability to sense a public interest were the phenomena of the publishing world just before and just after the turn of the century. Once Curtis pinpointed these interests, as he did for the *Journal* and *Post* audiences, he had sense enough to find and hire brilliant editors and leave them alone. "Make good or hang yourself," he told Bok and Lorimer constantly. Only one story survives about a Curtis attempt to influence the editorial content. He once told Lorimer his wife didn't think a short story was "a very good piece to be in the *Post."* "I'm not editing the *Saturday Evening Post* for your wife," Lorimer replied curtly. Curtis gave him a raise. "The editor is a pivot," Curtis said, "Get the right editor and you'll have the right magazine. Then it's only a selling proposition."

But freedom didn't mean lack of supervision and broad guidelines within which the editors worked. Curtis recognized magazine publishing as an integrated process, with advertising, management and circulation every bit as important as the editorial content. Bok cites Curtis' rules in the biographical *A Man from Maine:*

—*To editors:* "Give the public the best. It knows. The cost is secondary."

—*To circulation men:* "Keep the magazine before the public, and make it easy for the public to get it."

—*To advertising men:* "We know we give advertisers their money's worth, but it is up to you to prove it to them."

He also believed in promotion: When the *Post,* in its woeful early days, plunged $800,000 into the red, Curtis asked N.W. Ayer & Son, Inc., the big Philadelphia advertising agency, to start a $200,000 campaign boosting the magazine. "That'll bring it up to the million. Then we'll know where we are at," he said.

Curtis' early life is cut from the same How to Make Good Through Hard Work (and a Bit of Luck) pattern which served *Post* article editors so well for years. He was an enterprising newsboy who made his first business coup at age twelve by buying papers wholesale and peddling them at a premium to soldiers in a Civil War camp outside his native Camden, Maine. As a teen-age printshop owner he wrote and published a little paper called *Young America* for the town boys. ("Why is a man with a cork leg never to be forgotten by his friends?" "Because he is re-membered.") As a Boston dry-goods clerk he sold newspaper ads so briskly during his lunch hour on a free-lance basis that he left the mercantile world for that of publishing.

Curtis came to Philadelphia in 1872 after a fire destroyed the *People's Ledger,* a weekly newspaper he had been running in Boston. He computed that the $1,500 annual lower print costs in Philadelphia would cover his living expenses; also, "I figured, too, that a man can make a greater success a little away from a big metropolis, by throwing his light upon it, than by being in it and in all probability lost in the thousands of others."

With $2,000 borrowed from a brother-in-law, Curtis started a four-page weekly, the *Tribune and Farmer,* which sold for 50 cents a year. He contributed a column, "Woman and Home," composed of household tips clipped from other domestic magazines. "Who gets up this column?" Mrs. Curtis asked one day with a chuckle. "I do," grumped Curtis. "I don't mean to make fun of you, but if you really knew how funny this material sounds to a woman, you would laugh, too." Whereupon Curtis turned the column over to her: "If you think you can do it any better, why don't you try it?"

She did—first a column, then an entire page, which drew more fan mail than any other feature in the magazine. In December, 1883, Curtis enlarged it to a special eight-page supplement and sent the copy to the composing room, *sans* title. What should it be named? asked a printer. "Call it anything you like, it's a sort of ladies' journal," Curtis said. Thus was the first foundation block put under the Curtis Publishing Company.

In five years the *Tribune and Farmer* had gained 48,000 subscriptions; the *Journal* drew 25,000 its first year. Curtis had taken in an advertising agent as a junior partner rather than pay mounting commissions on the business spawned by his new publication. Never happy with the man, Curtis allowed him to leave in 1884 with the farm magazine, keeping the *Journal* as his share.

When Bok took over the editorship in 1889—Mrs. Curtis was by then ready for home life—the *Journal* was the leading women's magazine, with a circulation of 440,000. The dynamic Dutch-born editor was twenty-six and single; the only woman with whom he had any regular contact was his elderly mother. He admitted he knew little of women, and even less of their needs; further, he had no desire to know or understand them better . . . although this attitude did not keep him from marrying Mary Louise Curtis, Cyrus' only daughter, in 1896.

Flimsy credentials for the editor of a women's magazine? Bok thought not. As an editor his mission was to study trends and then select "from the horizon those that were for the best interests of the home." For the home was one thing that Edward Bok did understand. His target was the American home, not the woman in it.

One of Bok's first acts as editor was to offer prizes for answers to three questions: What did you like best in the last issue, and why? What least, and why? What would you like to see? Bok fed the women's answers back to them in articles and departments, but always on a slightly higher plane. "Come down to the level which the public sets and it will leave you at the moment you do it," he wrote. "The American public always wants something a little better than it asks for, and the successful man, in catering to it, is he who follows this golden rule."

Further, Bok had that peculiar precocity that transforms some teen-agers into scale-model tycoons while their contemporaries loll in the classroom. As an early birthday gift he received an anthology of biographies of famous men. Out of curiosity he wrote a letter to one, asking for clarification of an obscure point. The man responded. Then Bok wrote to General George G. Meade, who sent back a lengthy letter along with a sketch of the Gettysburg battlefield. Soon Bok had scores of such letters that were fodder for the Sunday newspaper feature writers. He haunted New York hotels ("In retrospect, he must have been a frightful little pest," a later-life friend said) and in one evening obtained signatures of Mrs. Abraham Lincoln, General U. S. Grant, and Jefferson Davis. A cigarette company gave Bok a contract for 100-word biographies of prominent Americans to go on its cards; so many repeat orders came in— at $10 per biography—that he was able to hire journalists for $5 each to do the writing; Bok wielded the editorial pencil. He founded a magazine for a church society and gradually extended it into a literary journal. Drawing upon his "autographic acquaintances," he obtained short articles from President Rutherford B. Hayes, William Dean Howells, General Grant, General William Sherman and Cardinal Gibbons. Rival editors were puzzled, not realizing the famed contributors didn't even receive an honorarium. Bok worked days as an editor for Scribner's; his own magazine was produced at night. The publication eventually became "Bok's Literary Leaves," a column which Bok syndicated nationally to newspapers. Editors liked it so well he added a weekly letter on women's topics. This, too, expanded, until Bok's syndicate supplied a full page of women's material weekly—the start of the "woman's page" in the American daily newspaper.

"Bok's Literary Leaves" eventually attracted the attention of Cyrus Curtis in Philadelphia. Ethics forbade Curtis from attempting to hire Bok while he worked for another publisher, so he came to New York and simply asked the young Dutchman if he knew a good man. "Are you talking at me or through me?" replied Bok. "Both." Friends warned Bok he would be "buried in Philadelphia." After a quick survey of competing domestic magazines he decided he could easily top anything in the field. He joined Curtis in 1889.

The mail told Bok that the American woman was in need of drastic improvement in the way she conducted her home, her family, and even her sex life. (So gloomy was he over his feminine readers' intelligence—or the lack of it—that he, as editor of the leading women's magazine, for years opposed suffrage.) Another conclusion was that the American girl didn't confide in her mother, or ask questions of her, but that she would have no qualms about trusting what was told her on the printed page —if done properly. Not satisfied with his staff's efforts at counseling, Bok himself wrote a column, "Side Talks with Girls." ("Learn to say no," he wrote in his first column. "There is in that little word much that will protect you from evil tongues." He cautioned girls about promiscuous distribution of their photographs to boys.) The response was so laden with intimate questions that Bok embarrassedly turned it over to a woman from his old New York news syndicate, Mrs. Isabel A. Mallon. During the next 16 years "Ruth Ashmore" answered 158,000 letters.

Another Bok decision was that the average woman was an idiot on the subject of child care. Over virulent objections from the medical profession a physician-columnist read new mothers' completed questionnaires and prescribed directions by mail for them to follow. Eighty-five percent of the women who entered the program asked for monthly advice until their children were two years old.

Bok was the nearest thing to a muckraker to enter the Curtis premises. He inveighed against public drinking cups (and they vanished); he campaigned against French fashions, pointing out that Parisian couturiers made for the American trade "gowns of the *déclassée* street women of Paris"; he published horror stories and pictures of the slaughter of herons for their feathers for women's hats—and watched in disgust as women quadrupled their purchases of the hats in four months; his debunking of alcoholically potent patent medicines was largely responsible for the Food and Drug Act.

In 1906 Bok took a deep breath and became the first "respectable" editor to publish articles on venereal disease—a subject then discussed in public only at medical meetings. When protests flooded the Curtis offices Bok told readers that even stronger stuff was to come; that those who didn't believe in his policy should stop buying the magazine at once. Curtis' best friends told of ripping pages from the *Journal* before allowing it in their homes. But Curtis never wavered. After 18 months, serious letters began to come in on venereal disease.

Other Bok series told women how to build and decorate their homes; scores of thousands of cottages built in the early 1900's followed plans published in the *Journal*. Under photographs of home furnishings Bok's captions said omnisciently, "This chair is ugly." "This table is beautiful." He inveighed about the ugliness of American cities; town councils condemned the *Journal* after their eyesores were put before the nation in picture stories. So powerful was the *Journal*, however, that the mere threat of publication stopped promoters from erecting the "world's largest billboard" on the brink of Grand Canyon.

In summary, Bok's main contribution was the banishing of sentimental mishmash, piety and preaching from women's magazines, and their replacement with practical services and answers to questions that readers couldn't find elsewhere.

This formula was so enthusiastically received by feminine readers that Curtis started thinking of repeating it for men. He was convinced that men would read articles about the thing most important to them—their fight for livelihood in the business world—if the authors were men who knew what business was all about. Curtis truly felt that business was a thrilling romance, with all the qualities of great drama.

Curtis' idea was to build a five-cent magazine that would meet newspapers financially without competing against them on news; a publication without class, clique or sectional editing, meant for every adult in the United States.

There was, in Philadelphia at the time, a struggling journal called the *Saturday Evening Post,* a motley collection of clipped items put together by a newspaperman in his spare time for $10 a week. Rarely did it have more than a column of ads in eight pages; it enthralled readers with such items as "For the Sake of Time, a Story for Daffodil Time." The owner, one Albert Smythe, despairing of making a fortune in publishing, went to Chicago to invest in a gasworks and died in 1897.

The heirs weren't enthusiastic about putting more money into the magazine; bills were overdue, and the printers unhappy. They dispatched an attorney to see Curtis to discuss either a sale or a loan. He offered $1,000—$100 down. The physical assets received in turn were no bargain even at the forced-sale price—a mailing list with 2,231 names and a wagonload of battered type fonts, which were hauled to the Curtis office and dumped in the corner.

Printers called the new magazine the "singed cat" and suggested that it be chloroformed. *Printers Ink,* the printing trade journal, thought Curtis daft; that his *Journal* was a "wonderful property" but now "he was blowing all the profits on an impossible venture."

Several generations of *Saturday Evening Post* readers have read on the magazine's masthead *Founded in 1728 by Benjamin Franklin,* printed beneath a silhouette of Franklin. This statement has been denounced as one of the most bald-faced promo-

tional frauds in magazine history, but debunking by historians
—notably Frank Luther Mott—hasn't shaken Curtis Publishing
Company's faith in it.

The Curtis version of lineage dates back to the *Universal
Instructor in All Arts and Sciences and Pennsylvania Gazette,*
founded December 24, 1728, by O. E. Samuel Keimer, a former
employer of Franklin's.

The next year Keimer sold the newspaper to Franklin and
a partner, who shortened the name to the *Pennsylvania Gazette.*
Franklin became sole proprietor in 1732 and retired in 1748.
The *Pennsylvania Gazette* expired, totally, on October 11, 1817,
after 87 years.

In 1821, a twenty-four-year-old printer-poet-sailor named Robert S. Coffin thrilled the maidens around West Chester, Pennsylvania, with such exciting verse as "On Presenting a Lady
with a Cake of Soap," and "Ode to Genius Suggested by the
Present Unhappy Condition of the Boston Bard, an Eminent
Poet of this County" (the "Bard," of course, being the afore-
mentioned Coffin). Rather than further waste his genius in
West Chester, Coffin came to Philadelphia and started a weekly
paper, *The Bee,* first published in the spring of 1821. He sold
is shortly to Charles Alexander, who changed the name to the
Saturday Evening Post, to distinguish it from the proliferation
of other weeklies in the city. Unlike the late *Pennsylvania
Gazette,* the *Post* was not a newspaper but rather a weekly mis-
cellany of fiction, poems, anecdotes and items clipped from
other publications—a typical "fireside paper" of the nineteenth
century.

The *Post's* only connection with the paper founded by Franklin was that it was published in the same printshop in which
the *Pennsylvania Gazette* had expired six years before.

Historical writers of the late 1880's, however, skipped over
this six-year hiatus and suggested there was continuity between
the two publications. The promotion-minded Curtis didn't ob-
ject. He put the Benjamin Franklin story in the hands of his

drumbeaters—and sailor-poet Robert S. Coffin wasn't the founding father singled out for exploitation.

On January 22, 1898, the *Post* printed under its name on the front page, *Founded A.D. 1821*—the same statement as had appeared there for more than 30 years. By the next issue, January 29, 1898, the *Post* had aged 93 years. The slogan changed to *Founded A.D. 1728* and the volume number jumped from 77 to 170. Within a year Franklin's name was added as founder.

Although historian Mott scoffed at the Benjamin Franklin claim, he was careful not to fault Curtis personally with the alleged fraud. "... It must be understood that neither Curtis nor any of his editors invented the remarkable fable of the identity of the *Saturday Evening Post*," he wrote. "They derived it from others.... Moreover, there is a real, though tenuous, connection between the two papers." (A latter-day Curtis promotion writer reports the word "tenuous" was once stricken from a piece he wrote on the history.)

His skirmish with history notwithstanding, Curtis knew what he wanted to make of the *Post,* and he found the man to do it. George Horace Lorimer, son of a famous Boston minister, had been lured from Yale by P. D. Armour, the Chicago meat-packer. ("Come with me, George, and I'll make you a millionaire," Armour told the youth, enrapturing him with business forever.) After working up to an executive position in Armour, Lorimer sought a way to combine his commercial love with writing; he reentered college, got a degree and within two years was acknowledged as the best reporter in Boston. Lorimer read one day of Curtis' purchase of the *Post;* he wired Philadelphia within an hour, asking for a job, and was hired as literary editor. Curtis wasn't satisfied with his first editor, William George Jordan, who relied upon imitation of Bok's *Ladies' Home Journal* and the *Post's* outmoded formula. Curtis fired Jordan, put Lorimer in charge and left on a vacation trip to Europe. Lorimer did so well the editorship was his when Curtis returned a few months later.

Lorimer was a devout worshiper of the free enterprise system; his finger was as sensitive to the throb of the American male's purse as Bok's was to the woman's. Because of their business backgrounds, Lorimer and Curtis knew a fundamental change was underway in American life, and they made the most of it for the *Post*. The two prime movers in making America a nation, rather than a collection of geographically and culturally contiguous regions, were mass production and mass transportation and distribution. Henry Ford's assembly lines and $5-a-day paychecks showed manufacturers that the more they produced, the less it cost; further, the more money in consumers' pockets, the more goods they could buy. The sudden infusion of consumer goods meant that the bulk of the people of all income levels was able to buy substantially the same clothing, food and household wares.

Curtis' success was through adroit application of mass production to magazines. Frank Munsey and S. S. McClure two decades previously had discovered you can afford to sell magazines at less than cost, even at the loss of millions of dollars, and still make money—provided they are popular enough to attract advertising.

In 1902, the *Saturday Evening Post* had an average circulation of 314,761 and advertising revenue of $360,125. By 1922, circulation had increased seven times, to 2,187,024. But ad income was up a phenomenal *seventy-eight* times, to $28,278,755.

Railroads and low postal rates for magazines enabled Curtis to distribute his magazines nationally rather than to a handful of consumers on the East Coast near Philadelphia. Chain stores leapfrogged across the continent, making it feasible for manufacturers to advertise Ivory Soap and Baker's Chocolate and know that readers in Maine and California would be able to find them on the street corner. A & P alone went from 200 stores in 1900 to 11,413 in 1924.

The vehicle that the *Post* rode to tremendous financial success was the automobile. The *Post* carried its first auto ad, about a W. E. Roach horseless buggy, in an issue in March, 1900. For the next two decades auto advertising expanded as rapidly as the industry; at one point it made up fully 25 percent of the total volume. The auto manufacturers and Curtis Publishing Company developed a kinship that lasted well into the 1950's, to the continuing chagrin of *Life* and *Look* salesmen who found it difficult to overcome the two-way loyalty. (There is a touch of irony in the story: The *Post,* which opposed credit buying in its own operations, found itself in the position of helping to foster an installment-buying revolution in the nation.)

"Do you know why we publish the *Ladies' Home Journal?*" Curtis once asked a gathering of advertisers. "The editor thinks it is for the benefit of the American woman. That is an illusion, but a proper one for him to have. But I will tell you the publisher's reason. . . . To give you people who manufacture things that American women want and buy a chance to tell them about your products."

Curtis saw nothing incompatible about the interests of readers, advertisers and publishers. To protect the interests of all three he laid down the Curtis Advertising Code. His suspicious Maine eye scrutinized dubious claims in advertising; although the patent-medicine manufacturers were among the first of industries to advertise nationally—the genus Curtis cultivated—he fought them bitterly and banned such material from his columns. He barred liquor ads in the *Post*—a rule that survived until 1960, when financial crisis took precedent over tradition. (A parallel ban on tobacco advertising perished quietly in 1930 during another fiscally tight period, when the Depression sent Curtis scurrying for every advertising dollar it could find.)

Curtis also wrought basic reforms in the agencies that brought him the advertising. There were two types at the turn of the century. The first had no discernible interest other than the dollar. They badgered publishers for the lowest price possible and gave secret rebates to advertisers. The second, just developing, based its appeal on service; it prepared the ads and then put them into magazines that did the best marketing job. Rightfully, Curtis saw the second category as a means of building new advertising for his magazines. The Curtis Advertising Code forbade dealings with agencies that gave rebates.

To make his magazines an attractive marketplace, however, Curtis had to make them something different. This factor was all important. American magazines tended to be insipid imitations of insipid contemporaries, a cycle of printed boredom. When Lorimer took over the *Post* in 1899, *Harper's* lead articles included "The Ascent of Illimani," about a South American volcano, and "The First American, His Homes and His Households." *Scribner's* was even worse: "The Modern Group of Scandinavian Paints," and the "British Army Manoeuvres." *Atlantic Monthly* ran a poor third with "Australasian Extensions of Democracy." To prevent contamination of his own editorial mind, Lorimer refused to read competitive magazines, even while on vacation.

Lorimer could talk about business without being critical of it—so much so that the *Post* had the not-always-complimentary subtitle of "America's largest trade journal." Still, for the American businessman this treatment was welcome at a time when Ida Tarbell and the other muckrakers tweaked the noses of Standard Oil and assorted big-business untouchables. Lorimer let the businessmen tell their own stories. Harlow N. Higginbotham, credit expert for Marshall Field, the Chicago merchant, was considered enough of a heavyweight to lead an issue. Millionaires lined up to write "How I Made My First One Thousand Dollars." "American Kings and Their Kingdoms" recounted the fiscal exploits of Astor and Rockefeller. The diet was steady: "The Business Side of a University"; "Why Young Men Should Start at the Bottom"; "Why Millionaires Can't Stop Making Money."

Lorimer's fiction also stressed the romance-of-business theme, although not as assiduously as did the articles. In his first year he gave readers Rudyard Kipling and Stephen Crane; before his career ended in 1936, a Who's Who in American Literature crossed his pages: Booth Tarkington, Owen Wister, John P.

Marquand, Joseph Hergesheimer, Jack London, Bret Harte, Edna Ferber, Sinclair Lewis, Thomas Wolfe, William Faulkner, and F. Scott Fitzgerald.

High pay and the chance for mass circulation attracted the writers; Lorimer also ingratiated them with what was at the time revolutionary treatment. He paid on acceptance; an author who sold a Christmas story in June got the check in the return mail—not on publication in December, as had been the custom. He paid on an escalating scale, giving authors an incentive to continue sending stories to the *Post*. Lorimer cautioned editors to handle manuscripts gently, so that if rejected by the *Post* they would go back to the author in fresh enough condition to be mailed elsewhere.

In a lighter vein, William Hazlett Upson for decades made a hero of Alexander Botts, resourceful star salesman for the Earthworm Tractor Company, pitted in combat monthly with rivals whom he always managed to outsmart for the Big Contract. Clarence Buddington Kelland's western serials were printed horse operas, beloved in the rural homes into which they brought eight weeks of congenial suspense—always with a happy boy-gets-girl ending. (Lorimer's criterion for accepting fiction was to the point: "Will the *Post* readers like it?" He was respectful of big names, and bought them for cash whenever he could to adorn *Post* covers. But if the choice was between a good work by an unknown or the mediocre offering of an established author, he took the unknown. He regularly turned down stories by Rudyard Kipling.)

For years Lorimer expunged references to women smoking or men drinking from *Post* fiction; these barriers lowered during the Roaring Twenties, and not all readers agreed. One *Post* serial installment ended with a businessman having a drink with his secretary at home; the next began with them at breakfast. To indignant mail Lorimer replied: "The *Post* cannot be responsible for what the characters in its serials do between installments."

The *Post* was by no means universally admired. Its detractors decried its "America without the warts" portrayal of life. They charged it stimulated the nation neither culturally nor intellectually, that it was a paper-and-ink manifestation of Coolidge blandness. Upton Sinclair said the *Post* "is as standardized as soda crackers," that "originality is taboo, new ideas are obscene." Bernard De Voto thought he heard carping sounds in the criticism. Writers who scorned the *Post* he put into two categories: those rich enough not to write for it, and those whose material wasn't good enough for Lorimer. The *Post* viewed the critics as narrow-visioned wreckers and was baffled that they didn't share the editors' belief in the infallibility of business and the Republican Party. Lorimer particularly didn't like the "smartness" of H. L. Mencken. The *Post* had a short-lived department called "Americana," to counter one of identical title in Mencken's *American Mercury,* which jibed Rotarians, "uplift," the culture dearth and assorted "idiocies." Lorimer said that Mencken and his co-editor, George Jean Nathan, sought to "prove everybody and everything in America rotten."

Lorimer was a domineering man, almost ruthless in his demeanor. The *Saturday Evening Post* had been molded in his image, by God, and he was satisfied with the product. He had a massive head from which jutted a thatch of sandy hair, with just a bit of gray mixed in it. He was a floor-pacer, and his heels thumped into the carpet with authority as he strode around writers and editors who nervously sat in his office.

Norman Rockwell, early in his days as a cover artist for the *Post,* once innocently came into Lorimer's presence with a copy of the *Atlantic Monthly* rolled under his arm. Lorimer bridled when Rockwell said he liked the magazine. "Do you realize," he said, "that every story in there was refused by me?" Next time, Rockwell was careful to carry the *Post.* His sentiments about the *Atlantic Monthly* and other magazines he kept to himself. If a writer or artist strayed to another periodical, his name went on Lorimer's mental blacklist; the idea of anyone spending his talent on a magazine other than the *Post* was anathema to Lorimer.

So keenly attuned was Lorimer's empathy with his readers that he made snap judgments on acceptance of covers and articles. His eyes would scan a pile of Rockwell paintings; in an instant he would reject or scribble *OKGHL* on the margin. He knew that a reader wouldn't dawdle all day over a questionable cover when the magazine reached the newsstand. "If it doesn't strike me immediately, I don't want it," he said. "And neither does the public. They won't spend an hour figuring it out. It's got to hit them."

Rockwell sold his first two paintings to THE GREAT MR. GEORGE HORACE LORIMER (to use the artist's emphasis) in 1916 for $75 each. Seldom did Lorimer make suggestions. One of the rare times he did was to complain he was tired of seeing "the same mutt" in all Rockwell's pictures; couldn't he find another dog? Without mentioning it to anyone else Lorimer loaned Rockwell a photograph of his pet spitz. The art editor, who was on speaking terms with the Lorimer pet, was surprised a few months later to find him grinning at her from a Rockwell cover. One Lorimer quirk which puzzled Rockwell the 20 years he worked with the editor was his refusal to buy more than three paintings at a time, regardless of the number or quality submitted. So Rockwell learned never to show more than three "good" covers in a single batch; once Lorimer had rejected a work, it was dead forever.

With Lorimer printing articles by and about heads of state and heads of corporations, businessmen hastened to put their advertisements on the same pages. To America as a civilization, the *Post* was both thermostat and thermometer: it encouraged, set and recorded the comfortable new middle class of the nation, neither proletarian, plutocratic nor aristocratic. Lorimer incubated "middle-class political thought." And in this respect he should be remembered by the Republican Party as one of its best friends in history. The Iowa corn farmer, the Cleveland industrialist, the Wyoming rancher, the Texas citrus grower, the New York banker, heard from Lorimer of the political issues of the day—where previously national politics were disseminated pretty much by word of mouth.

Lorimer prided himself as an "interpreter" of the country and its people, although, as biographer John Tebbel noted, it was sometimes difficult to tell "where interpreting America left off and telling America began."

Lorimer's theme was unbridled conservatism. "We are not crusaders or uplifters or muckrakers in our editorial policy," he said, "but we are trying to follow the dictates of extraordinary business sense to work for the best interests of all America over a term of years."

Because of Curtis' formula, and Lorimer's able execution of it, Curtis Publishing Company totally dominated the magazine industry in America during the first third of the century. In five of the years in the period 1918–1929, according to computations by Theodore Peterson, 48 cents of every advertising dollar spent in U. S. magazines went to Curtis. The "low" during the period was 39 cents in 1926. (At this time the magazines were the *Saturday Evening Post,* the *Ladies' Home Journal* and the *Country Gentleman,* the latter now out of the Curtis stable and dead at the hands of others.) The *Post's* share of the advertising expenditures ranged from 27 to 31 percent in the other years of the era.

These figures show the remarkable gains made by the *Post* both in circulation and in advertising revenue:

	CIRCULATION	ADVERTISING REVENUE
1897	2,231	6,933
1902	314,671	360,175
1907	726,681	1,266,931
1912	1,920,550	7,114,581
1917	1,883,070	16,076,562
1922	2,187,024	28,278,755
1927	2,816,391	53,144,987

The crest of the period was a *Post* issue of December, 1929, a paper monument to Curtis and Lorimer. It contained 272 pages and weighed almost two pounds. Sixty 45-ton presses rolled round the clock for three weeks to produce it, consuming 6,000,000 pounds of paper and 120,000 pounds of ink. The reading fare was enough to keep the average adult busy for more than 20 hours, *Post* editors estimated. And the issue—largest of any magazine in Curtis' history—put $1,512,000 from 214 national advertisers into Cyrus Curtis' moneybox. This grandiose effort was so mammoth in bulk that scrap dealers eagerly paid five cents to newsstands for the paper alone.

For Curtis personally the lushness of the magazine's profits meant wealth perhaps unparalleled in the publishing industry. In 1924 alone his personal income was estimated at more than $5 million—one of only five men in the United States to earn that much. His personal philanthropies before his death in 1933 were in excess of $10 million.

In a 1927 editorial, announcing that *Post* circulation had surged over three million for several issues (a figure reached on an annual average ten years later), Lorimer wrote:

> This is honest circulation, clean circulation, built on the merit of the magazines, without clubbing [group subscriptions], cut-rate or catch-penny methods. The *Saturday Evening Post* goes to the most intelligent, and progressive audience in America—the backbone of the community's buying power. It has been built up slowly and steadily by appealing to and reflecting the best and most vital things in American life. Its readers are those who support the nation's industries rather than its nightclubs.
>
> Its growth has not been based on sensationalism.
>
> It has not been based on an appeal to the morbid and prurient-minded.
>
> It has not been based on thinly veiled indecency. It has been edited on the theory that the tastes and standards of the American public are steadily growing better.

Alex J. McCaughey

JOSEPH C. GOULDEN was born in Marshall, Texas, and received his start in journalism on his hometown paper. After attending the University of Texas and serving in the United States Army counterintelligence service, he became a reporter for the Dallas *Morning News*. In 1961, he joined the staff of the Philadelphia *Inquirer* and THE CURTIS CAPER had its genesis in a 16,000-word series he wrote for that paper. Although only thirty-one, he has already won several coveted journalists' awards. He is married and lives with his wife and two children in New Jersey.

All in all, the *Post* was the type of magazine about which President Warren G. Harding could say, just before he rolled over and died of a blood clot to the brain: "That's good. Go on, read some more." (The last words heard by the lamented President were from a *Post* article, "A Calm View of a Calm Man," praising his support of the World Court.)

Chapter Two

IN 1936, during the brisk pace of social legislation under the New Deal, the *Saturday Evening* Post published, and with a straight face, an article advocating child labor.

"The surest prescription for starting an American boy toward outstanding success is to let him go to work before he is fully grown," wrote Boyden Sparkes in a piece entitled "Horatio Alger at the Bridge."

Sparkes' argument could have been buttressed by case histories from within Curtis Publishing Company itself. Founder Cyrus H. K. Curtis was a newsboy at twelve and had his own printshop at sixteen. Edward W. Bok, the *Ladies' Home Journal* editor, went to work in a bakery at ten and, as a sixteen-year-old newspaper reporter in Brooklyn, covered with distinction an affair featuring President Rutherford B. Hayes. Curtis, however, was born in 1850, and Bok in 1863. The *Saturday Evening Post* of 1934 was edited for another generation—one disgruntled with the abuses of mankind and his economy that had developed under the big business system that the Curtis Publishing Company loved so well. A new philosophy was afoot in the land, and the *Saturday Evening Post* was aware of it and resented and fought it.

Any quest for the "why" of the Curtis Publishing Company's present troubles goes right back to the doorstep of two of the three members of its founding trinity—George Horace Lorimer and Cyrus H. K. Curtis himself.

In the instance of Curtis, it was a series of financial decisions —seemingly sound at the time—that had a continuing catastrophic effect on the company's financial structure for three decades. The first came in 1925, when the company earned a then-record $16 million. Curtis was seventy-seven that year; the corporate setup was such that, had he died then, the family would have had to sell so much of his common stock holdings to pay inheritance taxes that control of the firm would have been lost. As a legitimate means of insuring retention of Curtis Publishing Company by the heirs, Curtis distributed 700,000 shares of preferred stock valued at $100 each to holders of common stock. By so doing, Curtis gave the preferred shareholders first call on future earnings of the company, with their dividends to be paid before a cent was handed to future common shareholders. Because of the turn of later events, Curtis created a monumental headache at the same time he created the preferred shareholder class.

In another area, meanwhile, Cyrus Curtis discovered that the Midas touch that turned the *Post* and *Journal* into neatly printed stacks of gold was not infallible when he applied it to other publications. The experiment was painful in three areas —to Cyrus Curtis' pocketbook; to Cyrus Curtis' ego, when he realized the rest of the nation wasn't particularly interested in a Philadelphia newspaper, even under his imprimatur; and to Philadelphia journalism, whose newspaper graveyard was considerably expanded by and because of Curtis.

Curtis' failures had a sobering effect upon his successors in management and contributed to a skitterish feeling about involvement in enterprises outside the magazine field. And lack of diversification receives a high percentage of blame from latter-day analysts for Curtis Publishing's present woes.

Curtis' dream of becoming a Great American Newspaper Publisher dated to 1873, when a colored lithographic picture of the Philadelphia *Ledger's* new building so fired his imagination that he came from New York and stood on Chestnut Street gaping at it, openmouthed. Forty years later Curtis bought the

Ledger—and the building he had traveled 100 miles to admire. His goal was to make the *Ledger* the *Manchester Guardian* of the United States.

Curtis then began killing newspapers in his own version of a journalistic urban renewal project. He purchased the *Evening Telegraph,* founded in 1864, and buried it to obtain an essential Associated Press contract. The *Press,* which dated to 1857, had newsprint contracts which Curtis decided he needed during the First World War. A clang of the cash register and the *Press* was dead, and the contracts were Curtis'.

The third kiss of death touched the cheeks of the *North American,* considered a competitive nuisance by Curtis. And, in 1930, Curtis rounded out his disposal of morning competition by purchasing the *Inquirer* and merging it with the morning *Public Ledger.* An afternoon paper he founded in 1918, the *Evening Ledger,* was pitted against the *Evening Bulletin.* The mergers and closings tossed thousands of newspaper workers— printing, editorial, advertising and administrative—into the streets.

Another afternoon paper, a tabloid called the *Star,* lasted briefly because, in the words of a veteran Philadelphia news-paperman, "you couldn't believe a single word that ever ap-peared in it." In 1926 Curtis purchased the New York *Evening Post* and made an overnight ideological conversion of its edi-torial stance from liberal to conservative.

To house the *Ledger,* Curtis constructed a virtual twin of the Curtis Building, adjacent to it across from Independence Hall. From a professional standpoint Curtis' dollars did much to make the *Public Ledger* a national organ. He spent lavishly in building a foreign service on a par with *The New York Times* and the Chicago *Daily News;* at its peak in the late 1920's, the *Ledger* service was supplied to more than 300 other newspapers. But the *Ledger* had a fatal flaw. It did not receive the local advertising essential to support a costly worldwide news op-eration. Further, national or even regional distribution was a logistical impossibility. The *Ledger* was caught in a journalistic backwash between New York on the north and Washington on the south. Despite their city's cultural and intellectual history, Philadelphians are peculiar creatures, more interested in the way their local newspaper covers a warehouse fire or a Phillies' baseball game than in the quality of a story from Paris. Late in the *Evening Ledger's* life, in 1939, the Curtis heirs sought to strengthen its local coverage by importing as editor-in-chief Stanley Walker, who made "city editor" virtually a household term while directing the New York *Herald Tribune* in the 1920's. Walker and Philadelphia greeted each other with boredom; the new editor showed interest in only one local landmark, Thirtieth Street Station, where he could catch a New York train on Thursday night for a weekend that lasted until Tuesday morning.

The *Evening Ledger* city editor met Walker after about eight months—when a constable called and suggested he tell Walker to pay a relative's department store bill under pain of court action. Walker had only one local crusade: Because of a pique unrevealed to anyone on the staff, he directed that whenever a prominent judge's name appeared in *Evening Ledger* columns, initials be used in place of his first name.

The newspaper venture did enable Curtis to solve a delicate personal problem. His first wife, Louisa Knapp, died in 1910, and he married Kate Stanwood Pillsbury, a Wisconsin widow, the same year. Her son-in-law, John C. (Jack) Martin, a machinery salesman, soon became a favorite of Curtis', and he and his wife moved to Philadelphia.

But Curtis met opposition from his family and executives—notably Bok and Lorimer—when he tried to squeeze Martin into the Curtis Publishing Company. To bypass them, and also to counter internal objections to purchase of the *Ledger*, Curtis set up the Curtis-Martin Company—independent of Curtis Publishing Company and with Martin as president—and went about his business.

Curtis took little interest in day-to-day operations of the *Public Ledger;* occasionally he would wander into the city room and halt the first staff member he encountered. "My, that's a fine suit," he said to one man, fingering the lapel. "I'd like to have one made just like that." Martin cared even less about the editorial side. A news executive still active in Philadelphia worked at the *Ledger* 12 years before Martin called him to his office. "I hear you're pretty good with the magistrates," Martin said, and handed the editor a traffic ticket.

So long as the magazines prospered Curtis could afford to lose money on the newspapers indefinitely and support them as appendages to his main company. But when Curtis died in 1933, trustees of his estate realized for the first time just what the Man from Maine's newspaper dream was costing. The New York *Evening Post* was dropping about $1,250,000 a year, or twice the profits of the *Inquirer* and *Evening Ledger*. For its $13 million investment in the New York *Evening Post,* Curtis-Martin Company stood to recover only $750,000, a $250,000 "nuisance value" payment from other New York publishers to remove the *Post* from the afternoon field, and a half million dollars for machinery.

Faced with a $4,000 daily loss for an indefinite period, the trustees were ready to take the $750,000 and forget about New York. Only Curtis Bok, Edward's son and then a Philadelphia lawyer, stopped the deal. J. David Stern, publisher of the Philadelphia *Record* and Camden (N.J.) *Courier-Journal,* quotes him as saying: "We must let no other newspaper die on our doorstep. The New York *Post* has the most distinguished history of any newspaper in America. We owe it to the memory of my grandfather to pass it into competent hands." The *Post* eventually went to Stern for $1.5 million.

The estate trustees quaked at the thought of attempting to make money from the *Inquirer* in the Depression and turned it back to the former *Inquirer* owners when payments could not be met. The *Inquirer* alone had cost Curtis $9 million.

Neither the estate nor Curtis Publishing Company has ever made public the extent of Curtis' newspaper losses. But trade observers have estimated that of a total investment of $42 million, only $13 million was retrieved after his death. This does not take into account the operational losses which on the *Evening Ledger* alone were staggering immediately preceding its ultimate demise in 1942.

George Horace Lorimer, meanwhile, had violated Cyrus Curtis' cardinal rule of tailoring an editorial product to an audience and its needs, in a fashion that would attract enough circulation to warrant high advertising rates. Succinctly, the audience changed; the *Post* didn't. Furthermore, it did not want to and resented vigorously and churlishly the switch in attitude of its readers.

For Lorimer the collapse of 1929 and the subsequent recovery measures taken by President Roosevelt and the New Deal were particularly galling because they represented the failure of his longtime friend, big business.

Lorimer's political involvement of the *Post* had taken some peculiar turns before he settled into the comfortable role of spokesman for Republican conservatism. In 1912 he backed Theodore Roosevelt's Progressives as a gadfly of the status quo. In 1916 he put the *Post* behind Woodrow Wilson because "he kept us out of war"—which to an isolationist like Lorimer was a great act of statesmanship. When Wilson's hope proved unattainable and the war began, Lorimer broke with the Democrats forever. The League of Nations disillusioned Lorimer further; although he despised Warren G. Harding as a man, he was articulate in his support of Harding's party.

In later years *Post* research people often wondered why their magazine couldn't achieve mass popularity in the big eastern cities. The answer lies perhaps in editorials by Lorimer on immigration which infuriated first-generation Americans in the 1920's. He advocated limitation of entry to "selected individuals from those races that are fitted biologically for assimilation. . . . The trouble with our Americanization program is that a large part of our recent immigrants can never become Americans. They will always be Americanski—near-Americans with un-American ideas and ideals."

Lorimer delighted in the big "Communist" hunt of Attorney General A. Mitchell Palmer in the 1920's. As biographer John Tebbel put it, he supported "all sorts of superpatriotic schemes for combating what the frightened conservatives believed was a Red plot to seize the United States, a nightmare that had been haunting them at intervals for decades."

Lorimer began boosting Herbert Hoover for the Presidency in the 1920's; he found Calvin Coolidge inarticulate but acceptable to the *Saturday Evening Post*. When the Depression caused Hoover to declare a moratorium on war debts, Lorimer chided him; however, this squabble over principle didn't preclude Lorimer from fighting savagely in 1932 to keep the hated Democrats out of Washington. In a post-election letter to Hoover he said he was "greatly disappointed at the outcome," and offered Hoover an outlet for any writings he wanted to do. To Mary Roberts Rinehart, friend as well as often-published author, he said, "I'll fight this New Deal if it's the last thing I ever do."

Hear his clarion call to battle in a 1934 editorial which is marked as the throwing down of the gauntlet between Lorimer (i.e., Curtis Publishing Company) and the New Deal:

> It is impossible to escape the conclusion that today we are having government by amateurs—college boys, irrespective of their age—who, having drunk deep, perhaps, of the Pierian spring, have recently taken some healthy swigs of Russian vodka. We cannot solve our problems with a discredited European ideology and a Marxian philosophy....

Again, in the same year: "When this Administration came into power, the country had a depression to liquidate. It begins to look now as if it has both a depression and a New Deal to liquidate."

And again: "During the past generation we have admitted many undesirable and unassimilable aliens to our country, but none so undesirable as those alien and un-American ideas that the New Deal Party has assimilated to itself."

If the New Dealers "are as a class competent to plan and run the business of the country," complained the *Post,* "then practical experience and training in industry have lost their meaning."

Cartoons depicted New Dealers as crackpots, Reds, misguided academists, rabble-rousers and vote-seeking politicians; arrayed against them were characters labeled the Harassed Rich Man, the Honest Businessman, Poor Taxpayer, the American People, and so on. Editorially, Lorimer called for a brake on the New Deal, saying, "It is better to be careful now than sorry later. It is safer to put over one sound plan than a dozen doubtful experiments."

The *Post* steadfastly refused to concede that perhaps the business community bore part of the blame for the nation's plight. "We might just as well say that the world failed as the American business leadership failed," opined editorial writer Albert W. Atwood. "Probably the failure of business to get fully back on the job has been due to the persistent attacks on it." This to a nation living in "Hoovervilles," working on Work Projects Administration jobs, and standing in breadlines. The patience Curtis had with big business didn't extend to the man in the street, and Curtis didn't realize it. Lorimer listened to his Main Line Republican friends, rather than the contradicting testimony offered by his research department, because his friends had "more standing" than the plumbers and bricklayers, ergo, they represented the true thinking of America.

New Dealers felt, justifiably, that Lorimer's attacks passed the bounds of fair political criticism. Although he never hit at President Roosevelt directly, he lambasted every recovery measure attempted, and further, let opposing views into the *Post* in a manner that had overtones of a sop. When a spokesman for the Democrats was let into the magazine, his article was clearly labeled "the other side"—and more than offset by attacks on the New Deal elsewhere in the magazine. In his early years Lorimer made the *Post* a true forum for all points of view, even when he found them politically repulsive. Clarence Darrow wrote on the open shop in 1904; Captain Joseph Medill Patterson defended socialism in 1906—there was even a place for Leon Trotsky's explanation of the Soviet Revolution. In the 1930's, however, New Deal criticism was an unceasing cacophony of ridicule. "After all," said an editorial, "it is *our* [emphasis added] country and not a laboratory for a small group of professors to try out experiments that bid fair to result in an explosion and a stink." As the 1936 election results clearly showed, the *Post* would be hard-pressed to substantiate the claim that the United States was its personal possession.

Lorimer constantly needled his editors with dire predictions of financial catastrophe when *Collier's* came out with a good story, or when the *Saturday Evening Post* newsstand sales showed even a minute dip. "Nothing ruins a magazine quicker than complacency," he said. The dire warnings, however, were strictly for staff consumption; Lorimer would start one of his imminent bankruptcy rumors on its worrisome course through the office and guffaw with visitors over the knurled brows it caused. Only in his last year, 1936, did he show any signs of worry, when he told Norman Rockwell that some editors felt the *Post* was losing touch and needed a more modern outlook on life and the world.

The effects of the crash—and of Lorimer's opposition to a new style of government that had proved acceptable to the majority of the American people—were not immediately felt at Curtis Publishing Company.

Some issues of the *Post* in April and May, 1930, contained more than 200 pages, and circulation went up a hair over 1929. But business failed the *Post*. As conditions worsened in the country, advertising began to slip away—slowly at first, then by huge chunks, pages at a time. Summer issues in 1931 for the first time since 1915 went below 100 pages; in 1932, issues of less than 60 pages, only a quarter of them filled with advertising, were commonplace. Advertising revenue had peaked in

1929 at $73 million; in 1933 it was down to $18 million, and didn't equal the 1929 high again until 1946.

Previously, Curtis Publishing Company had not found it necessary to sell advertising; manufacturers and agencies bought it, unsolicited and happily. In 1916 the advertising department had been able to rule that the *Saturday Eevning Post* would accept no ads that did not run at least every fourth week, thirteen weeks annually. A legendary *Post* story is of the advertising representative who, in advance of trips to Pittsburgh and Akron, would send postcards to steel and rubber manufacturers telling them he would be "available to receive calls" in his hotel on a certain date.

In the 1930's, however, there was a sense of urgency in the way Curtis salesmen went after advertising. They invoked the memory of Cyrus Curtis' friendship to business and the anti-New Deal philosophy of Lorimer in telling manufacturers that their place was in the *Saturday Evening Post*. But the comeback was slow, for now Curtis had new competition—Henry Luce's established *Time* Magazine and the newcomer, *Life,* which fought for advertising dollars with the ferocity of Dead-End Kids.

The problems in advertising were felt painfully in another area of the company—the balance book and the pocketbooks of stockholders, both within and outside management and among the Curtis heirs.

During the lush days of the 1920's, Curtis declared a dividend monthly—not quarterly as was the case with most corporations. The payments were either 50 cents or one dollar; in 1929 alone Curtis paid out almost $20 million in dividends. Common stock dividends in 1930 were $6; $7 in 1931. But in 1933 Curtis was so depressed (earnings $1.3 million) that no common dividend was paid. Nor was another to appear again until 1950.

What profits there were went to the preferred stockholder class which Cyrus Curtis had created in 1925. The company was committed to pay $6.3 million in preferred dividends each year before any earnings could be applied to common stock—and the preferred dividends were cumulative; if not paid one year, they were carried over to the next and built up to staggering proportions.

Another Curtis move that hindsight showed to be unwise was his permitting employees to buy company stock and pay for it through salary deductions. The company made loans to top executives so they could participate in the plan; Lorimer objected, saying any sudden change in value of the stock would be devastating to company and employee alike. And that is exactly what happened: The Depression cleaved the price of Curtis common from well over $100 to less than $10. Large blocks of unpaid-for stock worth a fraction of the purchase price were still around in the 1940's, to the distress of both company and employees.

A Lorimer letter to Curtis in 1933 indicates the depths of Curtis Publishing Company's troubles. "We had sufficient cash on hand both to meet our payroll this week and to provide the postage on our magazines for several weeks to come," he said. "We still have some cash for unexpected contingencies. . . ." That Lorimer thought it pertinent to write Curtis about money was a tip-off to the internal worry about finances.

To a stockholder griping about passing of dividend payments on preferred stock, Lorimer wrote: "You urge a continuance of dividend payments based on a 'faith in the future.' Unfortunately that quality is not convertible into cash, and it is cash which is necessary for the payment of bills and to meet current expenses."

Curtis took countermeasures. The ban on tobacco advertising was quietly lifted, and Curtis ordered one million dollars spent on promotion in the last six months of 1931 alone. New subscriptions were solicited via telephone, through newspaper advertisements and by newsboys in person.

Slowly Lorimer proved that his overall magazine, if not his politics, commanded the attention of the American reading public. Advertising revenue in 1936 was $26 million, a 17.2 percent gain over 1935. The rebound was considered by magazine historian Frank Luther Mott to be "one of the miracles of mass communications," because of the *Post's* sustained assault on Roosevelt at the same time he was reelected by a landslide.

This upswing in the face of public opinion was indicative of a fundamental, distinct shift of the *Post's* role in American life. It could be accepted as entertainment, but not as a guide to life.

Concurrent with his editorship with the *Post,* Lorimer had risen in the Curtis corporate framework—a director in 1903; vice-president and chairman of the executive committee in September, 1927; first vice-president two months later; president October 28, 1932; chairman of the board December 1, 1934.

In the early 1900's Lorimer had rivals both on the *Post* and in the company structure. The first consisted of the heads of the advertising and manufacturing departments of the *Post.* Lorimer won the struggle here by sheer dominance, but in a way that allowed the other men to continue to work congenially with him. The other rival was Edward W. Bok. In this instance, it was a case of the *Post* overshadowing the *Ladies' Home Journal.* Bok had made the *Journal* the nation's leading women's magazine, but in stature and ad revenue it was dwarfed by the *Post.* Bok eventually decided that he could find more interesting things than corporate politics to occupy his time; he resigned in 1919 and spent the rest of his life in writing and civic affairs.

From 1933 to 1936 Lorimer carried the crushing burden of both the *Post* editorship and management responsibility; he seemed to resent that business matters kept him away from the editorial desk and the half million words of manuscript he said he read weekly to decide what would go into the magazine.

Lorimer's hours in the business office, however, affected the magazine. He showed scant interest in improving the *Post's* physical appearance. Column after column of gray type filled the hulking magazine. Lorimer insisted on thrusting down the throat of the American people the same ideas he and Cyrus Curtis conceived in the early 1900's.

The Lorimer Dynasty ended with the last December issue of 1936, when he announced his resignation as editor and Curtis chairman in the only signed *Post* editorial he ever wrote. Voter endorsement of the New Deal that fall, says magazine historian Theodore Peterson, left Lorimer "crushed and bewildered, a stranger in a land he loved and understood so well for more than three decades." Besides, Lorimer was tiring. "For thirty-five years I've been in a squirrel cage," he told a friend. "I want to get out and climb some trees." He even talked about starting a new magazine "completely free of advertising influences," as if a publication could be more uninfluenced than the *Post*. But even before he left the office, Lorimer had been plagued by a cough and sore spot on his tongue. In August, 1937, a specialist diagnosed it as cancer; he died October 27.

Assessing Lorimer, Frank Luther Mott wrote, "The *Post* made its first spectacular success by a wholehearted devotion to material prosperity and by directing young men to that goal. But the loaf of materialism was, as a matter of fact, leavened by something more than patterned romance."

But for all Lorimer's fusty conservatism, he was an editor—even when he bore the title of president, chairman and chief executive officer. His sympathies were with the man who wielded the editor's pencil, not the accountant's pen. In 1937, however, when directors approved Lorimer's handpicked successor as chairman of the board, they put in charge of the firm a man from the business floors. Walter D. Fuller, who had been president since 1932, was more conservative politically even than Lorimer; he was an executive who peeked warily at unexplored paths and generally declined to set foot on them. Company old-timers also say he had some crippling blind spots about what publishing was all about. During his first year as chief executive officer Fuller called a staff meeting of editorial, circulation and production people. "We have in our files a gold mine of material," he said. "Put into paperback editions, these articles and serials will be best sellers. Everyone loved them when they appeared in the magazines and will want to read them again." A *Post* editor agreed the idea was a good one—as other paperback publishers later proved—but that Fuller's plan had one fatal flaw. When a magazine "buys" a story, all it obtains is first English-language publication rights; putting it into book form is something else again, and costs more money. With a series of *"hrrrms"* Fuller broke off the meeting and abandoned the idea.

The new Curtis leader claimed kinship to a company descendant who predated even Cyrus H. K. Curtis. He called Benjamin Franklin "my great-great-great-uncle." He was also a Horatio Alger prototype. His first job, at age seven in 1889, in Norwich, Connecticut, was selling copies of the *Ladies' Home Journal*. After school he started out to be a banker but tired of the profession after four years and went on the road, selling ladies' dress patterns. He switched to magazine circulation work with the S. S. McClure Company and joined Curtis in 1908 in the accounting department. He was successively comptroller, secretary, and first vice-president and president, all the while under the guidance of Curtis and Lorimer.

As president of the National Association of Manufacturers in 1941, Fuller brought into sharper focus Curtis' public image as an all-out foe of Franklin D. Roosevelt and the New Deal. He accused FDR of "coddling" labor unions; he decried employer taxes being used to support social security and unemployment programs; he was an outspoken isolationist—until Pearl Harbor. During the war he dropped cryptic—and unexplained—hints about government rationing of newsprint being used to silence FDR critics. Fuller thought frankly—and often loudly—that the Democrats were the ruination of the nation; when Pennsylvania got a Democratic state administration in the mid-1930's—ending decades of Republican rule—he threatened to move Curtis Publishing to Delaware to avoid "confiscatory" taxation.

Lorimer's successor as editor was Wesley W. Stout, a staff member for 14 years and, like Fuller, handpicked by Lorimer.

Stout made no significant changes in Lorimer's formula; his most striking innovation was an occasional photographic cover. Readers or advertisers weren't excited. Advertising revenues dropped from $26.6 million in 1937, his first year, to $22.3 in 1938, then recuperated and edged to $28 in 1942.

In editorial outlook, Stout was every bit as conservative as Lorimer; the popular support given the New Deal by voters in 1936 goaded the *Post* into increasingly vicious attacks on the Administration. President Roosevelt never answered directly, but he showed several visitors a large envelope containing what he termed the "dirtiest" attacks published against the government. The bulk of them were from the *Post*. The magazine's editorials were a cacophony of ridicule directed against organized labor, social reform programs, social security, the Tennessee Valley Administration—in sum, just about anything attempted by FDR.

Fuller professed admiration for Curtis' rule of leaving the editors alone; however, company old-timers say he constantly meddled with Stout in the editorship of the *Saturday Evening Post*. "Fuller thought some changes should be made; Stout wore Lorimer's mantle and wasn't up to a switchover," one former editor recollected. "Fuller kept him busy answering memos. Fuller is right in saying—as he did, frequently—that the business office and advertising people weren't allowed to interfere. But Fuller, as management, did interfere, and he thought like an accountant and bookkeeper. He didn't like to spend money. He constantly had his eye on the payroll and wanted to know why such and such a story cost X amount of dollars. You can't be a bargainer and an editor at the same time. Stout wasn't strong enough in the company to stand up to Fuller. Hibbs [Ben Hibbs, who became *Post* editor in April, 1942] was another story. I imagine the bristle in him stood up early, though, and he and Fuller had some sort of agreement about who would do what around the *Post*. They never had any open beefs, anyway."

Fuller's dissatisfaction with Stout was heightened by stock-holder unrest—both with the *Post* and with management. At the 1941 annual meeting, minority shareholders denounced management's "isolationism" and called for the opening of Curtis pages to opposing points of view.

The blowup came with the issue of March 28, 1942, which contained what was, up until then, the biggest boner and the biggest misunderstanding in Curtis editorial history. The boner was the title assigned the article, "The Case Against the Jew." The misunderstanding was that of American Jews who read no farther than the title and, sensitive because of Nazi persecutions, interpreted it as an anti-Semitic tirade. "Hell, it wasn't that at all," says Stuart Rose, who was *Post* fiction editor at the time. "Stout had been very concerned about the anti-Semitism in Europe and decided to tackle the problem head on. He thought that by discussing the causes of anti-Semitism rationally, in public, he could prevent it from spreading in the United States."

"The Case Against the Jew" was written by Milton Mayer, then an assistant to Robert Hutchins at the University of Chicago. The third in a series, it followed articles by Judge Jerome Frank ("Red-White-and-Blue Herring," an exposition of the Jews' historical role as scapegoat) and Waldo Frank ("The Jews are Different," on the cultural and religious enclaves Jews have in society). It is obvious that Stout anticipated trouble. In "Keeping Posted," an editor's note column at the front of the issue, Mayer described himself as an "adjusted Jew" who had adapted to life in a predominantly Christian society without violating his own religious principles. The "Keeping Posted" item continued: "When we asked him whether he was worried lest other 'adjusted Jews' accuse him of creating anti-Semitism with his present article, he wrote, 'Nothing anybody ever said created anti-Semitism, and nothing anybody ever will say will ever do away with any.'"

With that warning the *Post* plunged headlong into controversy. Mayer's article—written as a "Jeremiah" speaking to his own people—was a denunciation of the Jew's abandonment of his religion and culture in an attempt at assimilation into America; he took the position that only adherence to faith would protect the Jews from hatred and scorn. "He changed his name in New York and his nose in Los Angeles," Mayer wrote of the American Jew. "He had himself baptized a Christian Scientist and his children Episcopalians. He 'reformed' his ancient ritual and then abandoned it altogether, just like the gentiles, for the movies, the rumba and the nightclubs." He decried the self-abasement to which Jews would stoop to gain acceptance, citing payment by a man of $10,000 to join a Miami Beach club. "There was nothing that a gentile would stoop to that a Jew wouldn't do if he could. Shamelessly callous to their own 'self-interest,' Jews in the South exploited Negroes as callously as gentiles did. In New York's Harlem and Chicago's Bronzeville, tremendous anti-Semitism has developed in the last decade because of the Jew's tenement profiteering. The trade unions know that there are few employers as conscienceless as the Jewish sweatshop operator employing Jews." Jewish readers took this not as the words of a Jeremiah but as that of a Goebbels. Jews canceled subscriptions and advertising; they jerked *Posts* off the counters and hurled them to the street; in New York some Jewish-owned newsstands started a boycott of the magazine that persisted for years.

For Stout the furor proved fatal. Because of the *Post's* general decline (including red ink for the first quarter of 1942) he couldn't resist. "One spring afternoon he put up a notice for all staff members to meet with him at 4 P.M.," said Stuart Rose. "That was unusual; we never met at that time of day. I'll never forget his opening: 'Gentlemen, today I've resigned as editor of the *Saturday Evening Post.*'"

Minority stockholders in the company were glad to see Stout go, but they pressed for more fundamental changes in Curtis' outlook. A group went to court with a suit asking that they be permitted a say in editorial policies. "Law courts have decided that directors must direct a company with common sense," their lawyer said. "They must make money for stockholders. These directors have adopted a policy of ostriches, their heads in the sand, blaming their editors for policies in an attempt to duck responsibility." Management, the attorney charged, had permitted Stout to conduct an "anti-Labor policy, to pursue a policy against the [Roosevelt] Administration, a policy explaining the value of Naziism."

The suit failed, but management had it in mind at it threshed around for a successor to Stout. The job almost went to Rose. However, a few months earlier Rose, a World War One cavalry officer, had said to his wife, "I can't miss this war; I'm going to it." He obtained a commission as a major and was to join a division at Fort Benning, Georgia, late in the spring. While awaiting departure, Rose broke his back in a riding accident; not until the next spring did he learn from Adelaide Neall, Lorimer's longtime secretary, that had he 1) not been bound for war and 2) not been injured, he was in line for Lorimer's chair.

Public statements of both Curtis and Stout were vague about the reasons for the resignation, but persons there at the time say the Jewish article was the immediate precipitant. "There was not one point of disagreement but several," Stout said for the record. "It has been speculated that our differences rose from political viewpoints. That was not the case," Fuller said for the record. In May the *Post* apologized in an editorial, saying that Stout thought the three-article series "would be considered as a whole—that they would afford an intelligent basis for the discussion on a question . . . [and] a frank airing of the whole question would serve to clear the atmosphere in this country and perhaps help prevent anti-Semitism from gaining a foothold here." The *Post* expressed regret that the article had been "misunderstood."

Even without the Mayer article, however, Curtis' dilemma

was unmistakable. The magazine conceived by Cyrus H. K. Curtis, executed by George Horace Lorimer, and continued without change by Wesley Winans Stout, was no longer palatable to the American public or the American advertiser, and no longer profitable for the Curtis Publishing Company. A change was needed, and fast.

Chapter Three

IN the spring of 1942 artist Norman Rockwell nervously rode the train down to Philadelphia from his Vermont home to make friends with the new *Saturday Evening Post* editor and see if there would be any place for his cover paintings. He was shocked when he entered George Horace Lorimer's old office and found two gangly young men—editor Ben Hibbs, managing editor Robert Fuoss—in their shirt sleeves, their feet propped up on a desk that had practically been an American literary shrine when Lorimer occupied it. After a day's observations (during which Hibbs accepted nine cover ideas, three times as many as ever taken by Lorimer at one showing), Rockwell summed up the new editor in New England terms as "easygoing and quiet but with iron in his soul."

For survival the Curtis Publishing Company once again had put its faith in Cyrus H. K. Curtis' old dictum, "find the right man and leave him alone." Edward W. Bok had proven the theory valid in 1887 with the *Ladies' Home Journal;* Lorimer had proven it again two decades later with the *Saturday Evening Post.* Now Hibbs was to affirm it yet a third time, in twenty years of editorial brilliance which made the *Saturday Evening Post* as influential and respected in American affairs as it had been in the days of Lorimer.

The lesson of Hibbs is invoked by current analysts with an "I-told-you-so" mien. A magazine is a personality, not a collection of articles and features to fill the space around advertisements. In 1942, when the Curtis Publishing Company was in trouble, it gave an editor, Ben Hibbs, the responsibility of directing the journey back to soundness. In 1961, when the Curtis Publishing Company was in trouble, it looked in another direction for salvation—and found disaster.

An editor alone cannot save a company. He must be supported by enlightened talent in finance, in management, in production. Additionally, when an editor senses a revolution in a magazine's reading audience and alters his product accordingly, adjustments also must be made by advertising and promotion men. Hibbs wrought an editorial revolution in the *Saturday Evening Post;* beneath him, however, was a corporate structure permeated with dry rot and weakened by the accumulated, uncorrected mistakes of past decades—not the breeding ground for imaginative reform.

The term "easygoing" used by Rockwell might have been descriptive of Hibbs the man, but didn't fit Hibbs the editor. He, Fuoss and the rest of the staff labored seven days a week and at night for months converting the *Post* into a general family magazine. The change was both in content and in format, and a section at a time. The words "Saturday Evening Post" had previously been spread across the cover in two lines, in the same "Post Old-Style" type Lorimer introduced in 1904. Hibbs' redesign emphasized the single word "Post" just as *Look* and *Life* were an emphatic four-letter call to the reader at the newsstand. The rest of the magazine Hibbs inherited was almost as dated, the same basic "glamour of business" product Lorimer had found successful in the 1920's but which in the 1940's was weighty and tedious. Some "short" stories rambled on for 8,500 words. Lorimer's successor, Wesley Winans Stout, had not only disliked the modern world, he had ignored it—and with the blessing of Curtis management.

It took Hibbs three months to prove that a deft editorial surgeon can produce a svelte matron from the lamest of sagged-cheeked old bags. The *Post* of Lorimer and Stout had a narrow editorial target, the businessman. Hibbs broadened the *Post* to include the entire family. He liked to compare the *Post* Table of Contents to a restaurant menu: "We certainly don't expect the average reader—if there is such an animal—to read his way through every item listed, any more than the restaurant chef expects the patron to eat his way right through the menu. What we do try to do is to contrive our weekly menu in such a way that everyone who picks up the magazine will find a substantial number of things which whet his reading appetite."

The editorial smorgasbord served by Chef Hibbs insured continuity of readership. Sports articles were aimed at young men, and readership surveys showed their popularity went "right through the roof." But, more importantly, the young men graduated to more sober reading fare, both fiction and articles, and became confirmed readers of the entire magazine.

Hibbs spread his revolution over three months and kept quiet while it was in progress. The Contents page changed one week; new type fonts showed up the next, and finally the cover change. Not until the modernization was a *fait accompli* did he brag about it. There were some scattered complaints, particularly because he took Benjamin Franklin off the cover and moved him inside to the Contents page. A prominent Philadelphian wrote Walter D. Fuller, the Curtis president, complaining of a "disgusting young upstart and a barbarian from the Western frontier" who had blackened Franklin's name by changing type faces. (Actually the "Post Old-Style" type had been designed only in 1904, not by Franklin, although it was so firmly associated with the *Post* that few men outside printshops knew its true origin.) This man said that "within a year the *Saturday Evening Post* will disappear from the American scene," and that Hibbs would "go back to Kansas and punch sheep" (*sic*).

The *Post* of Lorimer reflected the years the editor spent as a businessman; the *Post* of Hibbs reflected the years the editor spent in small-town, Middle Western America. Hibbs was born July 23, 1901, in Fontana, Kansas, and grew up in the community of Pretty Prairie (population 400) where his father was a lumber merchant. Hibbs' ancestors, however, came to Pennsylvania even before William Penn. Forefather William Hibbs landed in 1678 and several generations of the Hibbs family settled in Bucks County, north of Philadelphia along the Delaware River. A grandfather brought the name west to Kansas just after the Civil War.

Hibbs was a Phi Beta Kappa at the University of Kansas and then worked on small-city newspapers in Colorado and Kansas. (A metropolitan rival once called him the "most quoted young squirt in the state.") When he left the job of managing editor of the Arkansas City (Kansas) *Daily Traveler* in 1929 to become an associate editor of the *Country Gentleman,* then a Curtis magazine, William Allen White—Hibbs' mentor and idol—wrote in the Emporia *Gazette*: "Philadelphia is taking from us the white-headed boy of Kansas journalism. He is blessed with great talents . . . he is cursed by the little gnarled demon of industry, which perches on his shoulder eighteen hours a day, digs its sharp teeth into his neck, driving him on to tremendous feats of work and enabling him to produce a greater volume of first-rate stuff than any other man in the state."

From 1929 to 1940, Hibbs wrote general articles and travel pieces for the *Country Gentleman.* He wasn't a chairbound editor; he stood in stifling dust alongside wheat farmers at harvest; he could swing a leg onto the fence and talk intelligibly about the farmer and his problems; he was more at ease at a churchyard picnic in Kansas than at a literary soirée in New York. He mildly distrusted the urbane and the suave; at one time he considered the word "sophisticate" a passable synonym for a worthless, empty-headed human being.

Hibbs hinted frequently that he thought the plain folk of Pretty Prairie to be the "most enduring part of America." In a 1941 editorial in *Country Gentleman* he said, "There are thousands of Pretty Prairies throughout this land, and herein lies my faith in America. I don't mean to say that there are not plenty of fine and patriotic people in our great cities and within the ranks of organized labor, I merely say that, in the country and the country towns there is still a stability of life and thought which is our greatest bulwark in time of crisis." Yet Hibbs also had the depth of intellect to comprehend the internationalization of the world during the mid-1940's, and to make readers as conscious of events in São Paulo and Budapest as they were of happenings in Pretty Prairie. As for his faith in the common man, however, Hibbs' *Country Gentleman* editorial would have meshed into his farewell message in the *Post* twenty years later without the change of a single word.

In September, 1940, Curtis Publishing Company made Hibbs editor of the *Country Gentleman*, and he did a revamping job that was a rehearsal of what he was to do with the *Post*. Hibbs professed to be dumbfounded when in April, 1942, Fuller offered him the *Post* editorship and said he wanted an answer within twenty-four hours. "I'll take it—may the Lord have mercy on my soul," Hibbs told Fuller the next day.

Hibbs' boyish, just-from-Kansas face seemed about ten years behind the calendar then, just as today. A former *Post* associate said, "Frankly, we didn't know what to expect. Here was a newcomer from a farm magazine. It took us about half an hour to realize that we were lucky—that our new boss had the heart of a human, the brains of a Phi Beta Kappa and the energy of a wheat thresher. If I were writing a profile, I guess I'd have to call Ben 'colorless'—that meaningless cliché we apply to anybody who isn't a brass band. I never saw him overstate anything or resort to drama just for effect; but he could state the goddamnedest ideas in his unexcited voice; sometimes I wanted to stand up and yell with joy on his behalf."

Hibbs' lack of braggadocio carries over into his personal life. His funniest stories have Hibbs as their butt. After a Sigma Delta Chi awards dinner he received a note saying his remarks were so high-minded they "were like a benediction." He made the mistake of letting editorial colleagues read the note. Fuoss later met the writer, who asked how Hibbs had received it. "Ben is taking it pretty big," Fuoss replied. "He's been showing your note around the office and right now the s.o.b. is having stained-glass windows installed in his office."

Another time Hibbs said of his profession: "If any sculptor ever does a generic statue of the subspecies *editor*, he should, if he is realistic, sculpt him with one arm akimbo, raised in front of his face, warding off the overripe eggs and decayed vegetables which are aimed at his head."

As an editor Hibbs considered dull writing and dull speaking to be among "the most powerful enemies of virtue." To keep freshness in his magazine he relied upon a bottomless manpower pool of free-lance writers, hundreds of minds constantly producing story and article ideas for the *Post*. "Each of these men was a specialist; it gave us a depth you could never have on a staff-written magazine," said a former Curtis editor. "If Ben wanted a piece on labor union pension plans, for instance, he wouldn't call a man who knew about labor unions, or a man who knew about pension plans—he would call a writer who knew about labor union pension plans."

Hibbs recognized the Second World War as "the greatest news story of our time" and covered the battlefronts with the thoroughness that a metropolitan editor applies to a city. The tone of the *Post* suddenly became more serious; Lorimer had built the magazine on fiction, even leading issues with short stories he thought to be particularly good. But, as Hibbs said recently, "things were happening in the world more exciting than what fiction writers could dream up." Hibbs put the war articles up front; the fiction content was only about thirty-eight percent of the magazine for the rest of his tenure.

An editor doesn't cover a world war by calling a New York literary agency and asking, "What do you have for me?" Hibbs had a rather fundamental problem right at the start. "Despite the fact that the war was already flaming on many fronts throughout the world," he said later, "I found we had only one foreign correspondent—and he was in New York." With foreign editor Martin Sommers, Hibbs recruited his own corps of war correspondents—among them Demaree Bess, Edgar Snow, Richard Tregakis, MacKinlay Kantor and Samuel Lubell—and dispatched them to every theater. "I knew we couldn't compete with the news magazines on immediacy, that our job was to put the events into focus and tell what they meant," he said recently. Demaree Bess and colleague Charles Rawlings did this for the Battle of the Atlantic in 1942, clearing fog from sea fighting that had raged for months, and telling what it was all about. C. S. Forester, the Englishman who wrote the Hornblower fiction stories for Hibbs, did a classic job of factual reporting on "How the British Sank the *Scharnhorst,*" the German warship. Hibbs also turned to the men who were making the events to interpret them to *Post* readers. Joseph E. Davies, U. S. Ambassador in Moscow, was prophetic in his prediction that the Russians would hold at Stalingrad and turn the tide of war on the Eastern Front. The admiral in charge of the U.S. fleet in the Asiatic in the early days of the war gave a report on that bleak period in *Post* articles in October, 1942—nine months after Pearl Harbor, but a story not then told in full by the news media.

To Hibbs, war coverage had a more important meaning than giving readers exciting stories of what was happening on the battlefields of the world. In a policy declaration he said, "I think the processes of democracy should not be suspended during the war. I believe that constructive criticism during wartime is not only patriotic but urgently necessary. The problems that confront the American people are staggering. It is our responsibility to weigh, analyze and explain these problems."

Of all his war coverage Hibbs seems proudest perhaps of the manner in which the *Post* told the human side of the conflict through the covers of Norman Rockwell. A series about "Willie Gillis"—with a hometown Vermont boy as the model—took the typical American youngster through the war: Rockwell showed him peeling potatoes as a recruit, exulting over a food package from home, sleeping late on leave. The eleventh, and last, had Willie sitting in a college dormitory room, reading a textbook. Hibbs' favorite was "the soldier's return," showing the neighborhood pouring from the rear of a row of tenement houses to greet a young man in an army uniform and combat boots; the mother's face is openmouthed, and her arms are flung out in anticipation; around the corner, a teen-age girl demurely waits her turn. Hibbs called this "the greatest magazine cover in history"; the original is now in his home in Penn Valley, a Philadelphia suburb.

In terms of public impact the greatest *Post* war effort was also a Rockwell product—the Four Freedoms paintings. Rockwell conceived the idea after reading Roosevelt and Churchill's Atlantic Charter proclamation; he took rough sketches to Washington and touted them to officials as his contribution to the war effort. But Washington wasn't interested in poster painters; a bureaucrat said he'd be happy, however, to permit Rockwell to do stick figure drawings for a Marine Corps calisthenics manual. Rockwell broke his spiritless train ride home with a visit with Hibbs in Philadelphia. The editor excitedly ordered the paintings for the *Post*. Rockwell worked six months; his results inspired a nation—the farmer speaking his piece in town meeting (speech); the family around the turkey-laden table (want); the child secure in his bed under watchful parents (fear); two old ladies kneeling at prayer (worship). The *Post* ran the Freedoms—not as covers but as inside features—in early 1943, with short pieces by writers saying in words what the paintings meant to America and the Free World. The Treasury Department borrowed them for a tour which sold $132.9 million in war bonds in sixteen cities.

Along with the *Post's* thorough war coverage, Hibbs pinpointed postwar problems which were becoming obvious to his staff. In the spring of 1943, Demaree Bess wrote a clear prospectus of what Russia expected as war spoils. He confirmed the Russian revelation to the British of their claims upon Poland and parts of Rumania, and continued: "Since they [the Soviets] have made their desires so clear in negotiations with the Germans and later with the British, nobody has any right to be surprised if the Russians move again into all the territories they occupied in 1939 and 1940 and incorporate them into the Soviet Union." Bess also said that the Soviets would avoid fighting in the Far East even when the European war ended; that the USSR would demand "a free hand in the postwar settlements in territories adjoining her borders and a full and equal partnership on world affairs when peace comes." What Bess wrote, of course, was an uncanny prediction of the course of the Cold War, still three years distant. The article was all the more remarkable in that it appeared at a time when the Soviets were our "gallant" allies, clean and brave and true as a troop of Boy Scouts. Publishing it took editorial bravery, especially for a man still feeling his way after less than a year in command of the *Post*.

Hibbs also had the spunk to publish articles by Edgar Snow which gave an other-than-official version of the intramural warfare between Mao Tse-tung and Chiang Kai-shek. Snow likened the Chinese Communists to the partisans led by Marshall Tito in Yugoslavia and said they offered "the only armed opposition to the Japanese in North China." Realistic interpretation of events—foreign or domestic—aren't always popular; Hibbs chose realism.

After the war, the serious fare continued, the "Now It Can Be Told" memoirs of generals and statesmen. The competition with Time-Life, Inc., and Cowles' *Look* magazine was stiff, but Hibbs signed his share of the war's important principals. Curtis paid a then-record $175,000 for "My Three Years With Eisenhower," the first intimate glimpse of the future President's wartime activities, written by Captain Harry C. Butcher, his naval aide for three years. The series was so popular that Hibbs followed with "Eisenhower's Six Great Decisions," by General Walter Bedell Smith, Ike's chief of staff, and later with Smith's own account of his ambassadorship to Moscow during the early phases of the Cold War. Both presidents Roosevelt and Truman recognized the *Post* as a respected, creditable medium of national communication. Thus it was in the *Post* (issues of May 13 and 20, 1945) that America first learned "What Really Happened at Teheran," by Forest Davis. Until Davis' article appeared, only scant details had been released of the last meeting of Roosevelt, Stalin and Churchill, at which the final war strategy was plotted.

There was good business sense behind the serials in addition to their proven popularity with readers. By splitting a "blockbuster" article into eight or ten parts, Hibbs insured high newsstand sales over an extended period. Ad rates are based on circulation averages: higher rates—more money. The most successful serial was the memoirs of Arthur Godfrey. Pete Martin, the Hollywood specialist, originally drew the assignment to write the eight articles for Godfrey's byline but couldn't establish a working rapport with the star. "I took over with the delusion I could handle Godfrey," Hibbs said with the pained expression of a man remembering a horrible experience. At any rate, the installments were written (by Hibbs) and scheduled for publication in the mid-1950's, when Godfrey was on the front pages for mass firings on his TV show and for buzzing the tower at Teterboro Airport near New York.

The previous high seller had been Bing Crosby's story, told by Martin, which sold 450,000 extra copies. The circulation department asked how many to order for Godfrey. "I couldn't conscientiously recommend more than a half million," Hibbs said. "I was a little low. By scrounging all over the plant and finding unsold copies in a variety of places, we finally managed to supply 800,000 extras." A *Post* circulation man in a Detroit suburb made the mistake of leaving a valued extra copy on the front seat of his auto just after an elderly dowager in a chauffeur-driven Cadillac had found the newsstand shelves bare. Returning, he found a one-dollar bill and a note on the seat, but no *Post*. *"My dear sir: This is the first dishonest thing I've ever done, but I had to read about dear Arthur.* THE LADY IN THE CADILLAC."

The *Post* editors weren't complacent about their magazine, even when circulation was rising. "One stinking hot summer afternoon in 1957," as Hibbs recalls it, he, Fuoss and Robert Lee Sherrod, another key editor, had a long talk about balance of the magazine. "All three of us had a feeling that we were drifting over just a little more each year to the lighter side. We weren't publishing anything of which we need be ashamed; yet somehow we were less than satisfied."

It would have been easy to rebalance the scales by shifting around the same old material. "I must confess that my initial reaction was we do just that. I am told that as one grows older, the familiar rut looks more and more inviting.

"However, Bob Fuoss, who can be frighteningly outspoken, promptly sat on my well-worn neck. If we were going to nudge the *Post* a bit more over to the serious side, said he, then for heaven's sake let's not do it in the same old way. Let's devise something new in the mass-audience field—something that will attract attention and redound to the glory and prestige of Benjamin Franklin's old magazine."

Three days later Fuoss dropped on Hibbs' desk a memo outlining the Adventures of the Mind series—one of the most successful in *Post* history. The basic idea was that a great chasm separated the thinkers and scholars and the man on the street; that the intellectuals conversed eruditely in rarified surroundings without communicating their knowledge to the ordinary citizen, who in turn lumped all such people together as unapproachable "eggheads," and ignored them and what they were saying. Fuoss' thinking was that the *Post*, a mass-circulation magazine reaching a large and diverse audience, could provide a bridge across the chasm. Hibbs budgeted $100,000 for the project, and two editors scoured the country for contributions. The eggheads at first were reluctant to leave their ivory towers. When the first article appeared, however, the intellectual community responded eagerly. "People who had sneered at the *Post* lined up to write," said Hibbs. Some of the results were baffling, even for Hibbs, Phi Beta Kappa that he is. "Oppenheimer sent in a piece that was completely incomprehensible. We finally decided to publish it as an example of how far out into the intellectual world a man can go—and let our readers grapple for it." Sixteen book publishers bid for hard-cover rights for Adventures of the Mind anthologies; Knopf, who won, sold them by the thousands through the *Post*.

"We made up our minds when we started that if we got 10 percent readership we would be satisfied," Hibbs said. "The project was something that needed to be done. To our gratification, we got around 20 percent." This compared with 40 to 50 percent readership expected on the average nonfiction article.

When Hibbs thought a subject was important to his readers, he gave it to them, regardless of whether it met with their approval. An example was the population explosion, which he still thinks to be the most important long-range issue facing mankind. "Some magazines were scared to death of this subject because of Catholics' ideas on birth control," he said. "We knew we would take an awful pounding, and the circulation and advertising people were scared when we started it.

"There were angry letters and denunciations from the pulpit and harsh editorials in the Catholic press, even veiled suggestions of a boycott. We didn't stop; we pursued the campaign. The denunciations diminished. By the time I left office, an article on birth control wouldn't even cause a ripple. The critics saw it was going to be published and that it did them no good to holler, squeal and roar."

Nor was Hibbs afraid to explore flaws in the American character. It was through the *Post* that the provocative *The Ugly American* was first presented to the public. "It is only by a free discussion of our errors that we can correct those errors."

The *Post* had considerable circulation strength in the South; nonetheless, Hibbs covered the civil rights issue with vigor, and in a manner that he knew would infuriate Dixie readers. The late Virgil Blossom, who was superintendent of schools in Little Rock, Arkansas, during the integration crisis in 1956 which caused the use of federal troops, told his story "with no punches pulled." Hibbs said, "Again, the circulation men were worried. Southerners wrote some pretty angry letters, but they didn't quit reading the *Post*. I guess they'd buy the magazine for Bud Kelland's serials and tear out Blossom."

Any aggressive publication courts libel suits; the *Post* under Hibbs had ten to twelve outstanding at any given time. Many the *Post* regarded as threats to drop a subject from further discussion. But Hibbs didn't scare easily, especially when his writers had documented their findings. "When we regard a topic as important, we don't tuck it under the rug simply because some lawyer may make a muscle," he once said in explanation.

One attempt at "making a muscle" came from Mickey Cohen, the West Coast racketeer. In the early 1950's, Hibbs read a short news item about teen-agers lining up outside the gangster's home in hopes of obtaining his autograph. "I thought this was a pretty lousy thing," he said. "I put Dean Jennings, a West Coast writer (and one of our best hatchet men, incidentally), to work on Cohen. He wrote a biting, sarcastic series. It told how Cohen, supposedly broke and not able to pay any taxes, was living in luxury with a mistress and running around with all kinds of gangsters."

Cohen sent word to the *Post* through a Philadelphia criminal lawyer that he wanted to read—and edit—the series before publication, that he had the "right" to do so. Hibbs replied, "If we were doing a piece about the president of General Motors, he wouldn't have the privilege of editing the manuscript." Cohen sued for one million dollars—and withdrew one hour before Curtis lawyers were to take his deposition.

The *Ladies' Home Journal,* meanwhile, had also undergone a reform after stagnating for years after Edward W. Bok retired as editor in 1919. The architects were Bruce and Beatrice Gould, two gregarious young Iowans who met at the State University of Iowa and married in New York City in 1923 while doing journalism work there. Bruce came to the *Saturday Evening Post* in 1934 as an associate editor after selling eight short stories to Lorimer. The next year, in what is regarded as one of Lorimer's best management decisions, he made the couple co-editors.

At the time, the *Journal* was second among six not-so-good women's magazines. Three editors who followed Bok had been unable to halt a steady decline. Gross advertising revenue plummeted from a peak of $16,627,000 in 1929 to a low of $7,242,000 'n 1935. Circulation hovered at two and a half million. The

Journal had middle-age spread in its editorial columns; in content it was barely distinguishable from the other fiction-and-service women's magazines. The Goulds restored vigor and originality to the magazine, viewing women not solely as females but "people up to their elbows in life, not just bread dough." The Goulds believed that "the working intelligence of the average American woman was far greater than generally believed." They set as their policy "to bring our readers not only the most accurate and honest information possible in the traditional areas —health, nutrition, education and the moral guidance of children; community social and cultural activities—but also to widen the boundaries of their traditional areas of interest." The bold thinking of Bok reappeared in stronger form. Bok had campaigned against woman suffrage, but the *Journal* plunged headlong into discussions of public affairs; the Goulds called for the cleansing of politics as well as the cleansing of maternity wards. They discussed mental health, birth control and divorce. The *Journal* wrote frankly about frank subjects, and told the world of it. A promotion ad during a venereal disease campaign showed a pretty girl saying, "Of course, I'll take a Wassermann." It was the first major magazine to run an article on Enovid, the little pink pills that revolutionized birth control.

Again in the Bok framework, but in modernized form, the Goulds gave the woman and her family practical advice. The remarkable "How America Lives" series performed a public autopsy on a family monthly for 20 years. Fifteen to twenty staff members researched, and wrote about, how the family handled its finances, food, budgeting, entertaining, internal problems. A former editor associated with the project recollected: "The series had a high degree of reader identification, and resultantly it was extremely popular. Finding subjects? It was easy. People believed in the *Journal* in those years and considered it an honor to be selected as a featured American family. Also, they felt they could help other persons by showing, for example, how they handled a long-illness problem. We drew a big mail. People are fascinated by money matters. They would criticize a featured family if it gave too little to charity, or allotted a large allowance to a daughter."

The Goulds tested their women readers with "heavy items" and found them begging for more. The *Journal* carried a condensation of Walter Lippmann's 1943 book *American Foreign Policy;* the war memoirs of Henry L. Stimson, President Roosevelt's Secretary of War; the papers of General Joseph Stilwell, U. S. commander in the Burma theater who was fired because he couldn't get along with Chiang Kai-shek. Dorothy Thompson and Mrs. Eleanor Roosevelt contributed regularly.

Yet the appeal of the *Journal* was distinctly feminist. The Goulds expected few men to read "Tell Me, Doctor," an intimate discussion of female affairs; "Dr. Spock Talks to Mothers," and "Can This Marriage Be Saved?" The *Journal* called itself, with justification, "The Magazine Women Believe In." And, to advertisers, it could say—also with justification—"Never Underestimate the Power of a Woman."

By 1943 the Goulds' *Journal* was dominant in the women's field, with 4,375,000 circulation; this reached 5,000,000 in 1953, and 6,000,000 in 1963.

In sum, the Curtis keystone magazines—the *Saturday Evening Post* and the *Ladies' Home Journal*—had established a cordial, affectionate rapport with its reason for existence, the American readers. All except for one segment of the audience: Madison Avenue, where pleasing a reader who is head of an advertising agency is worth millions of dollars to a magazine, instead of twenty-five cents at the corner newsstand.

Chapter Four

ON March 29, 1962, President Robert A. MacNeal soberly announced that for the first time since its incorporation in 1891 the Curtis Publishing Company had sustained an annual loss, $4,193,000.

Why? How could an experienced, established publisher produce 18 million magazines during a single year, take in revenues of $260 million and fail to show a profit? How could a firm with a continuous management chain of seven decades—including some of the most profitable years in American publishing history—fall into the hands of outsiders, as did Curtis a few months after MacNeal's announcement?

The reasons are complex and interrelated; some are directly chargeable to Curtis' errors; others are outside Curtis' control. Singly, none was necessarily fatal; collectively, they were devastating. Put simply, there was revolution in the communications world in the 1950's, both in the media and the selection of the media by advertisers. Curtis management recognized the changes so belatedly it had lost the resources and maneuverability to cope with them. The collapse of Curtis management during a crucial period stands as one of the most baffling in American corporate history, and it is one that can't be explained by the directors and major owners. During Curtis' period of paralysis:

—Television, in less than 20 years after the Second World War, built advertising revenues double those of magazines ($2 billion to $1 billion, rounding off the odd millions). These are not "new" advertising dollars above those generated by the expanding economy; they are dollars that, were it not for television, would have gone to the American magazines.

—Other magazines, particularly *Life* and *Look,* convinced advertisers that their editorial audience and reach were more potent than that of the *Saturday Evening Post;* that a dollar spent with them produced more sales than the same dollar would in the *Post. McCall's* did the same to the *Ladies' Home Journal,* and to a greater degree.

—Madison Avenue walked out on Curtis, calling their magazines shopworn antiquities that belonged in another era. Just why Madison Avenue felt this way has never been explained to the satisfacton of the former Curtis editors. Nor do they believe that there is a rational explanation that will stand up under stern cross-examination. However, they haven't had that chance of cross-examination. Madison Avenue silences critics by cutting the dollar out from under them.

A Philadelphia broker who had dealings with Curtis in the 1950's, when the troubles first were becoming apparent, said, "Walter Fuller and Bob MacNeal considered Curtis Publishing Company to be just like the Ten Commandments—you can't change them or else you are guilty of heresy. They felt the same way about Cyrus Curtis' company: he knew what he was doing, and they weren't the ones to say otherwise, even 25 years after the old man was dead and buried. What the company needed was bright new faces in management, who weren't afraid to innovate, to do things. But all Curtis had was high-button shoes and stiff collars."

Walter Fuller was successor in 1937 to George Horace Lorimer as chief executive officer of Curtis. He moved up to chairman of the board in 1950. MacNeal, his handpicked heir, became president at that time. Both were products of the Curtis business and production departments; neither had had a day's editorial experience in his life.

MacNeal emerges as a tragic—even pitiable—figure in the Curtis decline and subsequent upheaval, the man in charge when the final blowup came, the man who let Cyrus H. K. Curtis' company pass violently into hands of another breed of businessman. MacNeal grew up in Curtis, which he joined at age twenty in 1923 as a scheduler in the press and bindery; he took the helm of command at a time when the accumulated errors of the past and the new problems of the present were so overpowering that the only alternative to collapse was revolution. And revolution was something Robert MacNeal was congenitally unable to perform. A moody, brooding man, MacNeal was aloof and distant from other executives, confiding in no one, displaying little trust in colleageus above or below him. A longtime director said last winter: "The last five years we didn't know anything at all. We would ask Bob a question, and he'd sort of drift off, and we'd never receive the answer." MacNeal was wary of new managerial talent in the company, especially someone with enough energy and ability to be recognizable as a challenger; the reins of command he held firmly, unwilling to yield them even for a vacation if it meant leaving Philadelphia.

"Bob was a Scotchman who came up the hard way," opined Cary W. Bok. "He got there by himself, and he wasn't about to let go. What he was thinking about, all those years we sat there at the switch, the Lord only knows."

MacNeal was anonymous even in a city noted for unobtrusive, publicity-avoiding executives. At a civic luncheon he slipped into a vacant seat at the press table and introduced himself as "Robert MacNeal of Curtis Publishing Company." "Are you in the editorial side?" a woman asked. "No, business." "What do you do?" "Well, there was a manpower shortage, and they made me president." A former Curtis executive tells of his surprise in meeting MacNeal in a Germantown laundromat. "Here was a man making $130,000 a year, dropping quarters in the slot along with everyone else."

Three decades earlier George Horace Lorimer would have written a "romance of business" story about MacNeal's rise in

Curtis. (The story would have been *sans* sequel; Lorimer didn't like stories about men who reached the top through luck and pluck and then fell.) Son of a Medford, New Jersey, glassblower, MacNeal tried working in a glass factory across the Delaware River from Philadelphia at age thirteen and decided "there was an easier way to make a living." Holding part-time manual labor jobs he educated himself through home reading and night and business correspondence courses. His formal education ended at high school and he became an installer and tester of equipment for Western Electric Company. A friend told MacNeal that Curtis was "a wonderful place to work." So he went there, and he stayed there, 39 years, the remainder of his working life. ("Save my company," MacNeal cried to another officer, tears in his eyes, the summer day in 1962 when Matthew Joseph Culligan was introduced at a directors' meeting as the new Curtis president.) Since his dismissal MacNeal has steadfastly refused to discuss any aspect of Curtis, past or present. Last winter he agreed to look over a list of questions in writing but did not respond to them. He has also avoided numerous old friends at Curtis, turning down social invitations and shunning telephone conversations.

MacNeal's first job was making schedules in the Curtis pressroom and bindery. He attracted the attention of management by designing a folding machine that enabled the *Post* to print more than 200 pages, the previous limit. Walter Fuller moved the serious-minded young man up in a hurry—head of the standardization division in 1931, doing time and motion studies; corporation secretary in 1943; first vice-president in 1949; president in 1950 when Fuller became board chairman. MacNeal learned the language in every division in which he worked. Even when he became president he would go into the machine shops and, at the risk of soiled white cuffs, talk about and help solve mechanical problems. In his coat pocket was a little leatherbound black notebook crammed with facts and statistics about Curtis and its multitude of subsidiary companies. The information—even including the names and addresses of directors—

was typed on a "miniature Gothic" typewriter so more characters would fit on to a page. Why the notebook? MacNeal's superior in the scheduling division had carried a similar book way
back in the 1920's. "He was the fount of all knowledge, so we
had to have one, too," MacNeal explained.

MacNeal literally ran Curtis from that little black book; he
trusted its contents far more than he did his colleagues. He refused to delegate authority, saying once, "I'm all for it, but it
seems that every time I delegate one job, somebody hands me
two jobs to take its place." At one time he was head of not
only Curtis—the nation's second largest publishing firm—but
also thirteen subsidiary and affiliated companies. MacNeal set
a superhuman personal pace, working until 9 or 10 P.M. and
sometimes into the early hours of the next morning. Occasionally he saw the sun rise over Independence Hall. He considered
a weekend day at his summer home in Ocean City, New Jersey,
an adequate vacation.

Hard work, industry and dedication, however, weren't all
that Curtis needed. Under Hibbs and Bruce and Beatrice Gould
the tradition-bound magazines had been administered a jolt
of adrenalin; the rest of the company didn't keep pace.

MacNeal's satisfaction with the status quo was revealed in
a host of areas, some vital, others trivial. Curtis used five-decade-
old electric trucks, with clamorous iron wheels, for interplant
deliveries around the city—vehicles which elsewhere went out at
about the time of the Stanley Steamer. Inexpensive to operate,
admittedly—all the driver had to do was recharge the battery
overnight. But the next day the driver made his rounds at five
to seven miles an hour. Appropriately, Curtis seemed to be
moving at about the same speed, even though the jet age was
upon it. Philadelphia drivers honked at the electric trucks and
fumed; the rest of the publishing industry honked at Curtis
and whisked right by.

As a place to work, Curtis was as comfortable as an old shoe.
Once a person got on the payroll he had the guaranteed tenure
of a poorhouse inmate. Curtis had the reputation of a low-pay

employer, but a stable one, where only a major error or company blasphemy would put a person on the street. Lorimer had disliked firings and made no secret of his unhappiness when he decided that an employee had to be turned out of Curtis. He finally hit upon a system of writing the person a note, then leaving town for a vacation trip to the West and having the bad news dropped a day or so after his departure. In this way, all traces of the person had vanished by the time Lorimer returned, and he didn't have to bear the sight of an empty desk, or of a sad-faced man cleaning out his personal effects. The news, "I hear Mr. Lorimer is planning a trip," sent shudders and nerve-teasing rumors throughout the Curtis Building, especially in the middle-executive levels. "But Lorimer would leave town only maybe twice a year," a former worker recollected. "Many times he would swear to fire somebody and snort and roar and then cool off before he went west. He didn't take kindly to reminders, either. He was tough and stern; that was part of his façade and character. But there were soft spots, too, if you looked hard enough."

MacNeal had somewhat the same attitude about firings. A former executive said, "After three weeks at Curtis [he joined in the mid-1950's] I came home one night and told my wife, 'An efficiency expert would jump out the window if he walked into that place.' I would start at the top floor and walk down. Maybe five percent of the people would be doing something. It was sheer lethargy." There was a saying at Curtis: Nobody ever died, and few ever retired. (The overstaffing wasn't universal; for example, Hibbs produced the *Post* with a comparatively smaller staff than that of *Life* or *Look*, his chief competitors. A former promotion man also remembers the "take-your-briefcase-home" pace in his office.)

Among the professionals who have studied Curtis, the consensus is that the company's most glaring postwar error was its failure to diversify into new fields, such as broadcasting, as did Time-Life, Inc., and Cowles, the *Look* publisher.

Curtis put all its eggs into one basket—magazines. The diversification it attempted added only more eggs—mostly bad ones, with the exception of *Holiday*.

Curtis Publishing Company's skepticism of television as a competitor or possible side-investment began with Fuller. In 1949, for instance, he told a meeting of Curtis magazine distributors: "Television will not take the place of the written word. In former days we worried about the effects of automobiles and motion pictures upon the reading public. These fears proved unjustified, and our surveys show that television, while taking its own important spot in the national picture, will have no major effect on the changing reading habits." What Fuller overlooked was that the automobile and motion pictures weren't rival media capable of attracting advertising dollars formerly the sole property of magazines, radio and newspapers.

Although every sprouting television antenna meant more competition for his magazines—both for readership and advertising dollars—MacNeal maintained the same stance as did Fuller, even when the realness of the threat became apparent in the mid-1950's. "The trade today is television conscious," he said in a 1955 speech. "As more and more stations are opened and more of them added to the networks, the cost per show increases. The advertiser, instead of cutting down his time or the number of stations, has been cutting, instead, the size of his magazine advertisements. It's the easiest way out for him." Just as in the early days of big radio programs, MacNeal said, many of the television programs were influenced by the upper echelons of companies. "Once this phase passes, just as it did in radio and the programs are returned to the advertising and sales managers, where the question of cost of reaching per thousand individuals is paramount, then there will be a return to increased use of magazine advertising." But, MacNeal conceded frankly, he didn't know when this day was coming. It didn't appear while he was at Curtis.

Cary Bok recollected wistfully last winter: "Once we were offered Columbia Broadcasting System for three million dollars. You know, had we taken it, we might not even be in the magazine business today." This offer was made to Lorimer during the pit of the Depression, shortly after CBS' founding. But, Bok added, "There's always the danger of diversifying yourself into trouble. Success in publishing magazines doesn't insure success in other fields." Curtis also turned down a chance to buy the American Broadcasting Company immediately after the Second World War.

Had Curtis branched into other fields, however, it would have obtained the financial depth with which to keep pace with *Life* and Cowles in the circulation drives of the 1950's. The circulation drives are like a world war: perhaps they don't make any sense and you would like to sit them out and go about your business as you see best; but just as a war can obliterate an unresisting nation, a circulation drive can kill an unparticipating magazine. Curtis was forced into the fight; it ran out of dollars at a crucial stage and had to quit.

In fairness to MacNeal, analysts of the company point out, the scope of what he could have done under the Curtis organization was limited, even if he had been a man of action. In the area of diversification, for example, Cyrus H. K. Curtis had bequeathed his successors such a bizarre capital structure that raising the necessary investment funds would have been difficult, if not downright impossible. This was the outgrowth of the preferred stock clause, created by Curtis in 1925, on the basis of a $17 million profit. The company issued 900,000 shares of $7-dividend preferred stock as a sort of bonus to stockholders. By doing so, the publisher committed payment of $6.3 million annually to preferred stockholders before Curtis earnings could be passed on to common stockholders. When the Depression came, Curtis was able to continue dividends to common stockholders through 1932—then not a dime for two decades. As economic conditions worsened, the dividends were passed even on the $7 preferred. Since the dividends were cumulative (i.e., if not paid during a profitless year, they carried over to the next), the arrearages became staggering. When Fuller became chief executive officer in 1937, they amounted to $12,125,000. The scant profit eked from the troubled magazines—$1,279,000 that year—went immediately to the preferred stockholders.

Cary Bok gave this problem top priority in 1937 when he became Curtis treasurer. At his insistence and prodding, the company bought up much of the $7 preferred dividend stock at the $100 call price and paid off arrearages of some $60 on more. Restless stockholders had threatened a proxy fight unless they began receiving a return on their investment. Bok and Fuller persuaded them to approve an involved plan at the 1940 annual meeting which created a new preferred series, debentures and common stock with a lower annual total commitment (only $2.9 million) and no claim on previous arrearages. Last remnants of the $7 preferred were eliminated in 1956; the annual preferred obligation was dropped to a relatively workable $2.1 million—but still a significant share of the annual profits over the next years.

Among old-line Curtis employees one still senses a resentment of the Bok family for not paying more attention to the company during the 1940's and 1950's; had Cary Bok remained in Philadelphia during the 1940's instead of retreating to Maine, these people feel, the company might not have got into the trouble it did. But if Bok did nothing else for Curtis Publishing Company during his entire life, cleaving the preferred obligation is accomplishment enough. Of this, today, he says matter-of-factly, "It saved the company. We couldn't have gone on, piling up the arrearages, we'd have been out of business." (And, ironically, the persons most adversely affected by the changes were Bok and other members of his family. "The company was most important.")

Fiscally, Curtis was wary of indebtedness under Fuller and MacNeal. The company had a history of avoiding bank loans. In the early days, when the cashbox became lean, Cyrus Curtis looked to papermakers and other unconventional sources for loans. He even borrowed from N. W. Ayer & Company, the advertising agency. The conservative Fuller liked to tell how Curtis started his company "on nerve and a little money he borrowed. For years he went along, sometimes two or three hundred thousand dollars in debt before he turned the corner and began to show a profit. In the publishing business . . . you cannot get bankers to put up money. Publishing houses must be built out of the business." The *Ladies' Home Journal*, in Curtis' lifetime, called credit buying an "evil" and a "trap for the poor." Curtis Publishing Company paid cash for the 108-acre printing plant it built at Sharon Hill, outside of Philadelphia, after the Second World War. If a new facility was so expensive that Curtis would have to go to the bankers, Curtis waited until it had hard dollars in hand.

At the end of the Second World War, when paper shortages lessened and the *Post* and *Journal* started their great surges in circulation and advertising under Ben Hibbs and Bruce and Beatrice Gould, Curtis had to divert its surplus into plant expansion, into banks of presses capable of grinding out millions of copies of the magazines weekly. These were paid for out of profits—profits that under another philosophy of management could have been used for expansion into different fields.

(In an interview in the winter of 1964, just after he became president and chief executive officer of Curtis, John McLean Clifford was asked whether he felt nervous in view of the $35 million his company owed to the Serge Semenenko banking syndicate. Clifford seemed surprised that the question was even posed and said he thought it to be somewhat naïve. "Owing money is a good business practice," he said. "It's not what you owe that counts, but what you can earn because of what you owe. It's like a man saving all his life to buy a house. You can pay for things while you are using them; there's no sense in waiting. That's what bankers are for; they have the money to lend; if I need it, I believe in borrowing it and putting it to use.")

But Fuller and MacNeal took the view that the only way to build a business was to plow the profits right back into it, even at the expense of withholding dividends from stockholders. In a memo to employees in the 1950's, MacNeal put it this way:

> This fundamental ... is exemplified in the programs of expansion and reinvestment in our properties which we have instituted, particularly since 1945 [i.e., building of the Sharon Hill printing plant]. It was assumed in all our plans that we must be prepared ... to meet the challenge of the expanding postwar economy and also that we must build so soundly that future trends would neither disturb our financial health nor hinder the advancement of our position.... Such an extensive program during the last few years has naturally resulted in some curtailment of immediate profits, and in conservative dividends to our common stockholders. Clearly, however, this progressive overall program is essential to the basic interests of our stockholders ... our readers, our agencies and our subscribers.

Nonetheless, good ideas were offered to the Curtis management that it could have had for the asking, with a minimal cash investment. When it became apparent in the early 1950's that television was a real live competitor, not just a passing fad that would go the way of Chinese checkers and parchesi, some intermediate-level executives tried to turn the company in the direction of the new money.

Stuart Rose, longtime fiction editor of the *Saturday Evening Post,* had extensive talks with the William Morris Agency, and worked up tentative plans for a 26-week television series dramatizing *Post* short stories. The format called for the author to appear first and explain how he came to write the story, and what he meant. Morris liked the idea because it would bring name writers to television, both in person and through their works. The *Post* fiction vaults held enough material to keep all three networks running indefinitely. Rose saw the idea as a triple-header: a way to make money for Curtis, and Curtis sorely needed money at the time; a means of promoting the magazine's fiction content, traditionally its strongest selling point; and (not least) a definite way of improving television programming, which was an infant wasteland rapidly growing to vastness.

"Morris, a top agency, agreed to produce the pilot film at no cost to us," Rose said. "Of course, they wanted a share of the profits, but it was still a hell of a good idea.

"I took the idea to the president [MacNeal]. He said, in effect, 'Why split with Morris? They are OUR stories. Let's take all the money.' So management handed the project to some obscure Washington producer and spent a million bucks for something we could have had for free, from a top agency. What happened? The whole thing flopped, and Curtis received nothing. It died. Not a dime."

Curtis had mixed success with the new magazines it launched after the war. For months in 1946 and 1947 a group of editors tinkered with something tentatively called "Magazine X," which would have been the Curtis picture magazine answer to *Life*. Hundreds of thousands of dollars was spent on trial issues; Magazine X occupied a sizable chunk of the Curtis editorial offices. The project aborted after gloomy forecasts on printing and editorial costs. "Curtis chickened out," said Harry Sions, one of the editors hired to develop Magazine X, and who shifted to *Holiday* when the project was abandoned.

At the same time, however, Curtis found a winner in *Holiday*, begun in 1946 and a solid money-maker after five years. Its staff was buttressed by editors who were casualties of the Magazine X debacle. *Holiday* was consistently strong. For example, between 1955 and 1960, when the *Post* was sliding toward red ink, *Holiday* increased its revenue from $5,853,825 to $11,090,176, and its total advertising pages from 888.76 to 1,247.14.

It was hard for the trade to fathom Curtis' logic in 1954 when it launched *TV Program Week* after Triangle Publications' *TV Guide* was already a marked success. The magazine lasted only eight issues. Curtis tried to produce it centrally from Philadelphia, but found the variance in programmings and scheduling across the country made it essential that printing be done on a regional basis (as *TV Guide* was doing). Curtis couldn't move; it was weighted down in Philadelphia by the Sharon Hill printing plant. To decentralize would have siphoned too many key people away from the Curtis home office; the magazine was junked, and more scores of thousands of dollars went down the drain.

Bride-to-Be, started in 1955 for $1 newsstand sales, aimed at the regional and local retail companies, rather than big national advertisers. Dealing with these small operators proved a headache; also, the small businessman balked at putting his limited budget into a limited-circulation national magazine at the expense of alienating local media. *Bride-to-Be* rates were nowhere near the *Post* or *Journal,* but still high enough to cause second thoughts to the businessman with less than $10,000 to spend on advertising in a year's time. To cope with these problems—multiplied a hundred-score in every state—would have required an army of sales agents. Curtis decided the potential profits weren't worth the effort. The magazine was sold, in 1956, to *Bride's* Magazine.

Country Gentleman had always been a company pet, but an expensive one to maintain. Of its 45 years in operation, only 12 were profitable ones; the cumulative loss was $15 million. The chief competitor, *Farm Journal,* passed *Country Gentleman* in circulation in 1939 by buying the expiring *Farmer's Wife.* Curtis made a last-ditch overhaul of the *Country Gentleman* in 1955 and renamed it *Better Farming,* then dumped it. "If in forty-five years we hadn't learned to make it profitable," MacNeal said, "then I did not feel I was smart enough to change it in the years ahead."

In another venture, acquisition of the *American Home* put Curtis into the home-service magazine field. *American Home* was a steady profit-maker through the 1950's, then ran into trouble with three of the other four Curtis magazines at the end of the decade.

As the magazines shrank, the impact was felt throughout the Curtis empire. Curtis grows its own trees, makes its own paper, prints every issue of every magazine, circulates them through a wholly-owned subsidiary. Other publishers had always looked warily at such an arrangement. MacNeal, however, viewed the integrated operation as a source of strength, and while he was president did what he could to expand holdings in timberlands and paper mills. "A wholly integrated company gives you control of the quality of your supplies and insures you continuation of them," he said in 1958, just before the bottom dropped out. MacNeal did concede "one big disadvantage." He said, "We sell a part of the products our subsidiary companies produce outside. When the demand for them is high, so is our demand on the inside, and vice versa. So integration tends to accent the curve of profit and loss. The ownership of presses, however, is particularly important in maintaining the quality of production."

The printing and papermaking facilities depended upon the magazines to keep them busy; the decline had a domino effect on all phases of the operation. "Taxes and insurance go on, even if production does not," Cary Bok said last winter. The papermill equipment required expensive maintenance even when operating at less than full capacity; in slack times Curtis couldn't turn loose the entire work force because the men would be needed when full production resumed. The same held true for the Sharon Hill printing plant. Curtis always managed to avoid unionization of the printers by running its own version of a paternalistic welfare state; as father-protector it couldn't resort to layoffs for fear of having the printers show up some morning with a business agent in tow. During slack periods other magazine publishers let their printers and papermakers worry about the production problems; Curtis paid for its production problems.

Curtis' papermaking subsidiary, the New York & Pennsylvania Company, was so remote that many employees thought it to be a railroad. New York & Penn's two mills are in central Pennsylvania. One at Lock Haven was constructed in 1879 and expanded in 1922; the other, built in 1887, is 100 miles west of Johnsonburg. Cyrus Curtis bought an interest in them early in the century and gradually built his share to one-third. For $20 million Curtis Publishing became full owner in 1950. New York & Penn was allowed to stagnate over the years; it had only one major customer—Curtis—to keep happy, and its capital expenditures were negligible, an average of only $2.5 million annually from 1950 on. (A papermaking machine and its myriad accessories cost as high as $25 million.) Since New York & Penn didn't have to sell on the outside market, Curtis management felt it did not have to meet the competition. Other paper companies, meanwhile, poured millions into their plants for modernization.

When paper consumption of the magazines slumped beginning in the late 1950's—from 224,115 tons in 1959 to 177,000 tons in 1964—New York & Penn had to hustle to crack outside markets and dispose of its extra capacity. It cut prices and spent heavily on new equipment so it could produce the high quality papers offered by competitors. Not until 1963, for instance, was New York & Penn able to produce the coated paper that advertisers like because of its glossier reproduction of illustrations.

After the Second World War, Curtis had an opportunity to diversify its printing geographically, as did Time-Life, Inc., and Cowles Magazines and Broadcasting, Inc., the *Look* publisher. A management consultant firm, after months of study, recommended retention of a central printing plant in Philadelphia, and Curtis invested millions in the facility at Sharon Hill. Curtis magazines are printed there whether destined for sale at 8th and Market streets, Philadelphia, or Powell and Market streets, San Francisco. Hauling them westward requires a battery of railroad cars (Curtis rents refrigerator cars since they are empty, and cheaper, on the return trip west). Because of the time element Curtis magazines had a "closing date" 50 percent earlier than competing magazines; at one time *Post* editors closed out issues 19 days before they appeared on the newsstand.

Other publishers view printing, papermaking and electrotypography as completely separate businesses, each requiring different management skills. Under this line of thought an executive can't "publish" magazines and "print" them, too. Also each operation carries its own set of labor and production problems. In June and July of 1960, just when Curtis needed trouble least, a strike shut the paper mills for seven weeks. After the strike was over, Curtis had to pay costly overtime to mill workers to insure having enough paper in the fall, the busiest season. The overtime was cleaved from earnings, to an extent that MacNeal felt it worthy of mention in the annual report. The other publishers speak in moot terms, however, when they second-guess Curtis, because they didn't have the same opportunity to build expensive production facilities when they first went into business. *Reader's Digest* and *Time* were started by publishers happy to be able to pay the rent.

In the first third of the century the Curtis Publishing Company dominated the magazine world in circulation and in advertising revenue—as high as 43 percent of the total advertising volume—as no publisher had before, no publisher has since, and probably no publisher ever will again. Curtis editors created the modern magazine and by superiority alone were able to knock down newcomers. The tragedy of the editorial stagnation immediately after Lorimer's death is reflected in the rapid rise of the *Saturday Evening Post's* new competitor, *Life* magazine. Henry Luce began publication of *Life* in 1936 after months of experimentation and promotion. The first issue contained 96 pages of photographs—the most striking that of an obstetrician smacking the bottom of a newborn baby, captioned, *Life Begins.* The issue sold out within hours; people paid as high as a dollar for secondhand copies and put their names on waiting lists at newsstands. Within a few weeks, thanks to Luce's promotion (not to mention the photographic skills he assembled for his magazine) *Life* was selling more than one million copies weekly.

Previously, the other Luce publication, *Time,* had been a negligible competitor to Curtis. Founded in 1923, *Time's* gross advertising revenue was only $1,860,443 (one percent of the national market) in 1929, the year Curtis publications had $73,644,718 (38 percent, according to Theodore Peterson). With *Life,* Luce's fledgling empire closed the gap rapidly. Here's how Time-Life, Inc., marched up on Curtis Publishing Company:

	CURTIS	TIME-LIFE
Year	*Gross Ad Revenues*	*Gross Ad Revenues*
1936	36,316,597	9,301,508
1937	36,394,532	14,927,492
1938	30,869,705	14,489,497
1939	33,485,338	20,093,012
1940	36,659,454	27,660,546
1941	39,335,594	35,235,449
1942	35,438,845	39,624,927

Once in the lead, Time-Life stepped away vigorously. In 1947 it had a $10 million lead in revenue, $103 million to $93 million. In 1951, Curtis lagged even farther, $126 million to $102 million. By 1955, Time-Life's margin was $51 million—$168 million to $117 million.

Look Magazine (born 1937) started more slowly than *Life;* initially printed by rotogravure on cheap paper, it had trouble finding a reason for existence for several years. But as *Look* matured, the content grew more meaningful, with in-depth treatment of important subjects (mental health, redevelopment of urban areas) as well as entertainment. In 1944 *Look* had $5.6 million in advertising revenue; the *Saturday Evening Post,* $31.6 million; in 1964, *Look* had $75 million, the *Post,* $58 million.

What enabled the newcomers to surpass the leader? For one thing, the Gray Lady of Independence Square kept tangling her feet in her petticoats, from the advertising man's standpoint. A former Curtis advertising executive says, "Our management came up through the production side. The people at Time-Life had advertising backgrounds. Our men were quite capable in their fields, but they thought in terms of printing magazines cheaply, and how to save a dime here and a dime there. *Life,* meanwhile, was spearheading this concept of total audience reach. When *Life* sold Madison Avenue on it, the script was finished, it was just a matter of the string eventually running out on the *Post.*"

From its viewpoint of past superiority Curtis took a condescending view of television and its new magazine competitors. Curtis people scornfully called *Look* "the white man's *Ebony*" and couldn't conceive of a *Post* advertiser buying space there.

The Time-Life management showed signs of marketing brilliance. After the Second World War, *Life* sent sales trainees into the field to do missionary work for the magazine among merchants, to persuade them to feature goods tagged, "As Advertised in *Life.*" The tags cost a few pennies. The implicit message was that *Life* put its recognized editorial integrity behind the product and the man selling it. The retailers also received low-cost promotional material which a skilled young man would help convert into an attractive display, free of charge. The merchants, in turn, made their warm feelings toward *Life* felt all the way up the distribution line to top management at the manufacturer.

A *Post* adman tells of calling on National Biscuit Company and trying to lure away part of the hefty advertising budget being spent in *Life.* The *Life* sales trainees beat him without even coming into the office. "*Life* moves cookies, and I have 150,000 dealers to keep happy," the *Post* man was told. "They like what *Life* does for them, and they give us good shelf space."

Another Curtis alumnus said, "I've had ad managers tell me, 'Gee, I'd like to help and buy some space in the *Post,* but I'm going to have dealers jumping all over me if I do. Now if you had something going as effective as *Life* . . .'"

The *Post,* in fact, had attempted a similar sales promotion program. But, according to company legend, the result was an embarrassing disaster. In the mid-1920's the *Post* promotion people took a full-page Bulova Watch ad, printed it in stiff cardboard-poster form and distributed it to jewelers across the nation. The idea was to stress the quality of *Post* advertising; Bulova Watch got a free ride.

Watchmaker Arde Bulova took a different view, however. He exploded over what he considered to be an insult to the image of his company, sued the *Post* and forced withdrawal of the posters. He also boycotted printed advertising media for three decades to come. And the Curtis Publishing Company was nervous about any form of merchandising promotion for about the same period, even when *Life* was delighting the retail world with its "As Advertised in *Life*" program. When Curtis finally stirred, it showed it was capable of staging such a promotion. Curtis spent lavishly in 1958 on selling a tie-in with the National Association of Retail Grocers, a ten-day promotion involving 10,000 retail stores, 300 major wholesalers and 28 national grocery brands. Unfortunately for Curtis, by this time *Life* wasn't too concerned about competition from the *Saturday Evening Post*.

Curtis got into somewhat the same type of situation in advertising. Its competitors started playing the game by a different set of rules, and Madison Avenue and the manufacturers went along. The game has two titles—"numbers," and "audience reach."

Magazine men began to bandy the latter term about in the late 1930's in self-defense. Radio estimated—or guessed at—how many people listened to Amos & Andy and Jack Benny and the other popular nighttime radio shows. The resultant endless strings of digits were put before advertisers as a basis for proving radio went into far more households than other media, and therefore would be the most effective seller. All the magazines had to offer in return were circulation figures—and these were minute compared to radio's listenership claims.

Somehow it dawned on the magazine publishers that their raw circulation figures were no more indicative of the total number of people who read magazines than the number of radios in the land equaled the number of people who listened to radios. *Life* Magazine, only three years old at the time, was instrumental in organizing the Committee for the Continuing Study of Magazine Audiences, later regrouped into the Magazine Audience Group (MAG), which included Dr. George Gallup and Archibald Crossley, both of whom were heavily involved in the radio ratings.

MAG checked to see just where magazines went, and who read them. *Life* immediately was happy because, as a quickly read picture magazine, it had a high "pass-on factor," claiming up to twelve or thirteen readers per copy. A man in a barbershop could go through an entire issue of *Life* in the same time it took him to read a *Post* short story. The text magazines—*Post* and *Collier's*—were retained longer, and hence circulated less, because they took longer to digest.

But vagaries cast doubt on the entire concept of "audience reach." The Audit Bureau of Circulation pointed out a claim of one magazine that it had gained nearly 150,000 readers in an area where its proven audited circulation had decreased almost 10,000 in the period in question. The text magazines, through their sales and research departments, asked whether advertisers could rightfully base advertising schedules on such "flimsy" evidence as the Magazine Audience Group was providing.

Yes, said the persistent *Life* Magazine. It also had the foresight in the late 1940's to anticipate that if the "numbers" game was dangerous to magazines when the top hand was held by radio, the television newcomer posed an ever greater threat. *Life* saw, correctly, that television would give advertisers access to a mass audience by the mere flick of a switch. *Life* engaged Alfred Politz, who had a reputation for scientific accuracy and responsibility. Politz came up with a finding that 5.2 persons read each issue of *Life*—and *Life* multiplied this times its circulation, and its digits matched those of radio and television. Next, *Life* underwrote a study of *Look, Post, Life* and the *Ladies' Home Journal.* The resulting "Study of Four Media" showed *Look* to be second to *Life* in almost all categories, which Cowles was quick to emphasize in its competitive selling. The finding staggered the *Post* in the mid-1950's; some admen still believe it was the *coup de grâce* for the wobbling *Collier's,* whose direct competitor was *Look.*

Post got some consolation from the Politz survey. It was proven to be a magazine bought for reading, not for "looking." But *Time-Life* and Cowles salesmen turned this point to the favor of *Life* and *Look.* "A young mother who needs to buy a refrigerator or a can of soup is the same young mother who is too busy chasing three children to settle down in an easy chair with a 6,000-word article on the Congo," a former Curtis space salesman said. "She might like to read it, but when? The only thing she could cover with a glance in the *Post* was Hazel."

Other studies pecked at the buying prowess of the *Saturday Evening Post* readership. The Consumer Magazine Report (CMR), issued every six months by Daniel Starch & Staff, a market research firm, broke down the circulation of each magazine into age groups, incomes, occupations, what type of household goods they owned and other information of interest to advertisers and manufacturers. CMR showed that *Post* ran behind *Life* and *Look* in the metropolitan neighborhoods with high-income families. The *Post* was hitting more readers than ever in its history, but in older age groups.

Madison Avenue wanted to cover the younger people (base age of 35 years) who make more consumer purchases; the suburbanites with extra dollars that give them discretionary buying power; and the above-$25,000-income audience that is the cream. In this last category *Life* consistently had almost twice again as many readers as did the *Post;* in 1964, even after the *Post's* tortured search for a new image, *Life* had around 600,000, the *Post* only 375,000. "Those are the kinds of figures that talk on Madison Avenue," said an agency official. "Who gives a damn about the ribbon-clerk readers? This might sound trite, but I'm putting my money where the action is."

Why wasn't Curtis reaching this market? Madison Avenue claimed it had the answer—that people were tired of reading about Tugboat Annie and the Earthworm Tractor Co., that Pete Martin had called on so many Hollywood stars he was a boring "Man Who Came to Dinner"; that the readers would rather have a sprightly photographic essay on South America than a detailed discussion by one or both of the Alsops; that the *Post's* "escape" fiction had been supplanted by television soap operas and situation comedies and went largely unread; that the *Post* should take away Norman Rockwell's easel and give him a camera and a model in a scant bikini.

This entire line of thought is disputed by Ben Hibbs, who was *Post* editor from 1942 through the last issue of 1962. Hibbs doesn't "defend" his record of the years in which Madison Avenue insists the *Post* "slipped"; he states it and stands by it. A prized possession in the basement office of his home is a framed card on the wall, signed by the Curtis circulation manager. It lists a figure of 7,085,000 for his last *Post* issue—double that of his first.

"There were never any serious ups or downs, either," Hibbs said. "It was a steady climb over the years. For nineteen of my twenty years, despite the so-called 'decline,' the *Post* earned as much money as any publication in America has earned in a similar period."

Twice monthly during his regime, interviewers from National Analysts, the subsidiary company which did all survey work for Curtis Publishing Company, went out with copies of the *Post* and asked a geographically balanced group of readers what in the magazine they read and what they liked. Copies of the results went to Hibbs, senior editors and selected executives with adhesive stamps on every item in the book, telling the readership percentage by age and sex groups. "This was something for internal use, not the kind of thing you would fake to make a showing. We would only have been fooling ourselves," Hibbs said. "If there had been a 'decline' or a 'losing of touch,' the surveys would have shown it. They didn't. We had the same percentages, or close to them, on a steady basis.

"The ad people were always hollering in my last year about the Norman Rockwell covers, that they were old-fashioned. Heck, those were the *Post's* most popular feature." There were other independent indices. A barometer of Hibbs' success in gauging his selection of fiction was *The New York Times* best-seller list, published every Sunday. "During a period in the 1950's there was never a week we didn't have three *Post* books on the list, and sometimes as many as five." (He meant books that had been either excerpted or serialized in the magazine before hardback publication.) "Dammit, we were hitting the American market—we had to be with that kind of record."

Hibbs recognized the surveys as a valuable guide, when hedged with an important "but"; to wit: "I think the greatest folly an editor could commit would be to follow such indices too slavishly," Hibbs said in a 1950 speech at the University of Kansas. "He shouldn't start turning cartwheels and jumping through hoops every time the index turns up or down on certain types of material. You can't edit a magazine by arithmetic."

In another speech, in 1959, Hibbs elaborated on this theme and warned against lowering standards solely to court circulation. "Every editor worth his salt knows that there are ways to reach farther and farther down the scale of human intelligence and emotions and pile in the readers. The temptation is always there. Yet in the end, if we go too far in this direction, we certainly will destroy the character of the publications we edit and betray the very people whom we really want as readers. And that, of course, would be the final disaster."

What about the assertion that *Post* fiction was vapid and meaningless? "It is a pretty grim world we live in these days," says Hibbs, "and those publications which deal with the current scene must, inescapably, mirror some of that grimness. Yet, after all, the world is not entirely composed of hydrogen bombs, juvenile delinquency, race riots, mental institutions, heart disease and cancer.... I can remember the time when people thought it *fun to read.*

"Why shouldn't we provide our readers with a bit of 'escape' —to use a dirty word—from the cares of daily life through the vehicle of a buoyant human-interest article or an absorbing story? It is one of our functions, and a highly worthwhile function, I think. There is nothing incompatible in intellectuality and the love of entertainment—in a man or a magazine." In a 1960 talk at a *Post* advertising sales meeting Hibbs also stood behind the serialized article and story, which competitors then were calling an anachronism. In 1959 the *Post* published 12 nonfiction and 20 fiction serials in from two to eight installments. "We did this not because we needed something to fill up the great open spaces but because we believed most earnestly that it was good editing and good business," he said. Some stories simply could not be presented in one installment—an exhaustive study of James R. Hoffa, the Teamsters' boss; a first-person account by the captain of the nuclear submarine *Nautilus* of its voyage under the North Pole cap; the archaeological and adventure story of the exploration of Aku-Aku.

Hibbs had this to say to the *Post* ad salesmen: "When some agency man, parroting the promotion of our competitors, tells you that the *Post* is old-fashioned because it uses the continuing feature, I beg of you to stand up on your hind legs and tell him —in a nice way, of course—that he is nuts."

From 1954, when the circulation race became a grim business, until 1960, *Post* circulation rose from 4,590,607 to 6,301,789, according to Audit Bureau of Circulation figures. Advertising revenue increased from $77,940,710 to $105,049,136, according to the Publishers Information Bureau. However, there was a meaningful dip in another column: total *Post* advertising pages slumped from 3,687.18 to 2,788.29.

Ad rates are pegged on circulation: as *Post* circulation soared as Curtis sought to keep abreast of *Life* and *Look* (whose owners could draw upon outside television revenues), the ad rates soared along with them. This created a problem for the *Post* peculiar among the Big Three magazines.

A former *Post* advertising executive said, "We always depended a lot on the small manufacturer, the buzz saw factory type of guy, for instance, who liked the prestige of a *Post* ad. But our higher rates made it impossible for this type of business to advertise with us. They switched to *Business Week* or *U.S. News & World Report.*

"*Life* and *Look,* however, had a higher percentage of the packaged goods advertisers, such as food firms, the companies who had the financial depth to pay high rates."

Another factor was television, whose revenues were negligible until the late 1940's. Fuller and MacNeal viewed TV as a passing fad; advertisers, however, saw it as a medium through which their messages could be put before an audience far more vast than that of any single magazine. Here again circumstances harmed the *Post*. National TV ad rates are so high that the medium draws heavily from the big corporations—such as the auto manufacturers—with which the *Post* formerly had been strong. In 1953, advertisers paid more money for magazine space ($667 million) than for television time ($606 million). A decade later, television had surged far ahead, $2,032,000 to $1,034,000 for magazines. Its annual rate of gain slackened perceptibly in 1963 and 1964, but the central fact remains: television is the major advertising media.

An official of N.W. Ayer & Company, the Philadelphia advertising agency which is next door to Curtis Publishing Company both physically and emotionally, commented, "The advertising-dollar pie is about the same size. But there are more slices to cut, and consequently, some of them are smaller. Part of the new money, of course, came from the expansion of the economy. If it weren't for television, however, where else would it go but magazines?

"Advertisers spread their budgets just so far. You don't count on a single advertisement to be effective. First you must establish a 'presence' in a magazine, so that your familiarity soaks in with the reader. Rates got so high in the late 1950's that manufacturers simply couldn't afford to do that in every magazine. The growing tendency is for advertisers to pick two or three of the four general family magazines—*Post, Look, Life* or the *Reader's Digest.* Thus, somebody is left out, and unfortunately for Curtis, that somebody has been the *Post."*

This wasn't serious as long as the higher rates kept the money coming in at an undiminished volume. For six of the seven years from 1954 through 1960 the *Post* managed to produce increased revenue with a lesser number of advertising pages. Here's a breakdown on circulation and advertising figures for the period:

	ABC Circulation	Revenue	Ad Pages
1954	4,590,607	77,940,710	3,687.18
1955	4,702,729	83,731,203	3,686.81
1956	4,905,850	86,873,786	3,508.26
1957	5,301,042	90,899,031	3,300.81
1958	5,745,145	87,606,491	2,891.71
1959	6,115,878	97,598,552	2,816.55
1960	6,301,789	105,049,136	2,788.29

In the circulation race all participants cut subscription rates and newsstand prices drastically to attract new readers, and spent lavishly on promotion. At one point *Life* sold for 19 cents —about a dime under the cost of production. One Curtis official estimated his company spent as high as $10 for each new subscription obtained during the late 1950's; former *Post* people, however, view this figure as high. Whatever the cost, or the reasoning behind the scramble, MacNeal didn't like it. His temper finally snapped in 1961 when *McCall's* startled the industry with the announcement it was giving advertisers a "free million readers." By this, *McCall's* meant that although its actual circulation was eight million, it would base its ad rates on seven million. *McCall's* could do this because its pockets were lined with a freshet of new dollars supplied by West Coast industrialist Norton Simon, a new investor in the company who knew the magazine would have to have top circulation to surpass the *Ladies' Home Journal* and who achieved it with heavy promotional spending. Afterwards, MacNeal called the offer "hocus-pocus" and a "form of ego-satisfaction." Advertising rates already were "unprofitably low" in the women's field, he said, and *McCall's* decision was "obviously a hurried move calculated to preserve the illusion of leadership." A. Edward Miller, *McCall's* publisher, chidingly reminded MacNeal that his magazine had gained 27 percent in ad linage through mid-year while Curtis' *Ladies' Home Journal* was off 6.1 percent.

As Curtis magazines lagged farther and farther behind, Mac-Neal complained bitterly of what he called the "follow-the-leader" philosophy of advertising agencies, saying, "There is such a widespread tendency to assume that the magazine with the largest circulation is the best, a very substantial percentage of advertising linage goes almost automatically to the magazine with the most circulation in the field." He tartly suggested that the Audit Bureau of Circulation raise its standard of what constituted a "paid subscription" from one-half the regular subscription price to at least one-half of the newsstand price. Otherwise, MacNeal said, "It seems to me only a question of time before the Federal Trade Commission cracks down on this practice as fictitious pricing or a deceptive practice." As an alternative he suggested that the Post Office Department move to stop cut-rate subscription solicitations that "flood the mails with half-price offers."

MacNeal quit the circulation race in the spring of 1962; Curtis had lost $4.1 million the year before; it was well on its way to more substantial losses. In defeat, however, MacNeal sounded as if he dropped out of the race solely for the preservation of the subscription system and the U. S. Post Office. "We are all training the reader not to pay full price," he said. Mac-Neal's stated reasons were commendable, even vital to the industry, but he left one thing unsaid. Flatly, Curtis didn't have enough money to continue the promotions and cut-rates; rising production costs, unmatched by circulation revenue, were contributing to the losses. The Curtis public relations people, to save company face, had to sound virtuous in defeat. MacNeal's statement, however, was correctly interpreted in the trade as an admission of deep trouble; advertisers simply don't buy the story that a magazine strengthens itself by not seeking new readers.

As advertising pages slipped away, the *Post* became thinner—noticeable first only to the professionals, the media men in the advertising agencies. Then the drop began to snowball. Why? "We're a bunch of sheep," David Ogilvy, of Ogilvy, Benson and Mather, said candidly. "One agency leaves a magazine, we all wonder why and follow. The magazine thins again, and more of us leave. Suddenly there's nothing left. No one wants his copy in a thin book."

Paradoxically, Ogilvy points out, advertisers would be better off putting their ads into a small book. "George Gallup at Princeton discovered that ads in a thin magazine have more readership than those in thick magazines. But all the advertising is bunched up between Labor Day and Thanksgiving; no one bothers with it in the summer and in January—yet people are so anxious for prime season advertising space that the *New Yorker,* for instance, has to turn away business because it doesn't have room. Like I say, we're a bunch of sheep."

Former Curtis executives who saw their magazines melt like a parfait in a hot banquet room have a less complimentary zoological term than sheep for Madison Avenue. They are in the unfortunate position of having to keep their mouths shut about it in public, however, for they are now with publishers dependent upon the same Madison Avenue dollars which once were in the *Post, Journal* and other magazines. What they say after a couple of Scotches, however, follows the same general outline, something like this:

"It's a pretty sinister thing for four or five men to have life or death control over the major magazines. They treat magazines like they do television shows—you're either the winner, or you're dead. If you are third in the ratings in your time slot, you're out in the street, regardless of whether you are enjoyed and accepted by six million families. Some other horse opera has seven million fans, ergo, you're no good. Of the new shows started in the fall season of 1964, 61 percent were off the air before March 1. Madison Avenue is attempting to do the same thing to magazines.

"The pressures aren't as crude as they were years ago, when an advertiser or an agency would demand that stories be run, or not be run, but they are just as effective. The tragedy is that one little crew-cut executive, sitting in a Manhattan office surrounded by mysterious charts, graphs and surveys whose validity is subject to question, decides that a magazine which he has never read consistently is good or bad. He flips through the pages once a week and finds nothing that appeals to his superficial intelligence and throws it in the corner.

"It's what is called the 'New York reflexive action,' found in people who go to Manhattan and think what people do and say there is indicative of the entire nation. Because they're from Denver or Dallas they have to be even more 'Manhattan' than the natives. They're like a flock of turkeys, running across the field after a bright attractive grasshopper, gobbling at the top of their voices and not thinking about whether what they're chasing is even good to eat. Everyone else is running and gobbling, so they must run and gobble, too, to prove they're real 'Manhattan.' The *avant-garde* on the cocktail party circuit says the *Journal* and the *Post* are dated and unpopular, and Madison Avenue picks up the chant. The pressure is applied to ad salesmen, the people who have the face-to-face contacts at the agencies. 'Why don't you brighten up your magazines and run more pictures, or more arty covers?' It's demoralizing to the salesmen, and they bring the stories back home. Because they are demoralized, they don't work as hard; they have a scapegoat —after all, they're trying to sell an 'outdated' magazine."

One former Curtis executive told of meeting a corporation president in the Midwest and hearing loud praise for the *Post*. "I love your magazine, I read every issue and so does every member of my family. Tell your people back in Philadelphia to keep up the good work. You've got more substance than *Life*." The Curtis man asked an advertising representative later, "How much business do we get from these people?" "None, their agency won't recommend the *Post* or any other Curtis publication."

There was a slogan in the Curtis office in the late 1950's: "Love me less and buy me more." Not surprisingly, the reception to *Post* representatives was coolest in New York. "But the farther you got away from Madison Avenue the warmer it was. In Indianapolis and Chicago it was downright hot, even when we were being snubbed in the East. Unfortunately, the bulk of the dollars were back in Manhattan. Or the people who said where they were to be spent, at least."

By 1961 Curtis was in the peculiar situation of ruining itself by success. Improved circulation caused higher manufacturing and delivery expenses not offset by additional advertising revenues. From 1959 to 1961, postal expenses alone increased $6 million. The hunger for magazines to meet circulation-race obligations kept presses rolling around the clock, hampering preventive maintenance and resulting ultimately in costly breakdowns. After repairs were made, Curtis had to pay printers premium overtime to get the magazines into the mail on time.

Despite the shortcomings that were rapidly catching up on it, Curtis Publishing Company continued profitable through the 1950's by reason of girth if nothing else. The expanding economy threw advertising riches in all directions, and all media shared in the bounty. Television, of course, got the largest share of the new spending; its revenues increased by as high as 16 percent annually, three times the growth rate of the magazine industry. But Curtis received enough money to keep its empire inflated, even if leaky.

It was inevitable that the spiral end. At the close of the decade, even though total revenues continued to increase, the combination of inefficient management, increased advertising rates, lower number of advertisers and lack of outside income crashed down on Curtis with a resounding bang. Here's a rundown on revenue and profit for the period:

Year	Revenue (millions)	Profits (in millions)
1950	149.5	5.3
1951	153.8	4.8
1952	163.0	4.4
1953	174.7	4.8
1954	173.3	4.5
1955	179.8	4.0
1956	186.5	6.2
1957	202.6	6.2
1958	197.1	2.7
1959	243.0	3.9
1960	248.6	1.0

The narrowed base of advertising support made the Curtis Publishing Company top-heavy; the recession of 1960 shoved over the entire flimsy structure. "It was a geometrical loss of money," says a former *Post* advertising executive. "Eventually, the lines crossed, in 1961. When you're in that situation, the loss of a single big advertiser who decides—because of whim or because of logic or whatever—to go elsewhere is devastating. Some manufacturers and agencies plain like to experiment. They'll pull out of a magazine for six months and try spending their money elsewhere, just to see what happens. In the *Post's* situation by 1960 that could mean a loss of maybe three or four percent of your revenue." In the recession of 1961 *Post* advertising pages dropped to 1,574.28—less than half the 3,678.18 of 1954. Revenue plunged from $105,049,136 in 1960 to $86,539,596. Curtis doesn't break down profits and losses of individual magazines in its annual reports; however, 1961 marked the first year since 1942, at least, that the *Post* operated in the red. The *Journal* also experienced its first loss in two decades.

On total revenues of $260 million in 1961, Curtis had an operating loss of $8,831,356, cut to $4,193,585 because of a tax credit of $1,188,151 and a nonrecurring profit of $3,460,620 from the sales of securities. Advertising income was off severely —$130.9 million compared to $151.7 million.

From then on Curtis Publishing Company was on a greased toboggan.

Chapter Five

In early 1960, the Curtis management yielded to the cacophony of criticism from Madison Avenue and decided to "do something about the *Post*." If the advertisers insisted on a "modern" magazine, keyed to the younger American, that's what the advertisers would get. A task force set to work in secrecy under the command of Robert Fuoss, Ben Hibbs' managing editor, and Kenneth Stuart, the art director. A section of the sixth floor—the editorial offices in the Philadelphia building—was blocked off. "It was a Project X sort of thing, locked doors and the whole rigmarole," said a former editor. "You'd have thought it was the CIA building an atomic bomb—covered easels, locks on the desks, tight mouths." Close at the elbows of Fuoss, Stuart and the other changeover architects was an eager young chap named Clay Drewry Blair, Jr., who had been hired by Hibbs in 1957 as an associate editor in the Washington bureau and brought to the Philadelphia office about the same time the new format planning began. In terse memos he offered suggestions on how to "put some jazz" into the layouts; he argued and fought for his ideas, to the point of raised-voice rows with others on the team. For months the group worked—photographers, "idea" men such as Blair, a group of newly hired layout artists who had designed, among other things, record jackets and movie titles. Trial issues were produced, studied and condemned; in all, about six versions of the "new *Post*" came out of the Project X headquarters before the final selection was made.

In the spring and early summer of 1961 the advertising and promotional ballyhoo began. From June through September, Curtis pumped a hefty $1 million into the campaign to call attention to the "new *Post*." *Post* publicity men generated items and stories about the "exciting new magazine"; advertising salesmen were given sample pages for their briefcases, to show to agencies and clients as an example of the "magazine that's going to shake the world this fall." Teaser promotion ads screamed, "LIKE NO OTHER MAGAZINE YOU HAVE EVER READ BEFORE," and promised, "SUDDENLY READING BECOMES AN ADVENTURE." In August, Curtis rented the ballroom of a New York hotel and put the new *Post* on display before Madison Avenue. The theme in all the buildup was, "Look how wonderful we're about to become"; that the *Post* was now in the hands of "forward-looking staff members." Curtis president Robert A. MacNeal did his part to help further the atmosphere of optimism. Curtis advertising lineage, he said in June, had "hit bottom" and would show "substantial increases" in the months ahead.

"Keeping Posted," the editor's column at the front of each *Post* issue, advised readers of the coming change in the September 9, 1961, issue. The promotional buildup aimed at Madison Avenue had already caused expressions of concern from long-time subscribers over what was about to happen to "their" *Saturday Evening Post.* The editor's note gave assurances that "fiction will not evaporate," as had been hinted, but "we will be sifting it through a finer screen, averaging three stories and one serial per issue." The column pictured 22 new staff members, averaging twenty-eight years of age. This issue was 68 pages, a shadow of the 200-page toe-crushers produced regularly by George Horace Lorimer; a stripling compared to the 150-pagers of Ben Hibbs. In somewhat of an understatement the *Post* promised that next week's issue of the new *Post* "will be quite an eye-opener."

And indeed it was. The September 16 issue was 148 pages;

and about the only familiar thing on the premises was a Norman Rockwell cover depicting an artist at a board surrounded by *Post* covers dating all the way back to Benjamin Franklin's old *Pennsylvania Gazette*. The words "Saturday Evening" in the title were crammed inside the "O" of "Post." Even Rockwell's signature had been modernized. Somebody with sharp vision, a steady hand and a lot of patience counted 22 type fonts and sizes on the title page alone—a scrambled mess confusing to the mind and the eye, with no discernible pattern or logic.

Internally, the *Post* was editorial anarchy—a bastard conglomeration of splashy modern art, starkly graphic black-and-white photographs, article titles as jumbled as a child's bowl of alphabet soup. Photographs "bled" off the end of pages, with no white-space margin. Previously, *Post* makeup called for a cartoon or short feature—even a one-paragraph quotation or *bon mot*—to break the monotony of pages of type. The new *Post* put the cartoons and jokes into a single section. Only one portion of the magazine appeared untouched by the revolution. The articles themselves, beneath the blatant makeup, contained few surprises—an article about divorcées, an article about the "new" Japan, a personality sketch of Broadway producer David Merrick, a continuation of the memoirs of Casey Stengel. A new column, "Speaking Out," had been billed by Fuoss as "a forum for oddballs to pop off." The forum, however, proved no more Cassandraish than the Letter-to-the-Editors column of a daily newspaper. The "oddballs" denounced dirty books, dirty movies, husbands who won't go to the doctor, the Parent-Teachers Association, with humdrum indignation.

Readers howled even louder about the new *Post* than Madison Avenue had about the old one. Some sample letters in issues immediately following the change:

> If Benjamin Franklin ever saw this new magazine, he would come back and electrocute you with his kite. If you people need money so badly, I suggest you pump gas weekends rather than clutter up *every page* with ads.

Please change it back. There are hundreds of "new," "shiny," perky tabloid-type magazines on the newsstand—but only one *Post*. Would you put fingernail polish on the Statue of Liberty?

The *Post* makes a gaudy corpse. . . . I do not wish to view the remains. . . . Please . . . cancel my subscription.

. . . It was like seeing a wonderful old friend with whom you felt very comfortable and knew very well, turned into a slick, dressed-up and not very interesting copy of something you have never liked or enjoyed having around.

If you are trying to confuse your readers, you have done it. Norman Rockwell and Hazel are the only old-time friends I found.

In an editors' note, the *Post* claimed that "a poll of readers shows that a solid majority approves the change." Not exactly true. For a while, angry mail cascaded into Independence Square at the rate of 10,000 pieces a week; editors sighed wearily at the pouches of abuse left three times daily by the mailmen. The mail was a small percentage of the six and one-half million readers. But, when weighed in the framework of the number of people who were mad enough to put their feelings on paper, it was tantamount to a resounding, unmistakable indictment of the new format. The *Post* threw some of the approving ones into the Letters to the Editor column and gave the impression that public opinion was balanced. The *Post* didn't fool even itself. The voice of the people drowned out any attempts at phony optimism. The critical letters were furious for weeks, especially from the forty-to-fifty-year bracket out west of the Alleghenies, the *Post* heartland forgotten by the *Post* when it put on rouge and lipstick in the hope of attracting an affectionate pinch from Madison Avenue. Readers griped about the dropping of Hibbs features such as "You Be the Judge," in which readers matched wits with lawyers on a given set of facts;

and "The Perfect Squelch," where readers told weekly how they got in the last word. Cartoons lumped together on a single page were "like hitting a sizable piece of undiluted nutmeg in a pumpkin pie—UGH," wrote a man in Sonora, Mexico. "Why junk almost everybody over forty? I have been betrayed—and many others with me," said another reader.

The *Post* kept its audience off balance. An October 14 cover was in a familiar, chucklesome mold: commuters running through a sudden shower for station wagons at the Gwynedd Valley station on the Pennsylvania Railroad's Main Line. The next week brought something best described as "shattered modern art," pegged to a novel excerpt, "The Peace Makers," by Marquis Childs. So striking was this cover that the *Post* dared not serve it up cold. A note said: "Although the *Post's* traditional cover painting will continue to appear regularly, we shall occasionally use covers of *pure design* and from time to time publish a photographic cover." The photographic cover followed shortly, of President Dwight D. Eisenhower, "only the fourth since 1943."

Norman Rockwell occasionally showed up outside, but confusion reigned between the covers. Four poems by Robert Graves were presented in such a typographical mishmash that on first glance they appeared to be part of an adjacent institutional ad. The makeup innovations were jarring. Deep in the midst of a short story a reader would find something like this:

"Dave got the fingers of his other hand into a crack in the wall and clung desperately as Garbo's

**voice came to him,
'Hang on,' it said
with furious urgency."**

A reader responded to this gimmickry:

"It is most idiotic and disconcerting to be

reading alone and
suddenly find
text which has

no reason whatsoever to be emphasized broken out in big bold letters. Is this supposed to make your magazine more interesting and readable?"

If so, the *Post* changed its mind on this innovation faster than on any other. The typographical shouts were quietly dropped before the end of the year.

Staid *Post* readers didn't like the intrusion of *Playboy*-scented artwork in their magazine. A picture of a buxom, bikini-clad girl romping on the beach in the November 4 issue drew protesting letters from Scarsdale, New York, Ann Arbor, Michigan, and Louisville, Kentucky. ("Disgusted and nauseated.")

As a sort of last straw, the *Post* managed to offend even its own contributors. Doubly unfortunate, because people who make their living with a typewriter are able to produce a disproportionate amount of noise when angered.

One victim of the razzle-dazzle was Cleveland Amory (*Who Killed Society?*), one-time "Postscript" editor who contributed an article on society to a December, 1961, issue. To his shock, Amory opened the *New Yorker* to find a $10,000 double-page center-spread promotion advertisement on his piece. Or was it a promotion ad? Amory wasn't sure, he told his *Saturday Review* column readers. "In fact, in the entire advertisement, the only favorable mention we found was the line, 'If you are an aspiring egotist, you will find this feature full of helpful hints.'" The approach left Amory with several questions. "Chief of these was the fact that though we could easily see what the advertisement was against—it was against us—we couldn't for the life of us see what it was *for*." He called the *Post* and found that not

a single editorial staff member—nor the promotion manager—
had seen the ad before publication, a radical departure from
past policy. Tracing the source further, Amory called Batten,
Barton, Durstine & Osborn, where he found not one but three
Post promotion departments—for single copies, for space sales,
and for a "promotion promotion department." One executive
told Amory that "we were dissatisfied with the old *Post,* product-
wise. It's getting wider and wider acceptance, pull-wise." The
promotion writer had a ready explanation for the deriding
treatment given Amory: "That wasn't an ad for you; that was
an ad to get the admen who read the *New Yorker* to read the
Post to put their ads in *that.*"

What went wrong with the new *Post?* In retrospect the reasons are obvious: by drumbeating the new format so far in
advance Curtis said implicitly that something was wrong with
the old *Post.* Why, then, should advertisers buy space in a magazine so decrepit that even its own publishers agreed it should
be renovated? The promotional campaign raised such expecta-
tions that advertisers and readers were foreordained to disap-
pointment, regardless of what Curtis produced. Suspicious
advertisers took a "show-me" stance and held back scheduling
of campaigns until they could see what they were buying. Reac-
tions to the *Post,* when it appeared, ranged from lukewarm at
best to coolness and downright dislike. Hibbs had proven in
1942 that it isn't impossible to make a change in a magazine's
format—provided an editor does so gradually, without scaring
the reader, giving him a new fillip each issue until suddenly the
entire magazine is spanking new. The Project X team, in effect,
tried to introduce an original magazine to an audience which
had been buying something diametrically different. The carpen-
ters overcorrected. Rather than painting and fixing a somewhat
run-down old house, they junked it, destroying the good features along with the bad. The *Post* strained to be similar to,
but not identical with, *Life* and *Look.* It fell short; in the
process it lost its own identity. Persons who previously bought
the *Post* as a "text" magazine found themselves shortchanged:

The issue of February 10, 1962, had seven full pages of photographs; there were two title pages filled completely with art—one-tenth of the content stolen from the reader to "pretty up" the magazine.

The magazine was reformed on orders of Madison Avenue. Confronted with what it had asked for, Madison Avenue didn't like it. A joke went through the trade, "A couple of designers had too many martinis at lunch and brought the new *Post* back to the office with them." Another criticism perhaps had more validity. "The *Post* sought to go, in one week, from small-town America to Park Avenue," said a man who was selling ads for *Post* at the time. "It was designed by art directors for a small core of advertising executives. Your average reader profile isn't that of the adman."

After a surge of lineage in the first issues, the advertising agencies again turned their backs on the *Post*—leaving it alone in the winter with its fancy new coat, its old friends alienated, the new friends it had sought unimpressed. By November 4 the *Post* was down to 82 pages.

Robert Fuoss ruefully referred visitors to a Churchillian quote mounted over his desk: *We conferred endlessly and futilely, and arrived at the place from which we started. Then we did what we knew we had to do in the first place, and we failed as we knew we would.*

Since Hibbs' name was on the masthead of the new *Post* as editor until he retired at the end of 1961, he muses now, "It was inevitable I see in retrospect that people say I was canned." This isn't true. In 1960, while Curtis was still profitable, Hibbs quietly told MacNeal that he wanted to retire, at the age of sixty, at the end of 1961. "I always said a magazine should change editors at least every twenty years. Also, a man deserves to save some of his older years for a less hectic life. Every night for twenty years I carried home a briefcase of manuscripts. During that time we never accepted a social engagement for a week night." Now a senior editor for *Reader's Digest,* he politely but firmly declines to discuss anything that has happened at Curtis since he left. In essence, Hibbs feels that Curtis was a loyal employer; that it wouldn't be proper for him to be drawn into the situation there now.

Slowly, inexorably, Robert A. MacNeal saw the Curtis Publishing Company slipping away from him. In January, 1962, advertising volume was off a full 25 percent; first-quarter losses were $4,727,337—an ominous harbinger of disaster. Late in March, Curtis stirred itself in a unique, 4,000-word "Statement of Policy" directed at the publishing world. The statement was intended to restore public confidence in Curtis by laying to rest rumors about its stability. To the discerning reader, however, the words were those of a man fumbling with the barn door lock while a prize steed galloped out of sight into the darkness.

"We believe that now is the time to adjust our entire publishing operation to bring it into line with modern needs and opportunities," MacNeal said. "Television, which barely existed a dozen years ago, has attracted hundreds of millions of advertising dollars, some of which might otherwise have gone to magazines."

Then MacNeal announced changes that revealed the word "adjust" in his statement to be a euphemism for retreat. The *Post* was cut to 45 issues by combining into biweeklies the issues for the Fourth of July through Labor Day, the last of December and early January. The *Ladies' Home Journal* and *American Home* were cut back to ten issues.

In an unconcealed bid for advertising revenue MacNeal also said the *Journal* would accept liquor advertising for the first time. (Excerpt from a 1938 *Journal* house ad: "It is common courtesy not to receive guests in your home who might embarrass other guests . . . influence some of them to their detriment. The *Journal* believes that every reader has the right to decide such questions for herself. *We will not try to influence you by taking liquor advertising.*")

Once again MacNeal sought to charge others for Curtis troubles. He blamed the 1961 loss of advertising revenue "partly from television competition with magazines in general, partly from a hesitance in the placement of advertising in several Curtis magazines during their reorientation period, but mostly because of rumors which cast doubt upon the survival of the company, or of its magazines, or both." The rumors to which MacNeal referred were legion: That the *Post* would be folded and its circulation lists sold to *Look;* that the *Journal* would be merged with the *American Home;* that Curtis itself would be put on the block for the highest bidder.

MacNeal called a slowdown on the drastic formation revisions. "A little less *avant* and a little more *garde,*" he quipped.

The statement was also a surrender to *McCall's* in the circulation race it had been waging with the *Journal*. Only a week previously *McCall's* had stunned Curtis by announcing that it would charge the same rate—$4.85 per thousand copies—for both black-and-white and color advertisements. The *Journal* then was charging $4.37 per thousand for black-and-white and $5.22 for four-color. MacNeal said the *Journal* circulation base would be dropped from 7,000,000 to 6,750,000 in summer, 1962, and 6,500,000 in the winter. Curtis would concentrate on "quality," MacNeal said, and use low-price offers "in moderation" in the future.

Curtis also decided it should try some of that newfangled diversification that *Time-Life* and Cowles had stumbled into in the 1940's and 1950's. Why? "To make our company less acutely affected by the cyclical and seasonal trends of the mass magazine business," MacNeal said in phraseology that could have been lifted from a *Time-Life* annual report two decades earlier. Just an idea, however, no action. The statement didn't mention any specific areas for diversification.

For twenty years, Robert Fuoss had been Ben Hibbs' right-hand man at the *Post,* patiently awaiting his succession to the editor's chair. When he got there he remained only three months before resigning. MacNeal's March announcement told of his replacement by Robert Lee Sherrod, onetime war and foreign correspondent who had joined the *Post* as a Far East correspondent in 1952, becoming managing editor in 1954 and then top assistant to Fuoss. Why did Fuoss quit? The formal statements said only that "irreconcilable differences of opinion with management on matters of policy" had arisen. Friends said Fuoss didn't like the idea of knocking the *Post* down to 45 issues, that he wouldn't edit a magazine under those conditions. Sherrod's new managing editor: Clay Drewry Blair, Jr., sprinting up the *Post* masthead past older, more experienced men.

Instead of bolstering confidence, the MacNeal statement shattered it. Regardless of the reasons, once the Curtis troubles became open and obvious, Madison Avenue had no choice but to appraise with candor its magazines—their chances for survival, and their effectiveness as advertising media. MacNeal and other Curtis executives later termed this stance as malicious; Madison Avenue, however, thinks "realistic" to be a more apt term. "If I recommend that a client spend $100,000 in a magazine, I want to know the magazine is going to appear, and what else is in it," said one adman. Conversely, a memorandum circulated in Cunningham & Walsh, Inc., read in part: "We are careful not to become involved in speculation in publishing futures. . . . We should point out that, in any turbulent situation, the individual magazines involved might perhaps be the victims of capricious trade comment. Many of us recall that, in those days when *Collier's*, *Liberty* and *Quick* were having problems in securing advertising, they were delivering to the advertisers maximum visibility and high value in respect to circulation per dollar."

Robert A. MacNeal's one attempt at revolution was a garish public failure, the impact all the more severe because the new format had been billed loudly as the salvation of the *Saturday Evening Post*. Instead, it proved to be tinsel and noise. The crowd attracted by the ballyhoo saw only the further degrading of the Grey Lady of Independence Square, and went away either chuckling sadistically or feeling shameful over her treatment. MacNeal kept trying—futilely, belatedly, and abortively.

He cut the company's contribution to an employee's pension plan; he closed an electroplating subsidiary and saved a thimble of cash on the annual payroll. Curtis dumped more of its securities to lessen the impact of the mounting operating loss.

But he was two decades too late. The pace of crisis now was to quicken at Curtis Publishing Company.

Chapter Six

IN the high-powered world of corporate finance, an ailing company attracts the attention of outside money as quickly as the scent of fresh blood draws packs of ravenous wolves. Curtis Publishing Company was no exception. The smell of trouble drifted northward from Philadelphia to Wall Street beginning late in the 1950's, carried in the annual reports which investment firms study as closely as a general does his daily battle dispatches. The intelligence buried in the fine type of the reports started the investor groups sniffing around Curtis Publishing Company.

What they sensed there was exciting—a treasure trove of potential profits, sitting unguarded and neglected on Independence Square. Here was a company with revenues of $250 million annually, yet far shy of proportionate profits. Curtis' assets were grossly understated; the 250,000 acres of timberland, for example, were carried on the books at only $3 per acre, whereas the actual value was $10 to $15. The recapitalization program of 1938–40 had left Curtis with two classes of preferred dividend stock; in the opinion of analysts, both were underpriced. The $3 dividend preferred was selling for $22 to $25 per share, yet in the event of liquidation, either voluntary or involuntary, holders were entitled to $65 a share and unpaid dividends prior to any distribution of assets on other issues. The 60-cent dividend prior preferred, being traded for less than $10, had a liquidation value of $25 per share. Even though in trouble, Curtis had a net working capital of $36 million at the end of 1960. Yet on the revenues of $250 million Curtis management came up with a deficit of 19 cents a common share after payment of preferred dividends.

Corporate raiders saw a multitude of moneymaking possibilities in Curtis:

—To modernize its woeful management and turn the rich flow of advertising revenues into a profit simply by overhauling the existing corporate structure.

—To streamline the company by selling off some of the physical holdings and perhaps one or two of the magazines and continuing the *Post* as a rejuvenated pacemaker for the remainder of the publishing empire.

—To arrange a suitable marriage for Curtis and another firm that could put to use its printing and distribution facilities and impending tax carry-over.

—To throw Curtis cold-bloodedly on the open market and sell it piecemeal for whatever price could be obtained. Under this thinking the tradition-rich *Saturday Evening Post* was nothing more than six and one-half million names on a circulation list and a file cabinet of purchased stories and articles.

For all its history, tradition and long skein of profit-making years through 1961, Curtis was in actuality an easy target when the corporate raiders hove alongside and sent up a boarding party. Working control of the company was in the hands of Cyrus H. K. Curtis' heirs. And persons long connected with the Curtis organization said the heirs apparently were content with a humdrum approach to publishing. "They seemed to think that making a lot of money was vulgar, that it would all go to the government in taxes," one man said. "They were also humane— a person worked for Curtis for life." (Cary W. Bok chuckled when apprised of the comment that he thought money was "vulgar." "We've always had the philosophy of taking all we can earn," he said. "I have no qualms about profits.")

Curtis Publishing Company has what might be termed an interlocking heirship. Cyrus Curtis and his wife, Louisa Knapp Curtis (the author of the first *Ladies' Home Journal* columns) had only one child, Mary Louise Curtis, born in 1876. At the age of sixteen she fell under the charm of Edward W. Bok, 13 years her senior. They married after a four-year engagement and had two sons, W. Curtis Bok, born in 1897, and Cary W. Bok, born in 1905. Mrs. Bok was widowed in 1930. In 1943, at the age of sixty-six, she surprised almost everyone in Philadelphia by marrying Efrem Zimbalist, the violinist and director of the Curtis Institute of Music, which she had founded. Zimbalist was 12 years her junior.

Both Bok and Cyrus Curtis made personal fortunes from Curtis Publishing Company. In addition to his $100,000 a year annual salary—highest then of any editor in America—Bok was given stock in the company, which Curtis had incorporated in 1892. Curtis rewarded the *Journal* editor with sizable chunks of the magazine's profits; and Bok also made a conventional fortune from the books he wrote in retirement. When Bok quit as editor in 1919 after 30 years, he said, "I am going to play. I went to work when I was thirteen years old and I have been working ever since. That means 43 years, and I have not been out of a job one day. Now I am going to enjoy myself while I can still enjoy a good time."

The rest of his life Bok devoted to writing, philanthropy, music and peace. His autobiography, *The Americanization of Edward Bok*, won the Pulitzer Prize for literature in 1920; he also wrote Cyrus Curtis' biography, *Man from Maine*, and four other books during the 1920's. Anonymously, he underwrote the Philadelphia Orchestra for $250,000 over five years, then ramrodded a campaign that insured its financial stability for years to come. He endowed, for $150,000, a Woodrow Wilson chair of literature at Princeton. At his winter home at Mountain Lake, Florida, amidst a bird sanctuary, he built the famed "Singing Tower," a gleaming marble edifice crowned with a 61-bell carillon, which was dedicated by President Coolidge on February 1, 1929. Bok died of a heart attack in the shadow of the tower the next year. His $23,713,981 estate included $17,445,839 in Curtis Publishing Company holdings; $2 million of the estate endowed the American Foundation, Inc., for support of the Singing Tower shrine and other philanthropies; the bulk of the remainder went to his wife and two sons.

Cyrus Curtis gave an estimated $9 million to charity before his death in 1933; in his lifetime he was called "Philadelphia's greatest asset." He raised $5 million to build the city's Franklin Institute, a science museum; with his daughter he bestowed $12.5 million on the Curtis Institute of Music, whose graduates are a Who's Who of American music—Leonard Bernstein, Gian-Carlo Menotti, Samuel Barber, Marc Blitzstein; almost half the membership of the Philadelphia Orchestra at any given time. Only one thing is required of an applicant: that he have a talent worthy of cultivation.

Curtis left his controlling common stock in a trust with a provision that the company continue along the course he had charted for it: "Believing that the success of the Curtis Publishing Company will be promoted and best insured by the continuance, as far as possible, of the present management and policy, it is my wish and I direct that during the continuance of this trust my common stock of the Curtis Publishing Company shall be retained by my trustees and shall not be sold *unless some extraordinary contingency shall arise* [italics mine] making it desirable to sell and then only in the event that my trustees unanimously agree." The trust was to continue through the life of his daughter and her two sons; the seven trustees, over the years, have been composed of the immediate heirs (now Cary Bok and Mrs. Zimbalist) and Curtis executives and employees who reflect the family's thinking (Bok's personal secretary, for instance, and Robert A. MacNeal). The trust holds 17.3 percent of the outstanding Curtis stock; another 14.7 percent is in the hands of the heirs individually or of persons or foundations associated with them—in essence, control of 32 percent of the company.

The logical successors to Curtis were his grandsons, Curtis and Cary. The reasons they were not involve some rather tangled family history. Bok encouraged the boys to be individualists—to choose their own schools, plan their own summer vacations, select their own careers. Stated with a certain simplification, Curtis went to the left, Cary went to the right. In an era when the *Saturday Evening Post* was the conservative organ of America, Curtis became a civil libertarian, internationalist, New Dealer, death penalty opponent and, for a while in the 1930's, a supporter of the Russian Revolution. Curtis quit Williams College before graduation to become a navy lieutenant in the First World War, then entered the University of Virginia law school. Penology, social work and the bar proved greater attractions than publishing. He came back to Philadelphia as an assistant district attorney, got himself appointed to the board of Eastern State Penitentiary, the State's toughest, and worked actively for reform. To see the conditions firsthand, he arranged with the warden to go behind bars as a prisoner—then had to call off the project when newspapers got wind of it and authorities were fearful the convicts would kill a prosecutor found in their midst. In 1927 he joined the information section of the League of Nations in Geneva; his interest in foreign affairs stimulated, he went to Russia in 1932 with his wife. After two months of an ordinary tour Bok decided he wasn't seeing the inner workings of the country. He sent Mrs. Bok back to Philadelphia, moved in with a lower-class Russian family, and got jobs in a candy factory and as a chauffeur for Intourist, the State travel agency. Bok came home three months later, traveling second-class, wearing workman's clothes and enthusiastic about the Soviets having "the answer to the future." George Horace Lorimer, by then the Curtis chief executive officer, made loud noises heard all over Independence Square. The mere mention of the Russian Revolution to him was anathema; praise for it provoked apoplexy. "That damned Bolshevik," a surviving friend quotes Lorimer as raging. "He'll never do anything in MY company if I have anything to do about it." Divorced and remarried, Bok returned to law.

In addition to Lorimer's latter-day opposition, there was also a mysterious clause in the will of Edward Bok—written in 1926, when Curtis Bok was a young Philadelphia lawyer—which has never been explained. The will provided for the sons and Bok's wife to share equally in the estate, then added:

> I have, however, with the assistance and guidance of said son [Curtis Bok], and my executors and trustees, prepared and signed a memorandum dated the same date as this, my will. And I request that he or they will, as nearly as circumstances in their discretion permit, carry out my will, as expressed in said memorandum. Said memorandum is not to be probated with my will, nor filed in court or elsewhere.
>
> I direct that my son and my executors and trustees shall place this memorandum in a safe-deposit box in a trust company in Philadelphia, and that they will provide for safeguards satisfactory to them for its preservation. . . .

The contents of the memorandum were, and are, a secret. But cryptic clues point to the conclusion that one salient point was that Curtis Bok disassociate himself from the magazines. In the middle 1950's, when he was a Philadelphia judge and an accomplished author of essays and novels, a *Holiday* editor asked him for a whimsical piece on the law. Bok's reply was to the effect that nothing under his signature could ever appear in Curtis magazines. He was a trustee of his grandfather's estate but never took an active role in company affairs.

But Curtis never displayed any signs of longing, however, for a career at Curtis Publishing. Urbane, sophisticated, intellectual, he served 20 years as a Common Pleas Court judge and later 4 years on the State Supreme Court. (His appointment to the bench was in 1935, after his support of George Earle, first Democratic governor of Pennsylvania in the century. "A judge is a lawyer who is friendly with the governor," quipped a fictional character in one of his books a few years later.) Prosecutors and police didn't care for Bok because he expressed more interest in reforming people than in imprisoning them. Frequently testimony so moved him that he would set a man free—and put money in his pockets. "The first offense is a regrettable happening," he said in one of his books. "Once it has been committed, devices should be applied so accurate and sure that it will not be repeated." He fought capital punishment as a jurist and as an author, putting into novel form in two books his abhorrence of the use of a mechanism as inexact as a jury to take a man's life. He also opposed censorship, making a shambles of a restrictive Pennsylvania obscenity law in the 1940's by reading, then approving for sale, novels by James T. Farrell, William Faulkner and Erskine Caldwell. "My New Deal brother," Cary Bok often said of the judge.

To the other brother, Cary, the seashore of his grandfather's native Maine was more appealing than a publishing house on Independence Square. Following graduation from Williams College in 1926, he studied at Oxford for two years and had rank-and-file jobs in the advertising and circulation departments. As treasurer from 1937 to 1940, he put through the recapitalization plan that eliminated the bulk of the preferred stock; as $1-a-year publisher of the *Evening Ledger* during its last years of life, he frankly told editors one day, sitting on a desk and swinging his legs, "Fellows, I know nothing about this part of the business; I'm counting on you." The years after 1940 he spent primarily in Maine; he built boats during the Second World War, coming to Philadelphia for board meetings. Several serious illnesses in the late 1950's effectively removed him from any active role in the company during the period when the blowup developed. Many company old-timers never see Cary Bok at all; but they know the name well: his signature is printed on Curtis payroll checks.

Cyrus Curtis had been a shy man, almost painfully so, and his sole relaxation came from music. Mrs. Zimbalist, tall, thin, and regal, shared both her father's snapping brown eyes and his love for a skillfully orchestrated symphony. For four decades Mrs. Zimbalist has been a bountiful supplier of funds to Philadelphia music. A few years ago she telephoned Eugene Ormandy, conductor of the Philadelphia Orchestra, and asked sweetly, "Eugene, darling, are you standing? Please sit down." Assured he had, she continued, "I'm giving you that pipe organ you've been longing for." The startled Ormandy said, "Do you realize how much it will cost?" "Don't worry about that," said Mrs. Zimbalist. She didn't either. The organ, purchased for an estimated $175,000, is now the center piece for the Academy of Music, where the Philadelphia Orchestra performs.

Ormandy reciprocates Mrs. Zimbalist's affection. One winter evening a few years back, stragglers were in the Academy lobby after a concert when they heard the orchestra suddenly burst into full voice again. A couple peeked back into the auditorium and saw Mrs. Zimbalist in her box on the orchestra floor, smiling contentedly as Ormandy conducted a favored piece for her in privacy.

Mrs. Zimbalist was listed as a director and a senior vice-president of Curtis Publishing Company but left the conduct of her father's companies in the hands of family retainers Walter D. Fuller and Robert A. MacNeal. In her later years, periodically Mrs. Zimbalist's mammoth closed limousine would halt outside the Curtis building and she would emerge, "two rather peculiar dogs on a leash," one man remembers it. Ben Hibbs was her favorite among the Curtis editors and executives, and she would politely request an audience with him, always insisting, "Don't disturb him; it's really not very important." At annual meetings she enjoyed a traditional jest with Fuller. "She would very respectfully ask Mr. Fuller that her salary as a director be doubled," said a retired executive. "Very gravely he would reply that economic conditions were such that this could not be done. She would thank him and sit down. Of course, her salary was only one dollar. But she and Mr. Fuller seemed to enjoy the byplay."

If the Curtis heirs were complacently content with the state of their company, another group of shareholders definitely was not. These were the common stock owners, who went from 1933 to 1950 without a dime of dividend on their investment. Here is how dividends have varied in the last four decades (adjusted to allow for splits in 1924 and 1929):

1924—$10.50	1931—$4.50
1925— 13.50	1932— 1.00
1926— 8.50	1933–50—nil
1927— 9.00	1951–56— 0.20
1928— 10.00	
1929— 7.00	1957–60— 0.35
1930— 7.00	1961–64—nil

The first stockholder revolt threatened in 1940 but was prevented when Cary Bok worked out the recapitalization plan under which arrearages were eliminated in exchange for debentures due in 1955 (and which were retired ahead of schedule in 1946) plus common stock.

This kept the dissidents quiet for ten years. In 1951, however, another uprising resulted in the seating of the first non-Philadelphian on the board of directors. A Massachusetts investor owning 1,300 shares of Curtis preferred and 85,200 shares of common waged a proxy fight among the 16,200 persons owning shares. His backers, banded together as the Independent Stockholders Committee, based their campaign on the nonpayment of dividends in common stock and lack of a program for retiring the remainder of the preferred stock.

In rebuttal Fuller pointed to the beginnings of a comeback: that $28.5 million in arrearages had been paid to preferred stockholders since 1941; that the way was clear for a common dividend; that preferred dividend requirements had been lowered by more than $2 million a year under Bok's recapitalization plan. Nonetheless, the dissidents elected Walter R. Reitz, an upstate Pennsylvania oilman, to the board. Curtis management and the heirs, of course, retained control with six other seats. Reitz' election had a psychological, but no practical, effect on the board. The other directors ignored him in consultations;

they were distinctly cool to the non-Philadelphian who had penetrated the Curtis inner circle.

Later in the 1950's the stockholders complained again; the board, they said, was so heavily laden with Philadelphians that it was parochial. New faces mean new ideas, perhaps even breakaway from the stagnation already pressing in on the company. MacNeal yielded—to a point. He increased the board in size and dropped from it Curtis executives who had *ex officio* seats; the new positions went to investment and insurance interests. But MacNeal vested actual working control of the company in an executive committee which included the same executives and editors who had been removed from the board in the reorganization.

The shufflings and realignments notwithstanding, Curtis had a pool of unhappy stockholders who felt no loyalty to a company which didn't give them a return on their investment. A former Curtis executive with reportorial training vows he can recollect to the syllable the answer Fuller once gave a little old lady who arose at a stockholders meeting and asked when she could expect a dividend on the common stock left by her husband: "In view of the improved competitive position, and unless there is some sharp convulsion in the national financial fabric, I believe we would be justified in saying that the prospects for any early upturn are viewed with a prudence not unfavorable." "Oh, Mr. Fuller," she cried, "that's what you have been saying for so long, for so very, very long."

In this climate the hard-nosed investor groups, the professionals whose business it is to appraise a company coldly, objectively and without sentiment, began looking at Curtis. They liked what they saw. They began accumulating Curtis common, quietly at first, so as not to push up the market price.

In April, 1960, the letters "CPC"—symbol for Curtis Publishing Company—began showing on the ticker tape of the New York Stock Exchange with increasing regularity. Between January and July, 1961, some 1.4 million shares of Curtis common stock changed hands, more than twice the volume for all of 1960 and about 40 percent of the existing common stock. Wall Street soon learned that the buying was being done by Carl M. Loeb, Rhoades & Co., but couldn't find the identity of the beneficial owners. Brokerage houses are not required to tell—and usually don't tell—for whom they are acting in such deals. But one thing was common knowledge about the Loeb firm: it specialized in finding sick corporations and making the most of them. Robert A. MacNeal couldn't, or wouldn't, tell what was going on. "I have heard," he said in the summer of 1961, "that people are accumulating stock and that it amounted to around half a million shares, but I don't know who they are." At this stage Cary Bok professed doubt that the take-over would succeed. "There may be some smart hombre trying to get control," he said, "but if he is, he hasn't been in touch with us about it."

The Loeb firm didn't have a clear field. Another syndicate organized by Lewis Strauss, the onetime chairman of the Atomic Energy Commission, also collected stock. More importantly, it dispatched Douglas Black, president of Doubleday & Co., the book publisher, to Philadelphia to look for ways to either buy or wrest control of Curtis from the then-powers. Strauss' group didn't have sufficient holdings to win a proxy fight, and it knew it. For a while, however, Curtis management didn't. Black became a familiar sight in the Curtis executive offices; Doubleday liked the prospects of a marriage with Curtis because of the company's printing and papermaking facilities and distribution system; additionally, the prospect of joint publication features, in magazine and hardback, were enticing. Curtis directors had a friendly feeling toward the New York house, too; under the tentative terms talked about by Black, Curtis could preserve its corporate identity—even perhaps as the dominant company.

In the meantime, Loeb continued hustling Curtis common stock, even while Doubleday talks were in progress. Other principals emerged—Treves & Co. and J. R. Williston & Beane, both brokerage firms. Treves often worked in tandem with Loeb in this type of deal so that the true power of each could be shielded as long as possible. Once they moved into the open, the symbol CPC danced constantly on the ticker tape. Curtis watched the rapid turnover with fascination—and also with curiosity about who would be the Curtis boss when it all ended.

The answer came in mid-spring. A brisk-walking, brisk-talking lawyer named Milton Gould called Philadelphia and requested an immediate appointment with MacNeal. His message was to the point: Gould represented Treves & Co. and J. R. Williston & Beane, interests which wanted a voice in Curtis affairs, and they would like to start with two seats on the board of directors. All very nicely put. No nasty talk about a proxy fight or anything like that. MacNeal listened silently and wrote neat notes to himself and was cordial when he bade Gould farewell.

When MacNeal told the Curtis board of his visitor, the discussion was desultory; the decision was to give the newcomers two seats by enlarging the board membership to thirteen. Just how much stock the combine had isn't known to this day. "I heard all sorts of figures, anywhere from six hundred thousand to a million," said Cary Bok. "That isn't very important. In a situation like that, a threat is sometimes as good as actuality."

With control of 32 percent of the Curtis stock, why didn't the Curtis heirs fight the intrusion? "There are many reasons," Bok said one winter morning in 1964, during a rambling interview at his seaside home in Maine.

"First of all, you never are assured of absolute control unless you have 51 percent. We have only 32 percent; we were unsure of what the other people had.

"Secondly, the Curtis board is elected with cumulative voting. The others could have pooled their votes and elected one director for sure; probably two, and possibly three."

Third, Bok said, the company didn't relish the idea of a public proxy fight during a time of internal stress. First-quarter losses that year had already touched $4 million—more red ink than went on the books during all of 1961. Curtis management had more important things to do than scurry around the countryside soliciting proxies from widows and small-time investors. The Wall Street groups, on the other hand, specialized in just this type of scurrying. Had Curtis chosen to fight, there was at least a 50-50 chance that Curtis would have been licked. Management and the heirs feared this, because they didn't know any more about the investors' long-range intentions than they did of the investors' holdings.

Additionally, Curtis by this time was so desperate for cash that it was ready to befriend anyone who came along and offered new ideas and fresh leadership. That spring it was forced to peddle two of its strongest sidelines to raise operating cash. Curtis sold part of its holdings in Bantam Books, Inc., and Treasure Books, Inc., to Grosset & Dunlap, Inc., for a $4.8 million profit. Both companies were returning a profit. But the need for immediate cash was overpowering and the book subsidiaries were something that could be conveniently cut from the empire.

The new seats went to Gould and to R. McLean Stewart, an investment banker. Gould was a member of the law firm of Gallop, Climenko & Gould; his small but bustling office represented Peter Treves and had an impressive record for corporate infighting. As general counsel, his firm helped straighten out F. L. Jacobs Co. after it was looted by promoter Alexander Guterma in the 1950's; it also was lawyer for the winning side in the protracted fight for the multimillion-dollar Mesabi Iron Ore Co. in 1960. The same month of the Curtis coup, investment groups represented by Gould also shouldered their way into power at 20th Century-Fox Film Corp. Gould became a director there almost simultaneously with his Curtis election. As a Curtis director he represented Treves and J. R. Williston & Beane.

Stewart, the second new director, was a former Wall Street banker then involved in oil exploitation and development through a Houston firm, Austral Oil Co., and also in two venture capital concerns, Burden, Fox & Stewart, of Houston, in which he was managing partner; and William A. M. Burden & Co., of New York. Curtis directors found Stewart to be a quiet, affable man with the knack of asking penetrating questions of company officers, and then making suggestions which when tested were found to be uncannily sound. Cary Bok, a man not prone to loose praise, says Stewart "made a real contribution; we were happy to have him."

The man to watch, the incumbents decided in a hurry, was Gould. In announcing the elections, MacNeal went out of his way to say that the new directors did not join the board "as a wrecking crew."

Gould, however, had the knack of making people uneasy, particularly the middle-echelon executives who had the most to fear from a merger or a liquidation. Some of these men are still convinced that the investor groups came into Curtis with the intention of liquidating it.

Soon after their election, Curtis held a luncheon for the new directors in the Downtown Club, adjacent to the Curtis offices, to introduce them to various executives. One official, his tongue loosened both by martinis and by anxiety over his future, got up enough nerve to ask Gould point-blank if he thought liquidation was the solution. "Gould smiled and said, 'No,' but he wasn't very convincing," this man said.

In an interview that spring Gould said he sought the directorship because the brokerage houses "had taken a substantial financial position [in Curtis] and then became alarmed" at the pell-mell acceleration of operating losses. Gould said in public what he was telling the directors in private: that Curtis' trouble was attributable to "an inability to adapt to changing markets ...new and energetic management is needed."

With that statement—a rough approximation of what he also said at the first directors meeting he attended—Gould signed Robert MacNeal's death warrant as Curtis president. All he needed now was to round up enough votes to fill out the firing squad.

Gould depicted himself as basically a litigator, a man who could get the facts and state them lucidly to prove his position. All spring he roamed through Curtis ledger books, noting an item here, an item there, looking for the key that would restore Curtis' vigor. He went about this task with a detachment that both impressed and stunned onlookers. ("He's the original man with ice water in his veins," says a fellow director.) Gould put the same sentiment into more polite, philosophical language: "It takes informed, articulated persuasion to overcome the superstitions, complacencies, outworked notions and old allegiances one can find in a company. But if I have any gift, it's for clear expression and lucidity." He also had the gift of provoking cold shudders among onlookers. "We're not liquidators; we breathe new life into companies," Gould said. "But if the wolves are chasing the sled, you may have to throw one baby off to save the others." He left Curtis guessing which baby was about to land in the snow.

The merger talks with Doubleday, meantime, continued even after the new money got representation on the board. The Strauss group talked both with management and with the Curtis estate trustees. But Doubleday balked at Curtis' asking price of about $20 per share for common stock at a time when the New York Stock Exchange price was in the $8 range. Several factors made Doubleday wary. Curtis had a liability for advance subscriptions estimated at almost $50 million. Also, Doubleday faced the same question as the existing management: Could it straighten out the *Saturday Evening Post?* Then came a tragic interruption—the death, on May 22, 1962, of Justice Curtis Bok. The talks were postponed, resumed again in the summer, and then broke off altogether.

(Doubleday wasn't the only publisher to express an interest in Curtis in 1961 and 1962, when it became an open secret that Curtis was amenable to discussion with a well-heeled prospective purchaser or merger partner. However, Curtis insiders say that Doubleday progressed farther than anyone else. Other prospects turned and ran after a peek at Curtis' tangled innards. Samuel Newhouse, the newspaper chain owner who probably could make a profit of a junior high school throwaway weekly, acknowledged in 1962 he made a tentative offer for Curtis.

Then he decided "not to touch it" because of the company's decline in advertising and circulation. "Only a fool or a rank speculator would walk into something that scared Sam Newhouse," said an executive of another firm that looked at Curtis.)

Twice during that turbulent spring of 1962 Robert A. MacNeal tried to quit as president. It was no secret to him that the search for a successor was underway; Gould said as much in directors meetings, and the progress of the recruiting drive was discussed openly among company officers. Gould had no opposition on the question of sacking MacNeal when the matter was brought into the open for frank, objective discussion.

"When a company gets into trouble," said Cary Bok, "the boss takes the blame. The boss, in this instance, was Bob MacNeal. MacNeal did enough work at Curtis for three, eight, ten men. But he ran the chariot all alone, holding all sixty-four reins. You just can't do that."

In the early summer, when even the elevator boys at Curtis knew the company was teetering on the brink of financial disaster, MacNeal left for a trip to Europe for the stated reason of looking for a new president. Management people who tried to find his whereabouts to consult on the almost-daily crises got nowhere. "That trip, I think, was the final blow," Bok said, "and it was obvious that MacNeal had to go." Bok had been in a Boston hospital that winter for major surgery; while recuperating at his Maine home, he fell and broke his leg. Under Curtis bylaws he was charged with presiding at board meetings in the absence of MacNeal. A phone call came the day before the meeting: MacNeal was out of town; should the Curtis plane be sent up for him? "Hell, I'm flat on my back in bed," Bok told Philadelphia. "I resign as acting president. Work something out." Walter D. Fuller, the Curtis chairman, and M. Albert Linton, insurance tycoon and chairman of the executive committee, stepped into the breach and ran the board meeting. The directors' decision: fire MacNeal. Because of his long service with the company it was decided to withhold the news until his return from Europe. The search for a successor was still in progress; there was no immediacy about making the announcement.

But the news got out. A Curtis executive said, "One of the newcomers was fearful that MacNeal would get back and sway the board to his side. So he leaked the news to the *Wall Street Journal* within three hours after the secrecy agreement. Of course, with publication the dismissal was a *fait accompli,* and MacNeal was out."

Chapter Seven

THE regime of Matthew Joseph ("Call me Joe") Culligan as president and chief executive officer of Curtis was an exciting one; even those persons who don't agree with what he did for and to Curtis agree that he wrought a permanent change in the character of the firm. Culligan himself claims without hesitation that he saved the Curtis Publishing Company's life, and that any analysis of his record as manager should use that "contribution" as a starting point. Firmly and with undiminished conviction, Culligan insists that "when all the battle reports are in," his position in Curtis history will be recognized—and, most important to Joe Culligan, appreciated. Twenty minutes' exposure to Culligan's defense of Culligan's presidency leaves the faint impression that Curtis directors are derelict because they have not erected a bronze statue of Joe Culligan in their own building or—the National Park Service permitting, as it undoubtedly would—across the street in Independence Square.

A strapping, handsome man with a black patch covering an eye wounded in the Battle of the Bulge, Culligan is a charmer with the frenetic, contagious enthusiasm found in a used-car salesman, an evangelical minister on tour in the hookworm belt or a junior college football cheerleader. Some of the big advertisers who heard Culligan's sales pitch on behalf of Curtis found him mesmerizing; he knocked on their doors in person, whisking around the United States like a jet-borne Flying Dutchman, driven by the compulsion for One More Contract before resting.

The messianic personality is one of the reasons Curtis directors chose Culligan as the Moses to lead them from their financial wilderness. A sharp change in Curtis' image was considered essential; the directors wanted a man who could infuse new vitality into Curtis' daily operations. Seventy years of conservative tradition had to be overcome, both internally and for public show. A 180-degree turnaround in a company's character isn't accomplished by anything short of shock treatment. Secondly, the directors felt that by tapping one of Madison Avenue's "very own," Curtis could reestablish rapport with the advertising agencies. Madison Avenue's discontent with Curtis was swelling daily. The "new *Post*" was a dismal flop, and advertisers showed no enthusiasm for returning even to a toned-down version.

Professionally, Culligan was indeed one of Madison Avenue's "very own," just about what a geneticist would expect Madison Avenue to produce after three generations of specialized inbreeding of mass-marketing ideas. To a man capable of generating sincere personal enthusiasm for a morning television chit-chat show, peddling a vast publishing corporation is only a graduated step forward. Culligan was born, reared and molded in a world where a man's standing is contingent on how well he sells himself and his ideas. His pre-Madison Avenue life is something interviewers have found Culligan passes over quickly, as irrelevant to the "real" Joe Culligan. Culligan was born June 25, 1918, in Eastchester, New York, one of five children of immigrants from County Clare, Ireland. His father, an agent for the alcohol and tobacco tax unit of the Treasury Department, died when he was ten. Culligan spent his childhood in Washington Heights in New York City; he played football, ran track and boxed at All Hallows Institute, run by the Irish Christian brothers; he also was a debater and the class valedictorian. Culligan's first sales-related job was as a greeter at the American Standard Radiator Company's building at the 1939 New York World's Fair. Culligan entered the Army as a private, went through Officers' Candidate School and ranger training, and in December, 1944, found himself a first lieutenant leading a heavy weapons unit in the Battle of the Bulge. In a skirmish a German hand grenade exploded at point-blank range; 22 pieces of shrapnel ripped through Culligan's left eye. Detractors who scoff at Culligan as a showman suggest that the black eyepatch he now wears is solely for effect, that were it not for the impression he made he'd trade it in for a more conventional glass eye. The truth is that the blast destroyed Culligan's eyelid and tear ducts; the eyepatch is not worn by choice. Nonetheless, the battle wound had a modicum of compensatory benefits. Without the patch, Culligan is another good-looking Irishman, ruddy complexion, wavy brown hair touched by bits of gray, lines beginning to show around the face and mouth. With it, he's the man who is remembered, as distinctive in a crowd as the Hathaway shirt man is on a magazine page. He has a confident, best-dressed-man poise and assurance which sets him apart from crowds around him.

Culligan spent seven postwar years preparing for the advertising big time. He sold space for *Good Housekeeping*, the Hearst magazine. He moved to Ziff-Davis Publishing Company and was assigned to *Modern Bride* Magazine, which was floundering hopelessly. In eighteen months Culligan transformed it into a money-maker. "I liked magazines but the glamour and excitement of the broadcasting business attracted me more. I wanted to get a taste of broadcasting." His first taste was another supposedly hopeless situation—Dave Garroway's *Today* show at NBC-TV, which was losing heavily. Culligan turned it around in less than a year, pulling its billings to $10 million in what *Billboard* termed "the greatest annual billing entity in the history of show business." NBC let Culligan run his own sales team; he sought out the bright and the eager, paid them well and gave them free range. Culligan personally went from NBC salesman to NBC vice-president in three years, from 1952 to 1955. During one twelve-month stretch he got 12 raises—and NBC thought him a bargain.

In 1956, General David Sarnoff, the NBC head, put Culligan

in charge of the NBC radio network, which was accumulating seven-figured red ink at the rate of $3 million a year. Culligan thought radio was an assignment to Siberia; he also thought he knew why: "The trouble with radio then was that we had lost the battle of the living room but refused to admit it. We made the mistake of fighting it." Through the market studies to which he pays worshipful attention Culligan located his audience physically—that there were almost as many car radios as home TVs, that the bulk of daytime listening was done by housewives too busy to sit before a TV. Culligan directed his attention toward this vast captive audience, concentrating on news and the same chitchat type of program which Dave Garroway had on TV in the morning. He put a premium on the split-second news scoop; on Culligan's New York desk was a little gray box. A push of a button sent a sub-audible tone over the air which activated a buzzer and a red light through the entire network, a warning that a news flash was coming. Culligan boasted that an NBC reporter could step into a phone booth anywhere in the country and be on network in two minutes. Conquering Siberia took Culligan a bit longer than his previous average—three years. A considerable chopping of deadwood was involved; old-time colleagues say Culligan was reluctant to turn anyone out until he had helped them locate elsewhere. But for overall managerial direction Culligan relied upon a man who later was to play an important role at Curtis—John McLean Clifford, a dour-mouthed California lawyer with a crew cut who watched costs as if the wasted dollars were coming out of his own pockets.

By 1962, Culligan was at Interpublic, Inc., the parent company of McCann-Erickson, the ad agency. His future was carefully mapped: With experience in all media he was ready for leadership in a major advertising firm. Curtis Publishing Company wasn't on Culligan's personal map. Until 1962 all he knew about the firm was that Benjamin Franklin started it (that's what legend and the *Post* masthead said, at any rate) and that it was in trouble.

Accounts of the mechanics of how Culligan met Curtis vary; the consensus says that the prime mover was Milton Gould, lawyer for broker Peter Treves and two other firms, J. R. Williston & Beane and Carl M. Loeb, Rhoades & Co. In the spring of 1962, after the "new money" representatives secured seats on the Curtis board and the decision was made to fire Robert A. MacNeal as president, a three-man committee was appointed to look for a successor. The members were Walter D. Fuller, former Curtis president and chairman; M. Albert Linton, elderly president of Provident Mutual Life Insurance Company in Philadelphia and chairman of the Curtis executive committee; and Moreau Brown, partner in the New York banking house of Brown Brothers, Harriman & Company, which also had sizable Curtis holdings. Gould was designated counsel— i.e., legman—for the committee.

One of the feelers put out by the committee reached Culligan through Gardner (Mike) Cowles, president of Cowles Magazines and Broadcasting. Culligan told Cowles he wasn't interested; that he was enjoying working at Interpublic, had been there for only 26 months, and had a five-year contract.

But the idea stayed in the back of Culligan's mind. He began accumulating more information on Curtis and ideas on what it would take to straighten out the company's affairs. He had three "saves" to his credit, each bigger than the other— *Modern Bride* Magazine, the *Today* show, and NBC radio. To summarize some rather complex reasoning, Culligan began to get the idea he could do the same with Curtis, provided he did obtain the presidency.

The next contact came through Bernard Gallagher, a publishing circulation and management consultant whose news letter, the "Gallagher Report," advises, goads and informs Madison Avenue with a sprightly mixture of agency and media gossip and hard news. Culligan and Barney Gallagher were friends, and Culligan occasionally fed the "Gallagher Report" a news item. In his issue of May 28, 1962, Gallagher listed Culligan as one of two "possible candidates" to replace MacNeal.

Some weeks later Gallagher suddenly found himself right in the middle of the Curtis-president-hunt. "Peter Treves and Gould had Bob MacNeal on the run," he said recently. "I owned a considerable amount of stock myself and had an interest that way. Gould called me on a Tuesday and said there was a directors meeting on Thursday; that they could get Mac-Neal out of the way if they came up with an acceptable candidate. I went through my executive files and Joe was the best I could produce in twenty-four hours." Gallagher brought Culligan, Treves and Gould to his office for their initial meeting, and the committee unanimously agreed the personable Irishman was its choice.

Fuller, who in retirement was running an executive placement service, was asked by the board to check Culligan. An eleven-year chairman of the Magazine Publishers Association, Fuller had the sources to do this task in a hurry. He called industry friends and asked what they thought; the report card was favorable; the committee recommended that Culligan be hired.

Culligan (who wouldn't be interviewed for this book, except for a 20-minute monologue on his managerial abilities) has been quoted on yet another version—that Fuller simply called "leaders of advertising and industry all over the country," said he intended to read a list of names, and "stop me when a name comes up that you think could do the job at Curtis." Culligan's name was the unanimous stopper, according to this version. (Fuller died in December, 1964; his former partner, who took over the executive placement firm, said neither the firm nor Fuller had any active part in the selection.) "Everything was favorable with Culligan in the check—no 'ifs' or 'buts' were put on it," said Cary W. Bok. "And," he added wistfully, in an interview two months after Culligan left the presidency, "for eighteen months it looked like a good decision."

But the Curtis board didn't approve Culligan before long discussion and more opposition than Gould and Fuller apparently anticipated. At a meeting on July 9 some objected that he was "nothing more than an advertising salesman"; these directors questioned whether he had enough solid management background to do the necessary corporate regeneration. They pointed to his lack of executive experience on magazines, saying that the Curtis Publishing Company, after all, was still the second-largest publisher in the nation. And Philadelphia Main-Liners had some openly expressed misgivings about putting a Roman Catholic at the head of the company.

The talent scouts had brought Culligan to Philadelphia for the meeting. For the two and one-half hours the directors met he paced the floor in the Public Ledger Building adjacent to the Curtis Building. Gould had the answers to the objections: Culligan's vigor and dynamism would more than cover any shortcomings he might have. ("So he's an advertising salesman! Anyone here have any objection to Curtis selling more advertising?" broke in a director at one point.) Time and again Gould cited Culligan's record at NBC, when he produced profits from two red-ink projects.

Finally the phone rang in the Public Ledger Building, and someone said to Culligan, "Come on over, Joe; the job's yours." The directors burst into spontaneous applause when Culligan entered the board room; he handshook his way around the table, meeting the majority of the directors for the first time. Within five minutes he was into his first pep talk: that his initial step would be that of "restoring confidence of America's business community" in Curtis. Culligan said he intended to "locate ten or twelve marketing people already in the organization, stimulate them into a frenzy of activity and help guide their selling activity."

The changing of the guard had some poignant moments. At the directors' table that afternoon was MacNeal, who had hurried home early from his European trip. He and the new president exchanged greetings cordially; two days later MacNeal gamely set up a meeting for key Curtis executives to meet Culligan. "Bob MacNeal has been a wonderful gentleman through all this," M. Albert Linton said later that summer. "He was obviously hurt. Who wouldn't be? But he couldn't be more helpful." To a friend, after his firing, MacNeal said forlornly, "I have nearly forty years of my life and hundreds of friends in this company."

(One of the first backbiting rumors circulated about Culligan began shortly after his election: that he got the job because his father-in-law, Joseph Dernberger, was a partner in J. R. Williston & Beane. Culligan met Dernberger's daughter, Doris, at an office Christmas party in 1946 at *Good Housekeeping* Magazine, where she was an assistant patterns editor. Insiders knocked this one down in a hurry with the indisputable answer that nepotism was the last thing Curtis needed at a time of crisis, and that the investors weren't about to jeopardize a multimillion-dollar stake simply to find a better job for someone's son-in-law, especially when the son-in-law was already gainfully employed.)

The formal statements after the meeting brimmed with confidence—both in Curtis and in Culligan. For the company, Linton said that Culligan's selection "signals a new era" and that "his broad experience ideally suits him for the challenge ahead." Culligan, unsurprisingly, was more verbose. "The Curtis Publishing Company has a great heritage and an even greater future," he said. "In accepting this position I recognize the responsibility I owe to the readers of all our magazines and the advertisers who use them. I also recognize the responsibility owed to the stockholders and employees of the company. My first aim is the prompt return of our company to profitable operations. We will continue to publish all the magazines in the Curtis line-up with new vigor." The job was particularly challenging, Culligan said, because "the world cannot afford to lose its great magazines."

Culligan's recovery program for Curtis can be broken into three broad areas: salesmanship and "image-rebuilding"; internal rejuvenation and reorganization; and finding enough money to stay in business while carrying out the first two items on the agenda.

The most pressing business was that of advertising. Culligan took over in early July, less than two months before the September 1 deadline by which most big advertisers like to complete their year's scheduling of space. Through July they had ignored Curtis, preferring instead to see if the company showed any signs of returning to stability. Advertising lineage in the *Saturday Evening Post* alone through the end of the second quarter was down an astounding 25 percent. Curtis was speeding through a year in which losses ultimately were to total $18.9 million. It was too late to do anything about the 1962 deficit, but Culligan realized that if he was to have a company to manage after the next six months, fast action was needed. Agencies considered his task a formidable one. The same month Culligan took over Curtis a confidential memorandum circulated in one agency, noting Curtis' decline in advertising sales, newsstand sales and offers of discounts to advertisers. It continued: "Time is a very real factor here, and it is not at all certain whether the discount [begun a month earlier] will be considered as a positive factor or as a sign that the merchandise is of questionable value. We trust that the former viewpoint will prevail."

The pace Culligan set for himself was furious even for a jet-age executive. He traveled 3,500 miles a week across the countryside. One remarkable spasm of salesmanship would have brought a shudder from the peripatetic John Foster Dulles. Culligan left New York late on a Sunday evening for Detroit, spent the day making presentations on Curtis to Chrysler, General Motors and Lincoln-Mercury (each a day's chore for an ordinary mortal) and flew back to Philadelphia for a 5 P.M. meeting. Then it was to Philadelphia International Airport again for a late-night flight back to Detroit for more selling.

To 120 executives Culligan told the same basic story: that Curtis was in business for keeps, as a voice of the free enterprise system, and that its magazines' editorial content was on the upswing. He told them to consider the magazines as a "marketing" medium, not an "advertising" medium. There's a difference, too: an advertising medium is simply a means of getting a commercial across to a vast number of people at the same time; a marketing medium is one that puts a certain type of message before a certain selected audience.

Culligan called himself a "marketing specialist" rather than an advertising salesman; yet his busy fountain pen signed contracts by the score: more than $30 million in new ads by the middle of August; $45 million by mid-October, 75 percent of it in contracts of one to three years.

The new Curtis leader found the trade and general press more than willing to help him beat both the Curtis and his personal drums. Culligan was exciting and quotable, and he did some things that ordinary persons don't do. Every morning he drove to the first tee of the Apawamis Country Club near his home in Rye, New York, and boarded a helicopter for a 50-minute ride to Philadelphia. He landed at a heliport at the foot of Chestnut Street on the Delaware River and rode the seven blocks to the Curtis Building. Culligan found nothing unusual about this mode of transportation at all; the train ride from Rye to Grand Central Station took the same amount of time. "It's the modern and economical way of doing things," he said.

A rather silly *Time* picture his first week in office showed Culligan with a phone clamped to each ear, his features tautly concentrated. "They say I'm psychotic," read the caption. Six weeks later *Time* had Culligan peering from the open door of a helicopter, his face set in the determined expression of a man who is going to intercept a Northeast Air Lines flight between New York and Boston and sell Big Advertiser Jones 40 four-color pages in the *Post*. All editors had to do was let Culligan talk and take notes, to wit: "One of the legendary things they say about me is this capacity for work I have. If I work eighteen hours a day, the others will work fourteen. You know how it is. Flaming leadership, that's what's really needed."

(Later that year Culligan griped bitterly about his press coverage in an interview with Pete Martin, who turned to free-lancing after being fired from the *Post*. The "psychotic" quote, he claimed, was ten years old, and the double-telephone shot was posed at the behest of the *Time* photographer. "I couldn't care less where the lunatic attacks come from so long as they attack me instead of Curtis and the magazines," Culligan said. "I have set myself up as a target which will attract the negatives, the assassins, and the poison-pen boys. I've got a coat of skin so thick those idiots can't get through it." Several paragraphs later Culligan conceded that the Time-Life management was not "destructive" and would be "distressed" if anything happened to Curtis.) The point he left unanswered was why he came back for seconds after one jab with the Lucian needle. Friends dispute his claim to a "thick" skin, also; one said, "Anything written about Joe that isn't nice becomes a hatchet job."

There was considerable minutiae about the go-go-go-go-ad-infinitum working habits which proved Culligan to be a real hustler: that he scheduled every minute of his 20-hour working day; that he liked to-the-second appointments, such as 9:26 and 10:04 (sometimes P.M., to the resentment of executives whose enthusiasm for Curtis Publishing Company wore a bit thin after 12 hours at the office). He could politely ease from the office of an advertising prospect in mid-conversation without offending—or looking at his wristwatch.

In a philosophical moment Culligan professed not to be scared by what he was attempting. He said, "Handling this company is like skiing. If you are standing looking down a great slope, as an experienced skier, there is nothing to it. It offers fun, adventure, a chance to use your skills. But if you haven't done it before, the prospect is terrifying. This is the fourth time I've attempted this kind of thing. In many respects, the other slopes were much tougher."

But such quiet moments were subordinated to brass-band optimism. "NUTS" shouted glaring black letters in a *New York Times* page in November, 1962. The Curtis promotion writer said, "The panzer divisions had the 101st Airborne Division surrounded in the little Belgian village of Bastogne. Cold gripped the fingers and toes of our soldiers, gripped their hearts as well. The German commander said, 'Surrender.' Tony McAuliffe said, 'Nuts.' And somehow from that moment, victory was never in doubt. . . . The Curtis Publishing Company says 'Nuts.' We are strong. We have faith. And the tide of battle has begun to turn."

The ad continued: "Earlier this year we were heavily shelled by rumors and guesses and bad press reports. The bombardment has stopped. The air is clearer, the sky is brighter. Tough men are in the front lines . . . the whole organization is hardened.

"Surrender? **Nuts.**"

The ad also contained "The Curtis Commitment," a for-the-record statement of what Joe Culligan intended to make of the firm. In the perspective of the *Saturday Evening Post's* history it sounds like something George Horace Lorimer wrote in the mid-1920's and stuck away in his desk in the Curtis editorial offices:

The Curtis Publishing Company is committed to the goal of becoming the voice and conscience of the competitive free-enterprise system, which is the foundation of a progressive economy and a democratic way of life. The editorial weight of the Curtis magazines will be applied to this undertaking and through text and photographic treatment we will present the voice and opinions of leaders of this country, this hemisphere and the entire Western World in speaking out on this subject.

It is our conviction that the competitive-enterprise system represents one of modern man's greatest achievements, and that it provides the framework not only for our economic well-being but also for the preservation of individual rights and the protection of minorities.

The pages of our magazines will provide a forum for all of the voices of the marketplace, including those of labor, business, politics, government and education, as well as those which speak for social forces and for the family group.

Reprints of "The Curtis Commitment" fluttered down on advertisers. Culligan viewed it as a blueprint for something more far-reaching than the mere sale of advertising space. David Ogilvy, of Ogilvy, Benson & Mather, who sometimes views with a cocked eyebrow the happenings on Madison Avenue, passed on a manufacturer's account of how Culligan used The Commitment as part of his sales spiel:

"Curtis has the only publications today that are committed to competitive-enterprise," the executive said Culligan told him. "Time-Life is only a predecessor to socialism. If you want competitive-enterprise to survive in this great land of ours, you had better help save Curtis. You can do so by buying 40 pages in the *Saturday Evening Post*."

"Get out of my office; I'm not interested in that sort of reasoning," the manufacturer told Culligan. ("Apparently only a few Goldwater types were willing to buy advertising to save the competitive-enterprise system," Ogilvy said. "It caused some good chuckles, however . . . by that old socialist Henry Luce, too.")

Culligan aides bedeviled Curtis editors about The Commitment. "Regularly I got phone calls—my secretary later learned how to fend them off—and some new vice-president would ask what I was doing to support competitive-enterprise in the next issue," said a now departed editor. 'I'm running a picture of the flag,' I finally told some guy. I suppose he was satisfied; I didn't hear anything else."

(Someone also asked Ted Patrick, the salty *Holiday* editor, what he was doing about promoting competitive-enterprise, saying, "I thought you ran a travel magazine." "Hell, so did I," grumped Patrick, who completely ignored the entire campaign.)

Hints of The Curtis Commitment could be found in the *Saturday Evening Post,* where Culligan urged frequent stories on competitive-enterprise. A May 25, 1963, article on the Chrysler Corporation ("Chrysler's Comeback in Detroit") heaped praise atop the new president, Lynn Townsend. The piece began, "With a low eerie whistle the new Chrysler turbine car flashed into public view last week. Chrysler officials, confident they have made the most dramatic advance since the industry turned from steam to gas, settled back in nervous exultation to gauge public response." The *Post* called the turbine a "radically new automobile that could revolutionize the entire auto and allied industries." It conceded that flaws could develop but Chrysler engineers are certain they have "won the fierce contest to produce a practical gas turbine for a passenger car."

Culligan viewed the Curtis magazines as a "network" suitable for package purchases of space. He asked advertisers to order in all five at the same time—in return for sizable discounts. The sales tally gradually rose: From July, 1962, through April, 1963, according to the company, Culligan and other salesmen signed contracts for $121,966,077 in new advertising orders. Companies such as General Electric, American Telephone and Telegraph, and Longines-Wittnauer Watch Company placed orders in the $6,000,000 to $7,000,000 range. But Curtis was on a treadmill. Huff and puff as he did, Culligan couldn't jar the *Saturday Evening Post* into action. In the first half of 1963, the *Post* gained 80 new advertisers—and lost 90 old ones. The *Ladies' Home Journal* gained 26 percent in ad pages in 1963 over 1962, and the *American Home* 25 percent. The *Post*, bell cow of the Curtis herd, was stubborn. Here are figures on Curtis magazine advertising for the period (with 1961 as a base to show the new regime's starting point):

THE SATURDAY EVENING POST

	ABC Circulation	Revenue	Ad Pages
1961	6,578,966	$86,539,596	2,071.02
1962	6,651,494	66,517,157	1,574.28
1963	6,601,358	60,723,905	1,462.01

THE LADIES' HOME JOURNAL

	ABC Circulation	Revenue	Ad Pages
1961	6,954,263	$27,136,697	745.16
1962	7,013,644	23,428,199	650.94
1963	6,440,512	27,783,139	818.66

HOLIDAY

1961	922,633	$ 9,980,175	1,062.48
1962	927,788	10,339,381	1,048.47
1963	933,738	10,302,693	1,045.62

THE AMERICAN HOME

1961	3,695,802	$ 8,318,034	442.23
1962	3,684,316	8,869,953	444.84
1963	3,366,015	10,431,130	551.01

During his first year in office Culligan estimated that he was away from his desk 85 percent of the time—rubbing elbows with corporation presidents, agency heads, even President John F. Kennedy. The latter visit provided Culligan anecdotal fodder for months; one associate says it was "two-thirds of his conversation until we looked openly bored at the repetition." Culligan seemed to think that, as an Irishman, he could somehow identify himself and the *Post* with the President. "I think the fact that the President granted a representative of our company a few minutes of his time will give a lift to the morale of the Curtis company and the staff of its magazines," said Culligan proudly. At a luncheon speech in upstate New York he even introduced himself as the "Number Two Man in the Irish Mafia." Jokingly, an editor asked, "Joe, when do you plan to run for President of the United States?"

A vice-president close to Culligan said: "Don't think it hasn't been discussed."

Culligan realized, however, that it would take more than salesmanship to salvage Curtis Publishing Company. "The notion you can sell your way out of trouble is foolish," he said. "You have to manage your way out, with cost reductions." He called Curtis "stuffy" and added, "A guy with a high stiff collar can put on a button-down shirt and not change his entire personality, you know."

To handle the internal reforms, Culligan imported two

friends from his National Broadcasting Company days who had helped him turn the radio division into a profit maker: John McLean Clifford, as executive vice-president for finances and operations, and Maurice W. Poppei, as comptroller.

"Let's get Curtis moving again," Culligan cried constantly, invoking the phraseology of President Kennedy. "We want the bright, the aggressive." Old-time employees used to the leisurely Curtis pace were "advance-retired"; so were the younger ones who "just didn't fit into Curtis plans." During the first nine months, pink slips appeared in an estimated 2,200—of 9,000—pay envelopes at all levels.

Culligan also sought to superimpose the broadcasting company structure on the Curtis organization to permit the advertising and business offices more say in how the magazines were run. Previously, the word "publisher" was anathema at Curtis. Morton Bailey, for instance, was "manager" of the *Saturday Evening Post,* with duties corresponding to those of a "publisher" at any other magazine. But he was quite satisfied with the title. If made publisher, he once said, "What would the editors think? They might feel I'm trying to lord it over them. Manager is good enough."

Culligan broke with this Curtis tradition. As publisher of each magazine he installed a former advertising man and gave each of them the job of telling the editors what kind of magazine was required for the type of people who would be reading it. Culligan didn't phrase the order quite that bluntly. He defined the new organization thusly, in late July, 1962: "It means a more vertical operation for each magazine with a chief executive responsible for the marketing and business aspect of his publication. The publisher is the man who interprets the magazine to the markets, meaning the financial community, advertisers, ad agencies and the reading public. He also interprets the needs of the market back to the editors. The editors, under the supervision of the director of editorial development, will still be responsible for what's between the covers of the magazines." That the publishers were all former admen, Culligan said, stemmed from the fact that "our main problem today is advertising." To doubters within the organization Culligan said firmly—and correctly—that under the old Curtis system no one had final responsibility for whether a magazine succeeded or failed (i.e., whether it made or lost money). The publishers, he said, would take either the fame or the blame, and "failure isn't acceptable." Culligan's "director of editorial development"—also a new job for Curtis—was Clay D. Blair, Jr., the hard-driving young thinker who helped design the ill-fated "new *Post.*"

Curtis editors watched in fascination as Culligan named the publishers. His selection as boss of the *Saturday Evening Post* was C. L. (Bud) MacNelly, since 1950 a vice-president of Ted Bates & Co., Inc., in the Madison Avenue heartland. After Mac-Nelly had been in office a few days, a staff member, in casual conversation, asked what had been his specialty at Ted Bates. "Food, drugs, soap, toilet articles, beer, I handled them all at one time or another," the editor said MacNelly replied.

Another pushed forward by Culligan was John J. Veronis, then thirty-four, advertising manager of the *Ladies' Home Journal* when the new regime came in. Culligan promoted Veronis to publisher of both the *Journal* and the *American Home,* shunting aside his former boss, E. Kent Mitchel, who was made "senior publisher" of the two magazines. Veronis had come to Curtis as a twenty-four-year-old ad space salesman. Curtis editors saw in Veronis the personification of all they had to fear under an advertising-oriented management. He was humorless, deliberate, driving, "a roaring, puffing freight engine bearing down on some innocent crossing," said one. "Veronis doesn't breathe; he pants. His lips move even when he isn't talking, with incessant and just audible 'e-yes,' 'e-yes,' 'e-yes,' as you desperately try to reach the end of your sentence before he starts talking again, grateful only that you finished it."

A mere suggestion from a source he trusted at the moment would sway Veronis on both persons and policies. But his opinions changed rapidly; in 24 hours the Veronis judgment could

go from "greatest salesman I know" to "*boy, he's a mistake.*"
He stunned a gathering of *Ladies' Home Journal* editors by
asking, without a trace of a smile, "I really wonder if the Goulds
ever were good editors." Sound, solid people under him were
viewed as threats to his stature and position. A *Journal* editor,
hearing enthusiastic praise from colleagues of a salesman who
was doing a good job, suddenly realized from Veronis' comments that he was becoming suspicious of the man's ambitions.
So the editors were told to "downplay the praise" when Veronis
was around.

Bernard P. Gallagher, through his "Gallagher Report," gave
Culligan a constant barrage of advice on how to revive Curtis.
He recommended, for instance, that Veronis be pushed—then
complained when Culligan made him publisher of two magazines instead of one. Gallagher gave the Curtis principals
Damon Runyonesque titles. Veronis, because of his boundless
capacity for work, was "Hungry John." Culligan was "The
Killer." Clifford, who was doing hangman's work reducing the
payroll, was "Mack the Knife." Blair was "Tiger." (Mused a
former Curtis executive now content elsewhere on Madison
Avenue: "For a long time I hoped Gallagher would give me a
nickname. It was almost like a promotion to a vice-presidency,
a status symbol that you were somebody at Curtis. I'm glad now
I didn't get one. Three of the four 'nicknames' are on the street
now." Only "Mack the Knife" survives, as president and chief
executive officer.)

Yet Veronis could sell advertising. He was a 20-hour-a-day
dynamo who brimmed with energy and ideas. Even persons
whose toes were left sore by his eagerly climbing feet recollect
with admiration his energy. "He worked his tail off trying to do
everything he was told and anything else he could think of,"
one Curtis man remembers. "He hustled ads, he hustled circulation, he came up with promotion ideas. It was a do-or-die for
Curtis. Being around him was exciting. He really tried." The
son of Greek immigrants, Veronis strove to become a first-
generation success story, and he was. The *Journal,* when he

became publisher, had been in a decade-long decline, editorially and financially. Veronis revitalized the advertising department and imbued salesmen with the same enthusiasm and confidence that Culligan was attempting to implant elsewhere in the company. The *Journal,* in 1963, increased its advertising revenue by $4.3 million, and its ad pages by some 26 percent. How much of this is attributable to Veronis, how much to Culligan, how much to Curtiss Anderson, the editor who replaced the Goulds? There are no existent yardsticks. But the mere fact that Veronis was aggressive enough to draw public attention is illustrative of a fundamental change in Curtis' prior image of advertising lethargy.

Being around Veronis was amusing as well as exciting. The adman admired and emulated Culligan, even to the point of taking on some of his boss' idiosyncrasies. Culligan boasted of arising each day to read a book before breakfast, but he couldn't always produce any recently read titles when asked, one former colleague said. Culligan also liked to summon spur-of-the-moment conferences at 11 o'clock at night at his home in Rye, calling older executives and saying, "Get on out here; there's work to be done."

Soon Veronis said, "Hey, I got up this morning and read a book, just like Joe. And the other night I had a meeting over at my place, just like Joe. We didn't get started until almost midnight."

Culligan made a point of letting luncheon companions know he didn't care for the adman's traditional two martinis. And sure enough, Veronis started coming back to the office with no gin on his breath—"Just like Joe."

Veronis took to heart Culligan's admonition that publishers should "interpret the market" back to the editors. And, as did Culligan, he viewed the magazines as merchandising media, rather than simply as periodicals which accepted advertising. Curtis editors felt pressures to lend support to advertising tie-ins; the *Journal,* for instance, designed—and put its name on —clothes for a weight-reduction ad. (When George Horace

Lorimer ran the *Saturday Evening Post*, advertising workers were tolerated, but not welcomed, on the editorial domain of the sixth floor. An adman once walked into the sanctum of the art department and admired a cover painting of a golfer. "Gee, that's fine," he said, "that'll help us sell some pages of advertising." He turned to find Lorimer behind him, stone-faced. "I'm sorry you said that," the editor said. "We can't use that cover." "It was a perfectly good lesson," said a former *Post* editorial worker who remembered the incident. "Lorimer scrapped it just to teach those bastards a lesson.") Under Culligan, however, there was no one "to teach those bastards a lesson." The one weight-reduction ad tie-in produced a flood of such requests, until the *Journal* pattern department was working part-time for advertisers. To editors and space salesmen alike any compromise with advertisers on free space and promotions opens floodgates that can never be closed. "Advertisers themselves soon lose respect for this practice," said a former Curtis editor. "They become cynical, disenchanted; they won't buy space unless you do more and more for them." Curtis editors were pressured into lengthy luncheon conferences—not with writers and photographers, but with advertising men, research and promotion executives. The end product of two hours of boredom: "There are 45,850,000 bathtubs in the United States."

In the pre-Culligan days Curtis editors ran their magazines unhampered by outside advice or interference; if they wanted consultation, they asked for it, from people of their own choosing. Veronis made no pretense to editorial genius (although he once suggested that a "publisher's column" would be appropriate for the *Journal*, since the *Time* publisher had one.) Under Culligan, however, Curtis crawled with consultants who were retained to tell editors how to edit and salesmen how to sell. One of the first was Dr. Peter Drucker, the famed management specialist, under whom Veronis was taking a course at New York University. Dr. Drucker appeared lost and hesitant when he met with *Journal* editors to tell them of "the future." For one thing, he admitted, he hadn't yet had a chance to read the *Journal* thoroughly, nor was he familiar with a new feature, "World We Want," an in-depth exploration of such weighty subjects as welfare, peace, medical care for the aged, and the racial problem. Nonetheless, Drucker opined midway through a three-hour conference that the *Journal* should do "more serious articles." (In other areas of the company, where he trod on traditional grounds, Dr. Drucker's ideas were valuable in guiding Veronis and other young executives who found themselves thrust into management positions.)

Another consultant was a child-care specialist connected with a child guidance foundation of which Culligan was a sponsor. He strode into Anderson's office one day and announced he was to check all copy pertaining to children, and said, "I understand you're going to get rid of Dr. Spock." Anderson said he would yield his right arm rather than Dr. Benjamin Spock, the Cleveland pediatrician who has raised millions of American youngsters via the printed page. The Culligan-supplied consultant made a crack about Dr. Spock's endorsement of SANE and said, "A lot of people question Ben's ideas." Rebuffed by Anderson ("Assigning him to check Dr. Spock's copy for policy would be like assigning Casey Stengel to review the Gettysburg Address for grammatical errors"), the doctor turned to other matters. He would be happy, he said, to be assigned a writer and photographer and tour the country, preparing stories for both the *Journal* and the *American Home*. "I know all the movie stars by their first names—I could get good stories on Art Linkletter, Loretta Young, Dale Evans, Roy Rogers, all those people." Anderson ignored the man, even after a call from Culligan's office that "something better show up in the *Journal* pretty soon or Joe is going to blow his top."

Culligan also supplied "consultants" personally. In Chicago for a speech to advertising executives he met on the street Dr. Frances Horwich, the "Miss Frances" of the *Ding Dong School* during Culligan's executive days at NBC. After a buss and an exchange of greetings, Culligan hurried her into a cab, saying, "You've got to come hear my speech; you'll be the honored guest, the only woman there."

Dr. Horwich settled back to listen to Culligan and heard him say: "This is a wonderful opportunity to announce that Dr. Frances Horwich is joining Curtis Publishing Company as a special consultant on children's affairs." When Culligan finished, he subjected her to a high-powered, arm-gripping dose of Culligan persuasion. "Your husband travels a lot—what does it matter if you live in Philadelphia or Chicago or wherever?" As it happened, Dr. Horwich's husband spent a good deal of time in Washington. Convinced of the travel time her husband would save by living in Philadelphia, Dr. Horwich agreed to join Curtis. Her assignment was to approve all articles on child care, and she didn't care for some that went into print around and over her. She objected, for instance, to a story, "Teach Your Baby How to Read?" Why? "Because I don't approve of teaching babies how to read," she said. Confronted with the research on which the articles were based—and a coincidental article in *Harper's* on the same subject that appeared almost simultaneously—Dr. Horwich beat a tactical retreat.

Dr. Horwich was more in her element at *Jack and Jill* magazine, which Culligan opened to advertisers for the first time since its founding by Curtis in 1938. Her task was to check products for their "suitability" in *Jack and Jill*, a monthly potpourri of stories in the four-to-ten-year-old bracket. Culligan had big ideas about using the *Jack and Jill* prestige to peddle merchandise to the kiddies—"Jack and Jill beach wear, bathing suits, kid games, milk fortifiers. . . . We'll have a whole line of Jack and Jill products which will be sold by others, with Curtis as part owner of these enterprises. In time, this activity alone could make more money than any of our magazines make today." Just what kind of ads would Dr. Horwich ban from *Jack and Jill?* "That's a professional secret," she said right after taking office. The first ad in *Jack and Jill* history ran in the May, 1963, issue—a two-page spread on World Book Encyclopedia, replete with a beaming picture of "Miss Frances," who lauded the books as "first in sales, quality . . . leadership."

Prompted by Culligan's recruiting of assistants throughout the company, Veronis decided he needed an assistant publisher to help him with *Ladies' Home Journal* business. The first was a disappointed man who was a holdover from the MacNeal regime. He is remembered chiefly for clutching the *Journal* to his bosom once daily and intoning, "I love this magazine." He lasted only a few weeks. The next assistant publisher, a space salesman brought in from the West Coast, floundered while trying to find just what in the dickens an assistant publisher was supposed to do. "Consult with editors," Veronis told him.

The third assistant publisher had been an airline hostess with Mrs. Veronis. Veronis considered her a personal listening post in the *Journal* editorial offices; she chatted incessantly with editors, seeking information on what was going on, and suggested that she be allowed to listen in on a telephone conversation with an advertiser who called the office.

Meantime, while Culligan roamed the corporate suites of the land, selling Curtis, Culligan and The Curtis Commitment, and Veronis, MacNelly and the other publishers "interpreted the market" for editors, a revolution of another sort stirred dust in the quiet Curtis halls. This was the cost-cutting program through which the new management sought to restore profitable operations.

J. M. ("Mack the Knife") Clifford was the man tapped for this project, and he carried it out with professional detachment. Whatever personal feelings he might have had about the unpleasant chore willed to him by Culligan and the earlier managements, he kept to himself. With pencil and pad he sat at department heads' desks, explaining how the firing of the lowest-ranking employees, collectively, would help Curtis. "This secretary makes only $4,000," one head recollects Clifford as saying, "But you have to learn to look further than that. First there's her social security, which we have to match. Then her retirement and her unemployment benefits, and all the fringes, and her cost in the office. A $4,000 girl actually costs us about $8,000. Double the salary—that's what a reduction saves us."

There was dissension, even an attempt at defiance. As an initial step all departments were ordered to cut payrolls across-the-board by 20 percent, either by reducing salaries or the number of employees. One department head flatly refused. "What alternative does management have in a case like that?" said a man still active in the company. "He was fired."

Cary Bok said he felt the firings keenly even though, in effect, he was a member of the management which ordered them. "People I knew for thirty years would ask for help, and I could do nothing. Saving the entire company, and the jobs of many, was more important than a few individuals."

Gags that might have been *Post* cartoons in the old days took on a new meaning: "If the boss calls, find out who it is." An office wag suggested that Culligan's booklet, "Know Your Management," be revised and issued daily.

The new management made a basic policy decision early in the firings which its spokesmen said later was prompted by humanitarianism. Older persons with pension rights were dropped in preference to a young man with children still in school. Why? A company spokesman says Curtis felt a fifty-nine-year-old man with a small established pension income had a brighter future than a forty-three-year-old man with family responsibilities who was suddenly turned into the cold. "It's hard for men in that age bracket to get relocated," he said.

This rankled the company veterans who had viewed Curtis as a combination professional and retirement home where they were content to stay as long as they were alive. For one thing, a person who retired early lost 6 percent of his pension rights for every year under sixty-five. A retirement five years in advance of the planned date thus meant a 30 percent cut in benefits— the difference between comfort and penury in some instances. Persons who had worked for years at Curtis' low-pay scales on the promise of a lifetime tenure and retirement were embittered

—the name Curtis was no longer immune from criticism in Philadelphia, where it had once been as sacred as that of William Penn.

The lost goodwill of secretaries, paper handlers and maintenance men in Philadelphia was insignificant, however, when put into perspective against the middle-echelon firings of advertising executives and editors—the anonymous professionals, unknown to the general public, who are the bone and sinew of a modern magazine.

"This is a tightly knit little community," David Ogilvy said one winter day in 1965, waving his hand in the direction of Madison Avenue. "You're an editor or an advertising man—who are your friends? Hell, they certainly aren't barbers out in Kankakee, Illinois.

"One of my vice-presidents had lunch with a Curtis publisher during the turmoil," Ogilvy said. "The Curtis man promptly told my man what a scoundrel he thought me to be. Then the Curtis man asked, 'Are you hostile to Curtis?'

" 'You're damned right I am,' my man replied. 'My sister worked for you bastards for seventeen years and was thrown into the street. Damned right I'm hostile.' 'Well, maybe I shouldn't be having lunch with you,' the publisher said. They arose simultaneously and stalked out without speaking to each other again.

"Each person fired has a multiplier of 100. For each one there are 100 friends mad at Curtis—and those friends are all in this little world of our people who can make their anger felt by sending advertising elsewhere, if they're in advertising, or by letting *McCall's* have the cream of the fiction, if they are editors. These aren't some anonymous Joes.

"What would happen if I suddenly fired twenty, thirty, forty percent of the people in my agency? They'd be out on the street, along with all their friends and relatives, telling everybody what a —— I am. Ads in the *Times* and promotion can't overcome that sort of ill will, either," Ogilvy said.

Just before Curtiss Anderson left as editor of the *Ladies' Home*

Journal (he lasted a year, from 1962 through 1963, before a fatal, climactic row with Clay Blair, Jr.) he established a panel of 20 distinguished communications people who were to select a woman who represented the ideals of the "World We Want" series in his magazine. After Curtis broke with Anderson, the new editor sent around a terse note dissolving the panel, without further comment. David Ogilvy, who had been on it, said, "We are big enough in our fields that a summary dissolution of something to which we had devoted time and thought isn't really important. But it was the spirit of the thing. I imagine that the affair left fifteen more people—and important people—disillusioned with Curtis."

After six months of Culligan's internal reform, someone ran a head count in the executive suite. When Culligan had first come to Curtis, he joked about MacNeal's top-heavy executive structure of 18 vice-presidents. The new count showed Culligan to have no less than 27. "Hell, in the first year he topped Bob MacNeal by ten," a former official said.

"Further, it was a great mystery what some of these characters were to do. They knew nothing of publishing—they were broadcasting men, many from Culligan's old crowd at NBC. We didn't even have desk space for all of them. They milled around as best they could, borrowing secretaries. They made a production of hustling advertising at a 'top-level' basis, and of always having big luncheon dates with big important people of some identity or another."

Many of the new executives played office politics with Machiavellian skill and ruthlessness. A division manager, just before the 1964 stockholders meeting, sought approval of a $250,000 appropriation to expand his operations. Culligan couldn't get the money immediately—he was having banker trouble by this time—and then, in passing, told the manager he expected an optimistic report for the stockholders. At the meeting several days later Culligan called on the manager, who launched into an oration on the $250,000 expansion as if it were assured. "Culligan chewed his tail out afterwards because the guy made him ridiculous before the directors, who knew what was going on," a former executive said. "But I think he secretly got a kick out of it, that it was the type of power play he would have used himself in a similar situation."

Within a month of his appointment Culligan confronted another problem just as pressing as that of the advertising situation—$22 million in short-term obligations to four banks. The decline in business in 1961 and 1962 had driven MacNeal to the bankers so dreaded by Cyrus Curtis to find the cash necessary to enable Curtis to meet current expenses. Because of their short term, the loans bore a high interest rate, and the dwindling dollar supply that Culligan inherited was by no means big enough to retire them. Had the bankers insisted on full payment when the loans fell due in August, 1962, they well might have pushed Curtis over the brink into bankruptcy, or caused a dumping of assets at forced-sale prices.

Culligan handled the bankers exactly as he did the advertisers: In a mixture of bluntness and optimism, he acknowledged that Curtis was in dire trouble, and that it could not raise the required cash for repayment. He also said he was confident that he could turn Curtis around if given enough time, that he had performed three similar financial rescues in his lifetime, and if the bankers were patient, they would eventually get their money back. And, most important, Culligan was able to reach into his briefcase and pull out a sheaf of multimillion-dollar advertising contracts as concrete evidence that he had Curtis on the move again.

The blend of salesmanship, charm and hard facts sold the bankers on Culligan. They listened to him at luncheon tables, they listened to him at conference tables. Ultimately, they granted him a year's extension on the loans—until August 16, 1963—so that he could work out a suitable refinancing plan.

The extension gave Culligan needed breathing room. No longer was Curtis in immediate danger of being heaved into bankruptcy. He also used the bankers' expression of confidence as a talking point in his advertising drive: "If hardheaded, realistic men like that are confident in Curtis, you should be, too."

The bankers, however, put an important stipulation into the extension. They elicited from Culligan a pledge that he would seek to obtain stockholder approval of the removal of a debt restriction in the Curtis bylaw. The rules required approval of two-thirds of the preferred stockholders before management could pledge any assets as collateral for loans. This provision protected interests of the preferred class in the event of a liquidation. It also effectively barred management from making any long-term loans for capital improvement.

And it was on this point that Culligan ran into his first serious trouble inside the company. Prior to the April, 1963, stockholders meeting, details of the debt elimination plan were made public. A minute but potent clique of preferred stockholders balked. In return for surrender of their veto power on debts, they said, they deserved something in return—a payment on the preferred dividend arrearages. Culligan argued, futilely, that the money wasn't available. Whereupon a Preferred Stockholders Committee—composed of persons holding only 1,900 of the 573,888 shares of preferred stock—filed a proxy statement with the Securities Exchange Commission and began soliciting proxies from shareholders with the aim of blocking the plan. Investors who had bought preferred stock as a speculation sided with the committee: If Curtis went into liquidation, their money would be protected. The $4 preferred, in liquidation, was worth $65 per share, although it was being traded in early 1963 for $22 to $25; the $1.60 preferred, worth $25 in liquidation, was selling for $9.

Culligan took a licking at the stockholders meeting when the issue was put to a vote. The $4-preferred shareholders voted the plan down, 181,000 to 67,000, even though it carried handily in other classes—2,672,000 to 43,000 in common and 197,000 to 9,000 in the $1.60 preferred. Culligan warned the preferred shareholders what they had done; he said removal of the debt limitation was "compelling" if Curtis were to retire or refinance the $22 million obligation.

Curtis Publishing Company was now in need of extraordinary banking help. Culligan found it, in the form of one of the world's leading corporate doctors, Serge Semenenko, vice-chairman of the First National Bank of Boston. In three decades prior to his involvement with Curtis, Semenenko arranged something more than $5 billion in loans for his banks and never had one go sour. From the mid-1930's through 1950, Semenenko's loans practically supported the film industry—$300 million went from First National of Boston to the Hollywood studios. The Russian-born Semenenko moved as smoothly amid California movie tycoons as he did among his Back Bay banker colleagues; his slurring Slavic accent, still pronounced although he had been in the United States since 1924, added to his courtly, continental air. Because of the nature of his business he cultivated the role of man-in-the-background. "People can get the wrong idea when a banker is in the picture." This gave him the title of "mystery man," which he doesn't like. Yet before he came to Curtis, Semenenko carried secrecy to the point of being a fetish. He cold-shouldered even the most routine of press queries; what items were published about him related to his charitable and social activities. The latter added to his aura of glamour, for he is host and entertainer to the restless jet set in New York, at his seaside home high in the hills above Acapulco, on a glistening white yacht in the Mediterranean. Interview requests submitted to his office and public relations adviser, the Robert Taplinger agency in New York, disappear as if stuffed into a bottle and hurled into the sea. The latter is a more direct route; conceivably, the bottle could wash onto the beach in Acapulco. After his emergence as banker for Curtis, and the resultant spate of publicity, Semenenko again retired into anonymity. The quotes below on his operating procedures were gleaned from two interviews which he gave *The New York Times* in 1964.

Semenenko was born August 26, 1903, in Odessa, Russia, son of a wealthy, philanthropic banker and large property owner.

His first ambition was to be a general staff officer in the Imperial Russian Army, and he entered the military college at Odessa. There he found history and economics more appealing and switched to the Classical College. The choice proved wise, for the Bolshevik Revolution the next year put the Imperial Russian Army out of business and forced the Semenenko family to flee to Constantinople. Semenenko finished his studies there and, on the advice of a professor, went to Harvard University's Graduate School of Business Administration in 1924. A few days before his twenty-second birthday Semenenko joined the First National Bank of Boston as a $100-a-month credit clerk. He established a ready rapport with the Boston Brahmins in charge of the bank; as a junior officer he argued that giving a loan to an ailing company unaccompanied by advice on what to do with it is akin to a physician prescribing medicine to an ailing patient without doing anything about the cause of the illness. First National of Boston let him try his theory on several companies, and it worked. Semenenko lapses into a metamorphical smorgasbord when describing his *modus operandi*. "The first thing I do is study the position of the company and its problems. I analyze the situation, see what 'medicine' is needed, determine what limbs have to be cut off, where 'injections' of vitamins are needed, how management can be reorganized and rejuvenated, how profits and loss can be brought into balance and how to open up new horizons. After my study, I submit a plan generally in a memorandum on only one page. The basic problems are usually the same in all cases; only the details vary."

Semenenko's list of corporate "saves" cuts a broad swath across American industry—Fairbanks, Whitney; the International Paper Co.; Minnesota and Ontario Paper Company; the Hearst publishing empire; the Kendall Co.

Why do First National of Boston and Semenenko always seem to be in the role of a financial fire brigade? "I do not believe in getting business by cutting the rate. I try to convince people that Boston money is the best money, for we stay with it through thick and thin." At one time, for example, Minnesota and Ontario Paper Company owed $65 million and had internal problems in proportion to the debt. Semenenko nursed it for 13 years; the company is now making millions annually in profits. As a banker he often has to make unpopular decisions: "I am not a liquidator, but if a company is to grow, then it has to get rid of the properties or the people that hinder it. If it can, then there will be more jobs available and higher profits for its stockholders." For this reason he is reluctant to take a seat on the board of client companies; if heads are to be chopped he wants them to be strange, impersonal ones so that he can order necessary executions without being swayed by his own feelings. "Where we have to eliminate losing properties, with persons losing positions, communities affected by closings do not feel kindly toward the banker. But balanced against these losses and hardships are the jobs, investments and opportunities saved for others. I am not interested in seeing any company go out of business. My idea is to save it and strengthen it."

For all his multimillion-dollar deals, Semenenko managed to keep his name even out of public records to a great extent. One exception was in 1963. Rep. Wright Patman, chairman of a Congressional subcommittee investigating tax-exempt foundations, found that Semenenko had obtained vast amounts of credit from tax-free charitable foundations to which he had access, and had used the funds for investment in the stock market. Patman also said Semenenko had bought shares in the companies for which he was acting as banker. David G. Baird, New York stockbroker and close business associate of Semenenko's, was in control of the foundations. Patman, an East Texas Democrat of the Populist school, said the Baird operations indicated that foundation funds such as those controlled by Baird afforded "boundless opportunities for lavishing favors upon business associates and friends," and that they constituted "taxable business activities operating on a tax-free basis." In 1956, Patman said, Semenenko borrowed more than $6 million from a Baird foundation to purchase 160,000 shares of Warner Brothers stock, which, Patman said "made him, at that point, Warner's second largest stockholder." He also borrowed to buy interests in Universal Pictures Company, the American News Company, and Olin Industries, which after a merger was a part of Olin Mathieson Chemical. The total borrowings from 1951 to 1961 were in excess of $20 million; the bulk of the investments were in companies for which he was banker.

Here are year-end balances on his account with the Baird foundations for a seven-year period, as reported by the Patman subcommittee:

1954—$1,517,143	1958— 5,313,320
1955— 855,957	1959— 1,249,537
1956— 6,070,448	1960— 1,208,035
1957— 3,744,570	

Baird told Congress that he did not make any profit from the foundations and has distributed grants of more than $35 million to educational, charitable and medical institutions.

Semenenko denied that any breach of ethics was involved; that he did not intervene to obtain credit for anyone else nor did he employ the foundations to gain any business advantages. Adequate collateral was posted for all the loans, interest was paid and the borrowings were frequently reduced. Actually, he said, the source was a handicap as well as a blessing. To get the maximum capital gain, he would have had to wait for the stock situations to "mature." However, Baird needed income to support the charities, so he was usually forced to sell before the optimum time came. Semenenko says he could have made more profit by holding the stocks longer; that he sometimes split the profits with the foundations and gave them outright gifts of $30,800 and $52,700.

Semenenko is a brave investor who occasionally puts his bank's money in places considered precarious by other financial institutions. Conrad Hilton, for instance, had the opportunity to acquire the Statler chain of hotels but lacked sufficient collateral to satisfy normal sources of credit. "But we had confidence in him. We put through a $100 million financing without security by providing the bottom $20 million financing and convincing the other banks to join with us. It is the bottom money that is the hardest." First National is Hilton's banker to this day, as are most of the other businessmen who found a friend in Semenenko.

It was another of the friends who matched Curtis Publishing Company with Semenenko. In the early 1940's, Semenenko made the unsnarling of the tangled affairs of William Randolph Hearst his full-time job. Where all others had failed, he persuaded the aging publisher to yield his money-losing newspapers and real estate. "We provided the credit and worked out a reorganization that eliminated the dead branches so that the tree might become healthy and survive," Semenenko says of this mission. Richard Berlin, head of the Hearst organization, knew Semenenko as his company's banker; he knew Culligan as an advertising and broadcasting executive. When Culligan made discreet inquiries about a banker capable of handling Curtis' refinancing problem, Berlin steered him to Semenenko. Their first meeting was in the late spring of 1963, and Semenenko was at first noncommital. For three months his agents investigated Curtis, providing the raw data which Semenenko digested into his one-page diagnosis of the problem. By the August 17, 1963, deadline on the extension on the short-term loans, Semenenko and Culligan had reached tentative agreement. The banks agreed to let the loans ride another few months so that necessary stockholder approval could be granted. Culligan's financial experts put together a revised plan which left the debt limitation intact, but permitted "specific borrowing" of $35 million. Of this, $22 million went to exchange the short-term loans owed by Curtis for five- and seven-year notes, and another $8.5 million for a similar exchange for debts of the New York & Pennsylvania Co., Inc., Curtis' papermaking subsidiary. The remaining $4.5 million was put into the bank as a revolving credit for working capital. Management was authorized to borrow another $5 million through 1970 subject to bank approval.

The deal was leavened with payments of $3 of the arrearages owed the $4.60 preferred shareholders, and 60 cents for the $1.60 preferred shareholders. With this lagniappe, stockholders overwhelmingly approved the loans at a special meeting December 10—98 percent of the preferred stockholders, 99 percent of the common. Semenenko's bank carried the heaviest part of the load, $10.5 million. Other participants were First Pennsylvania Banking & Trust Co., Philadelphia, $7.5 million; Philadelphia National Bank, $6.5 million; Franklin National Bank of Long Island, $5.5 million; Bank of the Southwest, Houston, $3 million; and Union Bank of Los Angeles, $2 million.

To the financial world the startling development in the refinancing was that a beaming, smiling Semenenko was in the Curtis Building auditorium when the shareholders voted, and later spoke to reporters for one of the few times in his life. He expressed confidence in Curtis and Culligan; he even speculated that Curtis might absorb smaller firms to get into the fields of hardcover and paperback book publishing and buy some TV stations. A day later Semenenko once again went out of the way to court the attention he previously had dodged. He and Culligan hosted a press luncheon at the Hotel Pierre in New York, and the banker talked even more lucidly about Curtis. "The real thing is not just to finance this operation," he said, "but to help it go ahead in its growth and diversification. It's not just a matter of providing funds, but I see a great opportunity for growth from within and without. I can see the pattern of a very important publishing empire in the making and I'm delighted to be part of it." He praised the "young and dynamic" management and the "phenomenal" cost reduction; seldom, he said, had he seen a company make such a fast turnaround.

By breaking his silence on Curtis and revealing his involvement, Semenenko willingly abandoned one of his chief assets, the freedom of silent movement behind the scenes. In Curtis' instance, however, he felt it necessary as a public vote of confidence. Additionally, he didn't want anyone to think his presence meant a liquidation was imminent. "I would not have wanted any publicity if the only solution was liquidation," he said. "I allowed my name to be used because I was sure that Curtis could be saved."

Semenenko doesn't sign blank checks, however, and especially when they are for $35 million. From Curtis he elicited a pledge that all management decisions be "reasonably satisfactory" to him, as the designated agent of the banking syndicate. As a service fee Semenenko's bank got ¼ of one percent of the loan ($87,500)—plus, of course, its interest, one percent above the prime rate on its share of the total loan.

There is conflicting testimony on just how active a role Semenenko took for himself in the day-to-day conduct of Curtis' affairs. One former executive maintains that Culligan "wouldn't push the elevator button without calling Serge." This is disputed, however, by Cary W. Bok. "All he asks is that he be kept informed of what's going on," Bok said recently. "So long as he is given complete information on what management is doing, he's satisfied." Bok had unconcealed admiration for Semenenko. "Were it not for Semenenko," he said, "Curtis would have been dead. . . . He is a quiet little genius who inspires confidence in everything he touches." Semenenko was careful to avoid even the semblance of interference with Culligan in the months immediately after the loan agreement. When Curtis moved into its rented space in the Saturday Evening Post Building at 641 Lexington Avenue, a woman familiar with the entire layout received a phone call one Sunday in Philadelphia, where she was visiting relatives. "Come on up, we have someone who wants to see the shop," she was told. The surreptitious visitor was Semenenko, who chose the solitude of a New York Sunday afternoon so that his appearance wouldn't cause a stir and more gossip.

Culligan's round-the-clock salesmanship, the cost-cutting and the internal reforms began to pay off for Curtis Publishing Company by mid-1963. Enough rank-and-file deadwood was chopped out of Curtis—2,500 jobs in all—to lower the annual payroll by

$13 million. Printing operations were streamlined; workmen disassembled the huge mechanical innards of the Curtis Building and packed the presses off to Sharon Hill. Fixed expenses dropped by $15 to $18 million annually, meaning the *Post* and the other magazines had a lower break-even point per issue. According to Curtis annual reports, selling, general and administrative expenses in 1961 were $62.6 million; this was down to $58.2 million in 1962 and $44.9 million in 1963. Production and delivery expenses dropped from $116.3 million to $106.5 and $103.2 million in the same stages.

Through the cost-cutting program the deficit of $18,917,000 in 1962 was arrested; the loss for 1963, Culligan's first full year as president, was $3,393,000. In the last quarter of the year, Curtis operated profitably for the first time since 1961—a net profit of $1.4 million. This was repeated in the first quarter of 1964, with operating profits of $96,000.

According to the 1963 Curtis annual report—which Culligan considers the best existent documentary evidence of his managerial prowess—all Curtis magazines showed substantial advertising gains for the last six months of the year.

Here's a breakdown, as listed by Curtis:

> *The Saturday Evening Post*—53 pages
> *The Ladies' Home Journal*—99 pages
> *Holiday*—23 pages
> *The American Home*—52 pages

For the entire year the *Journal* gained 168 pages, or 26 percent over 1962; *American Home* followed closely with a 106-page advance, 24 percent. As for the *Post*, "The second half of 1963 marked the first time since 1960 that advertising pages in this magazine were ahead of figures for the comparable period in the preceding year. This was significant, because it indicated that the *Post* had reversed its downward trend." Culligan said 93 *Post* advertisers used more space in 1963 than they did in 1962, and there were 190 new *Post* advertisers during the year.

Thirty-two advertisers invested more than a million dollars each in Curtis magazines that year. The gains of the *Post* and Curtis were told in the optimistic tongue known as *annual reportese*. To Culligan only the rankest of carpers would look behind his exclamations to point out that the *Post,* for the entire year, continued its sickening drop—in both lineage and in revenue. In 1962 it had 1,574.28 pages of ads worth $66,517,157; a year later, after The Curtis Commitment of Joe Culligan and the "sophisticated muckraking" of editorial director Clay D. Blair, Jr., the *Post* ran 1,462.01 ad pages with revenues of only $60,723,905. The *Ladies' Home Journal,* on the other hand, put out a "more Curtis" product under editor Curtiss Anderson and its lineage and revenue increased from 650.94 pages and $23,428,199 to 818.66 pages and $27,783,139, respectively.

Culligan also sought to turn Curtis in the direction of outside money. He established a development division to survey the parent firm's holdings with the view of making extra money from existing facilities. One profitable side angle was found in the magazines themselves. The dearth of advertising meant extra space that otherwise would have been filled with "house ads"—Curtis' own corporate messages. The development people approached manufacturers of mail-order goods and worked out deals under which Curtis went into the retail business. Curtis ran ads for the merchandise—using a dummy name to conceal its interest—and collected the orders and the money. The manufacturer shipped the items (of the do-it-yourself ilk) and received, in addition to its wholesale price, a one-dollar commission. Some *Saturday Evening Post* ads produced as much as $40,000 revenue on a full page—as much as Curtis would have received had it been sold to an advertiser. Manufacturers liked this because they would not have been able to afford the cost of a full-page *Post* ad; Curtis liked it because it added girth to their magazines, and a profit on space that otherwise would have been filled with promotional material.

But beneath the façade of recovery there remained weaknesses in Curtis. Culligan patched them over and forgot them while he worried about other matters. During his first hectic months, when literally only his salesmanship and charisma stood between Curtis and bankruptcy, Culligan was forced to delegate almost totally his responsibility for internal operations. He did so both of necessity and choice. The clock and human stamina limit what one man can do; on the basis of priorities, salesmanship came first, on the indisputable grounds that the immediacy of saving Curtis was more important than shifting individuals on an organizational chart. Yet the lack of internal stability in Curtis—attributable to the absence of an absolute boss on the premises—was ultimately to be Culligan's downfall. Curtis was sagging when Culligan came in; he temporarily inflated it, but didn't plug the holes. So all that he put into it leaked out again once he relaxed.

Culligan showed no signs of liking the day-to-day routine of running Curtis; this he put in the capable, but unauthoritarian, hands of Clifford—for the first 18 months, at least. For himself, Culligan took the role of "Mr. Curtis Publishing Company" in a year-long road show that played more stops than an over-nighter Southern circus. His wares were Curtis Publishing—and Joe Culligan. "No door is ever closed to the president of Curtis Publishing Company, not even Henry Ford's," he explained to other executives who suggested he might spend more time at Independence Square.

An editor now departed told of calling Culligan to say he had a problem and wanted a brief chat to clarify some policy matters. In the days of Hibbs or Lorimer the door would have opened immediately; Curtis was magazines, and management knew it, and gave the magazines the attention they required. The editor quotes Culligan as replying to him:

"I've had eight hours in the office in the last three months. If it's an editorial problem, take it to Blair. If it's an advertising problem, take it to Veronis. If it's a promotion matter, take it to that other guy. That's what those people are for. I can't waste time on detail work. That's what got Bob MacNeal in trouble." The editor never got the conference.

The lack of supervision was apparent to Madison Avenue agency people who saw Curtis where it counted—at the sales level—and from them came the advertising dollars which kept the company alive. At one time the *Saturday Evening Post* had 17 ad salesmen in New York alone—and 10 sales executives, not counting Culligan, who dealt with companies on "the Henry Ford level." Publisher MacNelly spent the bulk of his time on the street selling, rather than directing the force under him. The new regime had turned out the old so rapidly that continuity was lost; advertisers who spent scores of thousands of dollars annually told Bernard Gallagher they went for weeks without seeing a *Post* representative.

Culligan, meanwhile, angered his old Madison Avenue pals by bypassing agencies and advertising directors with his "Henry Ford level" approach to selling companies. "Joe can get away with that for a while," one agency executive said. "The manufacturers had read all about him—Lord knows, he got enough publicity—and they wanted to take a look at him. So he got some advertising.

"But this president isn't always going to have time to handle his advertising budget personally. Joe's going to find that front door a little harder to crash the second time. That puts it in the hands of the agency or the director again. Quite frankly, I have no qualms about cutting the guts out of a guy who goes over my head, or bypasses me. He's taking money out of my pocket and making me look like I'm not doing my job."

From the space salesman's viewpoint the Culligan regime was a continuing nightmare, interrupted sporadically by pep talks which, after a while, no one took seriously. The lack of direction left salesmen floundering on their own, and those at the top constantly changed the rules. The Curtis Combination was Culligan's idea on how to persuade major advertisers to take space in almost every issue of every Curtis magazine. But one former adman said, "There was no firm policy on the amount of discount we were allowed to give. It changed all the time, and often we in the field didn't know about it. But word got around in a hurry. It was damned embarrassing to have an agency man ask for the 'same deal X got' and have to sit there and hope you would winnow from him just what in hell somebody else had been allowed to give X in the way of a discount."

The Curtis Combination brought the magazines long-term non-cancelable contracts, but some advertising executives wondered if the price Curtis received was worth it. General Electric, for example, got a handsome discount on the four-color full-page rate for a three-year period. A man familiar with this contract said: "That's a lot of business, but that's also a lot of dollars we're letting get out of our hands."

The definition of The Curtis Combination also was vaporous. "At first it called for every issue of every book. As it worked out, however, everybody got 'favorable' rates—only some were less favorable, others were more favorable. Campbell's Soup, for instance, wouldn't go near *Holiday*. Their people figured readers weren't going to be thinking about tomato soup when they were curled up with the magazine dreaming about Bermuda or Capri. So they balked. What happens? They're let into The Curtis Combination without buying *Holiday*. Here we are, working our tails off in the field, trying to build advertiser confidence in the new management, and the new image, and all of a sudden the ground rules are changed."

When Culligan and Clifford cut costs, they concentrated on the so-called "service" departments whose very nature precluded them from contributing direct profits to the company. In a time of fiscal emergency these were considered luxuries which could be temporarily abandoned. The research department, which at one time had up to 100 workers, went to 12 overnight, and then down to one man.

"We were left without factual data on which to base our sales talk," recollects a former advertising man. "The art department formerly had prepared all sorts of sales material—charts, graphs—showing what Curtis magazines could do for them. This vanished."

The firings hit the sales force with bombshell impact. With

one swipe of a pen the entire Philadelphia sales office for the *Post* vanished. "From day to day you didn't know where you stood, whether you would even have a job the next morning. Morale was as low as the bottom of the Delaware River, and not much brighter. Hell, in self-defense, people started looking for jobs. They'd spend as much time in interviews as they did pushing the *Post*." Space salesmen were unhappy both in their own office and on the street. The constant turmoil in management reverberated around them. "How many times did I see an agency man lean back and say to me, 'Straighten out your own house and then come around again; I'm not very enthusiastic about what's happening at Curtis, and I'm not sure I want to get my clients involved.' A few statements like that—the burden of selling both your magazine and your management, and you really not believing in either yourself—saps whatever enthusiasms you might have been able to muster. Especially when you agree with the agency man, deep down inside."

The managerial chaos—a chain reaction started by the injection of volatile, eager new executives into a power vacuum—afflicted every Curtis office at one time or another during Culligan's early months. The revolution left isolated little empires vacant throughout Curtis, targets for anyone who felt powerful enough to grab them. Culligan, who thought in terms of million-dollar deals, gave cursory attention to the turmoil below him. Indicative of his attitude toward the detail work of corporate management was the collapse of Premium Service Co., which fell victim to what might be called "incestuous cannibalism."

Premium Service Company was a wholly owned subsidiary which had been a small but steady profit maker since Curtis purchased it in 1938. It offered coupon redemption deals to manufacturers of cigarettes, soaps and household products, and an independent trading stamp plan to small grocers. Twenty to thirty percent of its volume came through Curtis Circulation Company, another subsidiary, in the form of prizes for subscription contests and other promotions. The head of Premium

Service fell ill in 1963, and Culligan dispatched a consultant to Teterboro, New Jersey, the Premium Service headquarters, to make a survey. The consultant recommended moving the company to space in the Curtis Building which had been vacated by the printing division. He also said Premium Service had so much business it could get along without a sales force. So 150 white collar and sales people were fired, and Premium Service came south—to disaster. In Teterboro it had a five-year-old, one-story warehouse built for rapid shipping on a volume basis. In Philadelphia it was crammed into an upper floor of the Curtis Building, with sporadic elevator service and an antiquated floor layout that made a botch of the traffic system. The only saving was on the rent; further, anyone who knew anything about the premium business had been fired in Teterboro, and new managers installed. In 15 months Premium Service's volume dropped from $2.3 million to just over $1 million. Customer handling deteriorated so badly that clients left en masse; without a sales force, Premium Service was unable to replace them.

Even more incredible, Premium Service then got into a knockdown family fight with its sibling, Curtis Circulation, which was griping loudly about poor service. Premium Service took the offensive: If Curtis Circulation paid rates 10 percent higher, it said, perhaps Premium Service would continue to handle its business. The assertion of strength—especially where no strength existed—brought only a guffaw from Curtis Circulation, which signed with an outside premium company. At one swoop Premium Service lost 40 percent of its volume. That figure isn't exact. "We couldn't decipher our records," said a former executive. Culligan was furious, but the deal was final. Management gave curt orders: "Sell Premium Service off at the best price you can get." In 24 hours 80 to 90 persons received pink slips; the proceeds of the piecemeal sale were barely enough to cover the $300,000-odd debt Premium Service owed to Curtis Publishing Company.

Why didn't Culligan bang heads and keep one subsidiary from killing the other in fratricidal warfare? "Culligan was busy with bigger fish," said a former executive. "His lines of communication were poor, and he didn't have that knack of incisive questioning that brings out the truth of an involved situation."

Put more concisely, Joe Culligan was the boss of Curtis Publishing Company, but he wasn't controlling Curtis Publishing Company. The demise of Premium Service Company because of the intraoffice feuding among subordinates went unnoticed by the outside world. But to inside observers, the import was clear: Joe Culligan was administering creditable artificial respiration, but he had yet to put his subject into a position where it could breathe on its own.

Chapter Eight

HIS bushy black eyebrows screwed into a tight knot, Clay Drewry Blair, Jr., disrupted the afternoon calm at Curtis Publishing Company.

"Blair, you're an important man. Blair, you're wonderful," he extolled, hand jabbing the air as he gazed over Independence Square across from the Curtis Building in Philadelphia.

Below, unaware of the declamation in the sky, children and squirrels chattered across the grass.

A few onlookers suppressed snickers in the *Saturday Evening Post* office. Their managing editor had just bolstered his spirits with what secretaries jokingly—and oh so quietly—called "self-inflation."

But Clay Blair, Jr., seldom needed self-inflation. In 1962, at the age of thirty-seven, he became editorial director of all Curtis publications, the magazines that once constituted the most influential and affluent publishing empire in America. And, less than two years later, he and associate Marvin D. Kantor made a bold grab for control of all of Curtis by trying to oust Matthew J. Culligan as chief executive officer of the publishing house.

Blair failed—"painted into a corner by ambition," as one former colleague put it. But even in failure he left an indelible impression on Curtis' magazines and name. Just as Joe Culligan steered Curtis' corporate image 180 degrees from Philadelphia staidness and dignity, Blair made Curtis' editorial image one of controversy. And, although Blair has been out of Curtis since November, 1964, his influence lingers; the entire organization is seeded with editors brought in by him, and Curtis publications for years to come will reflect Blair.

Blair was frank about his Curtis goals—to a point. He said he intended "to restore the crusading spirit, the sophisticated muckraking, the exposé in the mass magazine. We're going to provoke people, make 'em mad." With six libel suits in the courts (two of which resulted in six-figure verdicts and settlements) Blair said, "We are hitting them where it hurts, with solid, meaningful journalism." The *Saturday Evening Post,* which Ben Hibbs once edited for the entire family, trumpeted exposés of vice and crime and sickening photographic layouts on Thalidomide babies (nine pages and the cover of a 96-page issue in 1962). Norman Rockwell, whose homey, comfortable paintings tickled the collective fancy of a generation (Blair called them "anachronisms,") was replaced with black-and-white "splash" photographs. Blair's *Post* was terse, muscular, journalistic; it abounded with life and its pages reflected the enthusiasm of the men editing it. From week to week the *Post* was uneven as it struggled through a second great transformation in two years' time; the surprises it offered delighted some readers, infuriated others. "One week we looked like *Life,* the next like the *National Enquirer,*" said a former editorial worker who didn't like the Blair style. "We were the hottest magazine in town for the entire year of 1963," says another who did like the Blair style. "We shook up the whole business. *Life* and *Look* had become fat and lazy; because of us they had to start doing enterprise reporting again. In that respect we were good for the magazine industry." Blair's *Post* was a modernized magazine, textually and graphically, and aimed at a younger and more urban readership.

But a cardinal rule of crusading is that the crusader must never fall off his horse. Once he does, he is a ridiculous figure whose future exposés are viewed with skeptically cocked eyebrows and disbelief. But that is exactly what happened to Blair and the *Post*, and often enough to shatter the reputation for trustworthiness that the *Post* had so carefully built and protected during the editorships of Lorimer and Hibbs.

Blair's unceremonious falls resounded in the publishing and legal worlds. They were doubly costly. The size of the libel payments was bad enough; the $300,000 given to Alabama football coach Paul (Bear) Bryant alone was almost half the advertising income of some issues of the *Saturday Evening Post*. But the public disgraces soured advertiser confidence in the *Post* at the very time financial wolves howled outside the Curtis door. For better or for worse, some advertisers don't like to be associated with a controversy—especially when a jury decides that the person stirring up the trouble is wrong, as happened to the *Post*.

Blair's life was turbulent even before he came to the *Post*. Through all his experiences runs a common strand: a preoccupation with bravery, and a frequent assertion of his lack of fear. In a *Post* promotion brochure issued in 1962, just after he began his meteoric rise, Blair said, "The real measure of a man is not how he performs in times of peace and prosperity but in times of adversity. I admire men who work and fight to the end under fire ... I am not afraid of anything, and I feel that fear is an indefensible emotion. Fear is something that a man feels when faced with an unknown, but he should probe the cause of his fear and learn what to do about it. Instead of provoking helpless frenzy, fear should be a call to action." A skin-diving enthusiast, he devoted long paragraphs in one of his books on the "psychological closet" he encountered on his first trip beneath the surface with artificial breathing equipment and how he conquered fear under water, even to the point of swimming *at* sharks to frighten them away. He was proud to be the first reporter to fly in a B-52 jet bomber, and the first reporter to be submerged on a Navy submarine when it fired a missile. A former co-worker recollects only two inconsistencies in Blair's professions of bravery. He refused to stay alone in his Philadelphia suburban home in the summer of 1962, while his family was out of town, "because somebody might take a potshot at me." ("We were in the firing period then—somebody REALLY MIGHT have shot at Blair," this person said.) Blair insisted on moving into a downtown hotel. Then, as later, he demanded a room on a lower floor, choosing street noise over height.

After graduation from high school at age eighteen, Blair volunteered for the Navy and spent 22 months in the submarine service, participating in two combat patrols against the Japanese. Off Hokkaido, northernmost island in the Japanese chain, Blair's submarine surfaced on a bright, cold night to charge its batteries. A Japanese plane swooped down, guns blazing, and the sub had to crash-dive. A lookout dropped a glove, which jammed under the hatch of the conning tower. As Blair told the story in the *Post* promotion booklet: "As we went under, torrents of water began to pour in. . . . It was one hell of a mess. I fought my way through a column of water to the intercom and ordered the ship to blow its safety tanks so we could get back to the surface before we all drowned." Again, off Kobe, a Japanese sub fired two torpedoes at Blair's surfaced craft. The helmsman froze. "I grabbed the wheel and gave it a turn," Blair said, "and we went between the two torpedoes. It was one of those moments when any action, right or wrong, seems better than doing nothing."

After the war Blair attended Tulane University and the Columbia University Graduate School of Journalism. At twenty-five he went to the Pentagon as a Time-Life correspondent, working under Robert L. Sherrod, later his superior at the *Post*. Blair was awed at Sherrod's constant contact with admirals, generals and cabinet members. "I would look at him and say to myself, 'This guy is a real pro.'" Blair, too, learned to talk the language of the military man; he was respectful of, but not cowed by, the stars on an officer's shoulders. Within a few months he broke a bureaucratic wall of secrecy and printed the first definitive story on the atomic-powered submarine and its builder, then-Captain Hyman Rickover. An even more controversial story developed: Blair found that tradition-bound

Navy brass, resentful of Rickover's achievements, were denying him a promotion to rear admiral. Over Rickover's objections Blair launched a crusade that prompted a Congressional investigation, a public furor and a White House edict that resulted in the promotion. Blair still believes this crusade to be one of the most important achievements of his life. The Rickover research team was kept intact, and, as the *Post* promotion booklet pointed out, "It has since turned out impressive numbers of nuclear-powered submarines, plus an atomic cruiser, destroyer, and aircraft carrier. Rickover's perfection of the nuclear-powered submarine made possible the development of the Polaris Weapons System, the only undisputed weapons lead the U.S. holds over the USSR." From this crusade Blair wrote his first book, *The Atomic Submarine and Admiral Rickover*. Rickover didn't like the publicity for a while and wouldn't speak to Blair; they became friends later, however, and, as Blair said, "Rickover calls me from time to time to ask one simple, needling question: 'What have you done for your country—lately?' "

By 1957, Sherrod was with the *Post* as managing editor; Blair came to him one day in Washington and said he'd like to join the magazine. Sherrod says he was delighted. "We hadn't been able to hire a new man in quite a while." Beverly Smith, then Washington editor for the *Post,* did some investigating and sent Hibbs an eight-page memorandum on Blair's impressive background. Hibbs says he hired Blair, on Smith's recommendation, because Blair "was a good writer, and he knew Washington and how to develop stories."

Blair right away displayed that he was eager to participate in any changes that might be made in Curtis. The Washington bureau was considering renting new offices; a month after he joined the payroll Blair grabbed a tapemeasure and eagerly crawled across the floor, computing how much space would be needed. Hibbs and Sherrod liked Blair's capacity for work, and the speed with which he ground out stories on the military. He wrote the first-person account of Commander William R. Anderson's voyage under the Arctic polar cap in the *Nautilus* (later expanded into a best-selling book, *Nautilus 90 North*); his friendships with admirals and generals sprinkled the *Post* with authoritative accounts of what was happening in the U.S. military establishment.

In the summer of 1959, Blair came to the Philadelphia office as an assistant managing editor. The format change was brewing, and those in the organization knew far-reaching changes were to be made in the near future. Blair wanted to be in on them. What he saw, he said later, "appalled me. I couldn't believe that this was a corporation in modern America. I was stunned—but I made a thorough investigation, as instructed, and wrote a 10,000-word report." Another person at Curtis at the time gives a different version. "He arranged the job as troubleshooter, convincing those in authority that a fresh look by someone from the outside would be helpful. He was frank in telling people around the office that his mission was to 'save the *Saturday Evening Post*.' He roamed the corridors for weeks, talking with people. He watched how often we sharpened pencils, he clocked when we came to work. His memorandum griped about the deadwood and the slow pace of the office. He didn't see why people should come to work fifteen minutes late and leave fifteen minutes early."

The newcomer at first impressed colleagues with his Southern congeniality. He would sit for hours, questioning, listening, discussing editorial problems. Some noticed, however, that their own ideas sometimes appeared in lengthly memos Blair wrote for Hibbs and Robert Fuoss, the managing editor and heir-designee. One man called him a "brainpicker, but capable of taking ideas and putting them to work."

Blair was publicly outspoken toward fellow editors. An editor once returned from a trip to New York and reported to Blair that "pickings are rather slim this time." Blair bridled. "For Crissakes," he said, "who are you working for—the agents or the *Saturday Evening Post?*" In times of stress he gorged on Cokes and coffee—eight or ten cups in a morning when a particularly troublesome problem was at hand. When he became managing editor, he hired a young Main Line debutante who wanted "publishing experience" and made her his "personal assistant." A colleague said, "Waitress would have been a better title." The girl did little more than trot to the cafeteria for Blair's coffee (which involved enough mileage to tire a track star) and to deliver his communications. Blair was dogmatic about his abilities. Questioned about a decision, he pounded his stiffened index finger on the desk and said loudly: "I never make a mistake. I am never wrong." He operated at breakneck speed, "always starting 22 projects at once," said an associate, "and not giving any single one much attention."

Blair found himself a spot on the team that was designing the new format. His role was that of the activist, who argued for "jazzy" photographic layouts. "Make the *Post* completely distinguishable from what it has been in the past," he said. "We've got to give the old girl a completely new face." When others on the team balked at the drastic measures advocated by Blair, the disputes were resolved with raised-voice arguments. Blair was candid about his intentions of "waking up this place." He bought a rubber stamp with the imprint Go Go Go CB and used it to sign his aggressive, confident—and often voluminous—memorandums.

When the "new *Post*" proved a dismal flop, Blair executed a deft sidestep—and then a major leap forward. Editorial workers who had watched him help mold the revamped magazine suddenly saw him shy away from responsibility with an "I told you so" attitude. When Fuoss quit as editor in March, 1962, Blair moved up as managing editor under Robert L. Sherrod. But Blair by now had more important things on his mind than an editorial chair in one magazine: He was thinking in terms of the entire Curtis Publishing Company.

During Blair's Pentagon days he made friends with Admiral Lewis Strauss, chairman of the Atomic Energy Commission. In 1954 Blair wrote a book, *The Hydrogen Bomb,* with Time-Life colleague James Shepley, which praised Strauss' role in development of the weapon in spite of opposition from the scientific community. Strauss at first was angered and offered to pay for nonpublication, for fear of aggravating the scientific community. Failing, his attitude changed and after he left public office and joined a New York brokerage house, he maintained close contact with Blair.

In the spring of 1962, when Strauss stimulated the merger talks between Doubleday & Company and Curtis, Blair did some corporate investigatory work which took him far beyond the bounds of the *Saturday Evening Post* office. Afternoons, nights, weekends, he conferred with production and advertising people, compiling facts and figures on virtually every aspect of the Curtis operation. He cross-examined accountants and department heads; he prowled around pressrooms and the bindery. When Blair finished, he thought he knew more about Curtis than most men in the building, and he had a reason.

Simply, Blair knew that Robert A. MacNeal was going to be fired, and in his thinking a good candidate for a replacement was none other than Clay Drewry Blair, Jr., managing editor of the *Saturday Evening Post*.

All spring Blair worked on his report. He sounded out support within the company; numerous executives gave him advice on needed reforms in departments.

The product of Blair's research was dropped on the Curtis executive committee in May, 1962. It was at once a management study and a revolutionary manifesto, and one which made Clay Blair, Jr., the maximum leader. The four-page, single-spaced report was entitled "Tomorrow Morning's Plan." Item one was "Appointment of new executive team."

    a. Clay Blair, President—(ready)
    b. William Buckley, Exec. Vice-Pres.—(ready)
    c. —

On and on the list went, twelve slots in all, seven of them with a name to fill it and the word "ready." Judging from the memo, Blair was satisfied with his immediate superior, Robert Sherrod, who was on the list as *Post* editor "(in place)". Only two spots remained to be filled: treasurer and comptroller, "to be supplied."

The most drastic recommendations were for discontinuing publication of the *Ladies' Home Journal* and the *American Home*. Here are Blair's reasons for junking the *Journal*, as stated in the memo:

    a. Direct and hidden costs, at least $14 million a year.
    b. Cannot compete with *McCalls* [*sic*], while *McCalls* subsidized.
    c. Would require outlay of $20 million to renovate *LHJ*.
    d. Historical odds against monthly magazine, women's specialty. (TV inroads)
    e. Forces full-bore press running, no maintenance time, costly breakdown.
    f. Forces operation of two binderies, two shipping departments, expensive duplication.
    g. Is hedge against rising postal bill, which will further cripple company.
    h. Will enable substantial operating cost cuts in Circulation Company, data processing, etc.
    i. Sale of *LHJ* subscription list to *McCalls* could yield $4 million in cash, wipe out fulfillment obligations of *LHJ*.

Blair's memo claimed that the *American Home*'s losses ("probably accurate") were $5 million a year, and that sale of the subscription lists would yield $3 million cash. This magazine, he said, had all the disadvantages of the *Journal*.

Blair advocated deliberately reducing the *Saturday Evening Post* circulation to 5 million and maintaining it at that level. Here's why:

    a. Lops off expensive unstable top 1½ million circulation.
    b. Gives *SEP* high quality, definable audience, noncompetitive with *Life, Look,* TV. Fulfills promotion policy of

high quality reading magazine for influential people, in class alone, like *New Yorker.*

c. Reduces greatly cost per thousand in ad rates, enables some advertisers to return to magazine, offers new opportunity for advertisers. Enables reduction of and dependence on costly, futile split-run [regional] advertising.

d. Enables better study of demographic profile, proof of audience, influence. Vital factor in selling advertising.

e. Enables trimming of costly subscriptions in arrears.

f. Immediately reduces postal bill; is a hedge against further crippling postal increases.

g. Greater availability of presses from this reduction, together with folding of *LHJ* and *AH,* enables *SEP* to cut week from editorial lead time, become more competitive, or "timely" on newsstands.

h. Enables reduction in data processing, commissions, subscription fulfillment, etc.

i. Frees some presses for rotational maintenance, thus avoiding costly breakdowns.

j. Permits greater use of regional editorial material, if needed.

k. Enables better quality paper, manufacturing.

Blair's plan called for consolidation of everything except printing and distribution services in New York. Cyrus Curtis' prized Independence Square building would be sold ("value $4.0 m"). What about Curtis Circulation Company? "Retire worthless people." What about the persons displaced by the closing of the *Journal* and the *American Home?* "Transfer worthwhile people of discontinued . . . editorial and ad divisions to *SEP,* to fill existing gaps, improve level of personnel."

Mechanical functions would have been brought under one roof at the Sharon Hill printing plant. Blair wrote: "It would require considerable expansion of Sharon Hill facility, but plant is built to accommodate expansion. Expansion could be completed in six months. Expansion costs could be covered by mortgage money on plant or on a sale-leaseback arrangement.

Entire manufacturing plant would then be more attractive to prospective buyer in event of liquidation."

But Blair was thinking primarily of salvation, not liquidation. His closing paragraphs, through which he hoped to convince the executive committee that its search for a president should go no further, said:

> The foregoing recommendations are designed to reshape Curtis in order to direct, emphasize and support the *SEP*, which is the only property held by Curtis capable of making large amounts of money. (The *SEP* is currently losing money at the rate of $12 million a year.)
>
> The suggested moves are drastic. But such moves are required to save the company. As an example, the current payroll of this company amounts to $51 million annually. The suggested reorganization and consolidation would reduce the payroll to about $30 million or perhaps less.
>
> The termination of *LHJ* and *American Home* would reduce direct annual losses of $7 million (*LHJ*) and $5 million (*American Home*), for a total direct savings of $12 million annually. The indirect savings here might amount to an additional $6 million for a grand savings of $18 million. The consolidation of manufacturing, shipping and data processing, it is estimated, might save an additional $10 million, including payroll. The reduction in circulation of *SEP* might save as much as $10 million, although this might initially be offset by the loss in ad revenue. (Stretching-out of schedules because they were sold on a guaranteed basis of 6.5 million circulation.) However, overall, it is expected that ad revenues to *SEP* will increase in response to these moves and/or to sale of the company.
>
> The sale of the subscription lists of *LHJ* and *AH* would yield, immediately, about $7 million in cash.
>
> The sale, within six months, of the 6th Street building [Independence Square] would yield an additional $4 million in cash.
>
> Total cash available within six months: $11 million.

The executive committee read Blair's proposals with interest. But it wasn't in the mood to accept the first item on the list—appointment of Clay Blair as president. A director said of the plan: "A lot of these things were obvious, like a rejuvenation of the Curtis Circulation Company. And we carried out some of them—like the move to New York—but not because Blair suggested them. The fundamental thing was that we didn't agree with Blair that all we had was the *Saturday Evening Post*."

Why didn't the directors look upon Blair favorably as a prospective president? "This young man had been in Philadelphia two years and he was a reporter, thirty-seven years old, bright and inquisitive but without a day's managerial experience in his life. If his competence had matched his confidence, we would have signed him immediately."

But the directors, mindful of Blair's relationship with Strauss, weren't about to do anything precipitous to disturb the Doubleday talks. After MacNeal's firing, M. Albert Linton, executive committee chairman, announced Blair would help run the company pending selection of a president.

Blair gave signs he thought himself still to be in the running. He was on the phone constantly with Strauss. The afternoon the directors were to pick a president he slipped away to the office of a Philadelphia stockbroker who was working with Strauss; before leaving, however, he alerted an office worker to "be prepared for the photographers and reporters." After Culligan's selection, Blair came back to the Curtis Building disappointed but not crestfallen. That evening he located Culligan by telephone at a dinner party and introduced himself. The directors had knocked Blair off balance, but not off his feet. As a consolation prize he was made editorial director and vice-president.

"How many people came in to congratulate me?" he asked a girl in the office. "One—that mousy little copyreader." Blair threw back his head and laughed uproariously.

Joe Culligan established an immediate rapport with the hardworking young Blair when he settled into the Curtis presidency.

The Curtis power structure, too, remained aware of Strauss' continuing interest in a merger. So Culligan gave Blair the job of again surveying the entire Curtis organization. From July 15 through Labor Day, 1962, Blair went through Curtis as a sort of management investigator, using a tape recorder and a battery of secretaries to transcribe interviews. One of the chief witnesses was the ousted president, MacNeal, who trudged daily to Blair's taping sessions, his pockets jammed with papers and notebooks, as inundated with bits and pieces of detail as ever. Blair treated him in a manner that infuriated others in the room. When a question came up about circulation of a competing magazine, Blair said, "Okay, Bob, you must have a little note on you somewhere with the figure." In an aside he said, "Bob even knows the price of doughnuts downstairs in the cafeteria." This continued for weeks; Blair started the interviews in the early morning and they dragged on until midnight. MacNeal was red-eyed and weary, but noncomplaining, when it all ended.

One of the directors totally unimpressed with Blair's "study project" was Cary W. Bok. "It was typical Blair," Bok said. "The report was antipathetic to everything that had been done before—stressing the weak points and ignoring the good. It made a nice fat book which I am sure is still secreted somewhere in a safe."

One part of Blair's Tomorrow Morning's Plan was approved that summer—the move of the *Post*'s editorial offices to New York. Sherrod, who had replaced Fuoss as editor in March, says the reason was elementary. "I had a staff to rebuild," he said recently, "and I couldn't persuade people to come to Philadelphia, the condition the *Post* was in." The decision delighted Blair, because he never liked Philadelphia. "This is no place to save a magazine," he once said. He had a long list of "barbaric" features about the town—the restaurants, the lunch hours, the accepted 9-to-5 working day. But editors comfortably settled in Philadelphia and Main Line homes thought Blair's talk about a move was another of the fancies which occasionally flitted through his head and away into nothingness. The decision caught them by surprise.

Post fiction editor Stuart Rose was vacationing in Cape Hatteras when a resort operator called him to the phone. Expecting a long-distance call from his daughter, he answered, "Hello, darling."

"Darling, hell, this is Sherrod," was the reply. The editor proceeded to tell Rose of the move. Stunned, Rose returned to Philadelphia to see what was to be done.

It was then that Curtis workers heard for the first time the full import of the title "editorial director" which had been bestowed on Blair two months previously. Culligan sent a memorandum to all editors and department heads on September 5, 1962, which read, in part:

> The office of the Editorial Director will be on the third floor of 666 Fifth Avenue, New York. On this same floor will be the editorial staff of the *Saturday Evening Post,* and it is hoped that the editorial staffs of *Holiday,* the *American Home, Ladies' Home Journal* and *Jack and Jill* can be housed on the same floor. Thus for the first time, the editorial products of Curtis would be consolidated under one roof and will have the benefits of sharing support services, sharing ideas and information, and of being able to get corporate decisions directly and immediately.
>
> The Editorial Director will be on hand and available to give guidance and suggestions. His responsibility includes the editorial content of the magazines, the operational staffing of the magazines, the public acceptance of the magazines. This responsibility will not be exercised on a day-to-day basis; the editors are still in charge of their publications. And this responsibility will not be exercised to make the magazines conform to each other; the separate personalities and identities of each publication will be preserved, in fact, encouraged.
>
> As a service to the publications, Blair will make himself aware of major upcoming articles in the Curtis magazines, act to prevent a conflict or duplication of content. He will keep himself

equally aware of the competition, passing along to the editors his information on where the other magazines seem to be headed. He will serve as a liaison with the new Curtis Special Projects Department, to help suggest and encourage books or one-shots from Curtis magazine material. Blair will attend the scheduling meetings of the publications, and will have responsibility for determining the final closing schedules and formulae.

Under the Editorial Director will be the New York Photographic Lab, installed on the same third floor of 666 Fifth Avenue to service the needs—printing, processing, photostating, duplicating—of all the publications.

Culligan's order—which was drafted by Blair—in effect made Blair editor of all Curtis magazines. As a managing editor, however, he was still technically subordinate on the *Post* to Sherrod. Sherrod's reaction was direct. "I picked up the phone and called Joe Culligan in San Francisco and quit," he said. "He begged me not to, that we couldn't stand the trouble. He told me to get together with Clay and talk about it." That they did, the next day at lunch. Sherrod says Blair agreed not to interfere with his duties as *Post* editor. An hour later Blair presided over a staff meeting called to explain his new role. Some 25 editors gathered in a barren conference room to hear him; the atmosphere was grim, for some persons were still unsure of whether they would follow the already-departed furniture north to the new offices in Manhattan.

Sherrod stood silently at Blair's side, arms folded across his chest, and listened to the new editorial director. "Shall we buy this radio station or not? . . . that's the kind of decision I will make," Blair said, according to three editors at the meeting. Pointing to Sherrod, his onetime mentor at the Pentagon, he continued, "Bob Sherrod is your boss, and I'm Bob Sherrod's boss. I reserve the right, if I think we need another editor of the *Post*, to get another editor."

Sherrod "looked downright black" at this point, recollects

an editor who was there. Blair finally turned and said, "You want to say anything, Bob?"

"We all thought he would quit on the spot," the former editor said. "He struggled a minute, then said, 'No, meeting dismissed, pupils.'" Many of the staff members went away feeling they had seen Sherrod humiliated publicly. Sherrod, however, gives a different interpretation—that his dark expression displayed anger, not humiliation. "It was a double cross. Blair went back on what he had said one hour earlier." Out of loyalty to the *Post,* Sherrod went ahead with plans for the move of the editorial workers.

Staff members received personal interviews from Sherrod and Blair about whether they were to be retained on the *Post* in New York. The implication was that anyone who wanted to move would be permitted to do so. However, Blair after each talk made a mark in red pencil beside each name on a roster— "g" for go, or "n.g." for no go. Some of the old-timers were given face-saving outs; after a not-so-subtle Blair hint that they weren't wanted, they were free to tell colleagues they didn't like the idea of commuting. One man fired outright was Pete Martin, who had been with the *Post* since 1925, first as art editor, then as author of the "Pete Martin Calls On . . ." series which took *Post* readers into the homes of scores of celebrities. At one time Martin's articles had been fabulously popular; now Sherrod considered them an outdated feature "we didn't need any more." Says Martin, "Sherrod told me, 'Well, Pete, we're going to attack the entertainment industry from another point of view.' And that's what they did, too—*attacked* the entertainment industry. I never did that—I wrote *about* the entertainment industry. I quietly eased out of the office. Shocked? Yes, in a way. But I was not leaving the magazine I had worked for. If it had been Fuoss or Hibbs who turned me out, I would have felt horrible. As it was, at any rate, I didn't get out of the house for about six weeks." Martin now uses his "calls on" technique for the Philadelphia *Sunday Bulletin* Magazine and writes special advertising supplements. Somehow, copies of the *Saturday*

Evening Post never make it to Birchrunville, Pennsylvania, his farm home at the end of the Main Line.

The *Post* celebrated its arrival at 666 Fifth Avenue with a reception for the press. Blair was ebullient, the man in charge of the spanking new quarters. Highball casually cupped in his hand, he told what he planned to do with the magazines. But first, he had to tell about some of the shortcomings of the past, and how they made his job all the more difficult.

For one thing, Blair said, Curtis lagged on fast-breaking news stories. Within six months, he said, Curtis would decentralize its printing plants and publish simultaneously in all regions of the country, and move its closing date to within a week of newsstand time. (Rule of office politics: Promote to the public what you can't sell to directors in private.)

Blair didn't like the previous *Post* artwork; photographs, he opined, were much better. "The old *Post* cover was an anachronism. They were just gags and we're no longer in a gag-minded era." The fiction? "Corny stories," said Blair. Excerpts from books that were "publishing events" would be much better—specifically, *Sand Pebbles,* by former sailor Richard McKenna, which the *Post* was serializing at the time.

Then he broke off the implicit criticisms of Ben Hibbs and Robert Fuoss, his former bosses. He'd rather produce than talk, Blair said. "We've worn out our welcome on that matter. But I will say this. Our U.S.P.—unique selling proposition [using words right from Joe Culligan's Madison Avenue vocabulary]—is going to be text, good text by the finest writers. This will be a compelling and timely weekly magazine."

In New York, Blair started remaking the Curtis magazines with his type of editors. Don A. Schanche, a former colleague at Time-Life, was put in charge of recruiting. He interviewed prospects by the dozens, young, eager men, all eager to make of the *Post* something which it had never been before. The *Post* had one thing to offer: a challenge. One of the men hired was William Emerson, a senior editor of *Newsweek,* then thirty-seven years old and with the magazine nine years. Emerson was well up on the *Newsweek* masthead; he was responsible for seven "back of the book" departments and at one time had edited all fourteen in the magazine. Why did he choose to leave this stability for Curtis? As did many men in the magazine field, Emerson felt keenly that the *Post* should be kept alive; early in his career he was a writer and editor for *Collier's*, and its closing cut him deeply. "I had two offers from the *Post*," Emerson said, "to be articles editor in New York or to write out of Atlanta, my hometown. I decided there had better be a *Post to* write for, so I chose New York." Of those early days at the *Post*, when Curtis was in the midst of its $18.9 million loss year, Emerson says, "It was a real whaling voyage."

The newcomers liked the frenetic atmosphere of Blair's *Post* because they could put their talents to work immediately and watch the results appear in the magazine. Another editor who had been with *Time* said, "Most of us were tired of group editing. We were happy to get into the personal type of journalism that Clay encouraged." The tempo at the *Post* increased. "News magazines teach a fearsome discipline," says Emerson, "because they are written in the space of a few hours. You sit down to write a piece on closing day and you don't get up until you finish it. We didn't go exactly that far, but we cut all the dawdling out of the process." The new *Post* editors "intensified" editing, to use Emerson's term. "A senior editor presided over an article from its conception to its inclusion in the book. He helped research it, he critiqued the process, he gave instructions on rewrite or did it personally. He was responsible for captions, cover blurbs, overlines, all the way into the book. It's a matter of putting the greatest talent where the steam hits the wheel."

To clear the way for newcomers Curtis ran an editorial guillotine at full speed. An early victim was Harry Paxton, sports editor for two decades, who had scored many editorial coups for the *Post*. In 1961, for instance, Casey Stengel gave the *Post* his memoirs for less than *Life* had offered him "just because he wanted them to be handled by Paxton," a former staff member said. Paxton moved to New York, bought a home in the suburbs, worked in the new office a few months, then was called in one day and informed: "You no longer will be acceptable to the managing editor." Paxton was left holding two mortgages, one in Philadelphia, one on his new home.

Stuart Rose, fiction editor since the mid-1930's, tired of two weekly round-trip train rides to his home in Chester County, 35 miles south of Philadelphia. He also tired of Blair's cracks about *Post* fiction. "Blair was a brilliant journalist but an ignorant man," Rose commented. "The only comment I recall his making on literature was 'Why don't we run any Ernest Hemingway short stories?'" One of Rose's chores when Blair first came to Philadelphia was to introduce him to writers and agents. Fiction editors, assuredly, do not entertain writers in the Automat. A crack by Blair about "that racket Rose has" drifted around the office. "I think he resented people who knew important persons," Rose deducted. "He didn't understand the first thing about editing fiction." Yet Blair never criticized Rose directly; although he is twenty-five years older and 50 pounds lighter than Blair, old cavalry officer Rose said, "I always had the idea he was afraid of me, that I wouldn't take some of the things he tried on other people and got away with." Rose quit after several months and threw away his Pennsylvania Railroad timetable in relief. (Of eight senior editors on the *Post* masthead, four didn't make the trip to New York; none of the eight was on the masthead in the spring of 1965 ... nor was Blair, for that matter.)

Comfortable in his New York quarters, Blair set out to fulfill his aim of "making the *Post* the most talked-about magazine in America" through muscular, hard-hitting journalism. Sherrod's name adorned the masthead as editor for only five months after the move from Philadelphia, and friends said his face was not that of a happy man. During the day, Editor Sherrod was

Managing Editor Blair's boss, giving orders which Editorial Director Blair was free to rescind at night. "Sherrod was pale and dazed," said a former associate. Sherrod had first attempted to resign in September, 1962, to protest Blair's designation as editorial director. Three more times that fall and winter he gave his resignation to Culligan. Finally, in January, 1963, he made it stick. The formal announcement said Sherrod would become a roving editor because he felt "pent up in the office." Blair took the title of "editor-in-chief"—a new position in the Curtis organization; Lorimer and Hibbs were content with the simpler "editor"—and said Sherrod would head a "task force" of writers, artists and photographers to prepare articles on "the most important events in the world, wherever they are happening." Thus Sherrod returned to his first love, foreign correspondence.

Blair roamed the *Post* editorial offices restlessly. "Jazz it up, we need some jazz," he barked to makeup men. He would grab a heavy copy pencil and slash angrily across a layout. "Jazz it up, jazz it up, you've got to put some jazz into it." He considered himself an expert both on artwork and text; he had a liking for "blur" photographs—of a glob of unfathomable orange that was a man on a motorcycle, of a fantasmagoria of objects that the caption said was a football game.

Blair's aggressiveness took on new dimensions. Prudish souls —male as well as female—cringed at his scatological vocabulary, both written and verbal. He specialized in four-letter opinions, and loud ones, in the presence of red-faced secretaries. A Blair relic still preserved as a curiosity in the *Post* office is his red-penciled comment on an author listed among others on a memo: "Not this ———," using a five-letter obscenity. More delicate workers were shocked because Blair sent such communiqués across the office—secretary to secretary—without an envelope. As his tempo of 18- and 20-hour days increased, Blair often worked with an uncorked whisky bottle on his desk, available to all who needed stamina to match his driving pace.

(In the daytime this was replaced with a whisky-filled thermos jug.) Staff members learned to expect late-at-night phone calls from Blair at Toots Shor's, his favorite hangout. Blair lived in a $100,000 home in Greenwich and rode to work in a limousine; yet secretarial-level problems could put him into a fury. One girl came into his office late one Friday evening and said she would be leaving in two weeks to take another job. "Leave tonight," Blair ordered; within fifteen minutes she had cleared personal effects from her desk and was gone.

There was yet another Blair: a man who could, in a philosophical mood, talk untiringly about his fears that America was caught in a moral decline. He spoke earnestly, and frequently, about the corruption he observed as a reporter in government, in politics, in business. He is still quoted deridingly around Curtis as remarking, "I was in church when I decided I had to save the *Saturday Evening Post.*" But his friends are insistent that Blair's moral sense guided the *Post* into controversial areas, and that because of it he sought out stories that spotlighted shortcomings in American society. In an editorial on April 20, 1963, the *Post* said it intended to act "as a conscience—as an abrasive—for the competitive-enterprise system. We would point with pride to the achievements of that system, and we would relentlessly expose its failures and its weaknesses." It continued:

We live in an extraordinarily difficult era. The danger to our society is mortal. We have grown so fat, so lazy and complacent that we are peculiarly ill-equipped to respond to the challenge. We are preoccupied with the frills, with TV sets, extra cars, cabin cruisers, and other appurtenances of an affluent society. The signs of moral sickness are all around us: crime, dope addiction, juvenile delinquency. The economy is stagnated. Unemployment continues to rise. The legislative branch of our government, grown old and arthritic, is unable to cope with our problems. . . .

As a national magazine the *Post* has a responsibility to prod, to goad, to do what is necessary to awaken people to their responsibilities. The *Post* has an enormous power for good; and we intend to use it. If we infuriate individuals, or make them uncomfortable, that will have to be.

To Blair, the *Post* could become a reincarnation of *McClure's* Magazine, the first of the early-century muckrakers. He distributed copies of a biography, *Success Story: the Life and Times of S. S. McClure,* to everyone in the office with a covering memo: "McClure was perhaps the greatest magazine editor in history. Peter Lyon, who writes for *Holiday* occasionally, has done a fine job, I think. I hope you will enjoy the book as much as I did." Blair found rakable muck in Congress, in sports, in schools, in business. Writers Ben H. Bagdikian and Don Oberdorfer, in a lengthy article on outside interests of Congress, documented, among other things, how Rep. Emanuel Celler (D., N.Y.) used Congressional stationery to ask the Port of New York Authority to grant concessions to private law clients, and how Rep. Francis B. Walter (D., Pa.) used official stationery and government-paid telegrams to badger the Treasury Department in a case against a private law client. The *Post* delved into underworld influences in boxing. An article by Peter Maas detailed the peculiar public relations connection of Igor Cassini, the "Cholly Knickerbocker" society columnist for the Hearst syndicate, with the Dominican Republic. Maas then turned his material over to the Justice Department which, with the subpoena power he lacked, was able to delve even further into Cassini's affairs. A grand jury indicted Cassini, two months after the article appeared, for failure to register as an agent of a foreign government. In pre-trial motions Cassini contended the "prejudicial" *Post* article came from federal investigative files which were fed to the magazine. Confronted with evidence that Maas had given material to the Justice Department, rather than vice versa, Cassini pleaded *nolo contendere* and was placed on probation. In an editorial the *Post* said Cassini made some mistakes, then compounded them. "One of them was to try to pressure the *Post* into killing Maas' article.

He frightened us so much that we rushed the article into print —but only after rechecking our facts. We found them okay. So did the Justice Department."

The new *Post* delighted in the bombshells, the type of article that sets an entire nation to talking. And that it did indeed with a piece in the December 8, 1962, issue entitled, "In Time of Crisis," by Washington correspondents Stewart Alsop and Charles Bartlett. The article purported to be an inside account of the deliberations of the National Security Council during the Cuban missile crisis early that fall which resulted in the jaw-to-jaw confrontation of President Kennedy and Premier Khrushchev. It was also a public decapitation of United Nations Ambassador Adlai Stevenson. An inside-page headline ran, "An opponent charges, 'Adlai wanted a Munich. He wanted to trade U.S. bases for Cuban bases.'" This was opposite a full-page picture of a pensive Stevenson, finger against pursed lips; in juxtaposition with the anonymous accusation against him, the ambassador looked like a weak-willed nelly-nelly anxious to duck from view. The caption said, "Stevenson was strong during the UN debate, but inside the White House the hard-liners thought he was soft."

Only a few weeks earlier, Stevenson had stirred the nation when he stood over the USSR's Valerin Zorin in the Security Council, pointed to aerial photographs of Soviet missile bases in Cuba, and dared him to deny their origin. "I am prepared to wait . . . until hell freezes over for your reply," Stevenson said, brimming with indignation when Zorin demurred. The *Post* article, however, detracted from Stevenson's Finest Hour at the UN. The Ex-Comm (executive committee of the National Security Council) had agreed to blockade, first, and if Khrushchev didn't back down, to maintain the option of "destroying the missiles, and even of invading Cuba." The piece continued:

> Only Adlai Stevenson, who flew down from New York on Sunday, dissented from the Ex-Comm consensus. There is disagreement in retrospect about what Stevenson really wanted.

"Adlai wanted a Munich," says a non-admiring official who learned of his proposal. "He wanted to trade the Turkish, Italian and British missile bases for the Cuban bases." The Stevenson camp maintains that Stevenson was only willing to discuss Guantanamo and the European bases with the Communists after a neutralization of the Cuban missiles. But there seems to be no doubt that he preferred political negotiation to the alternative of military action.

The *Post* then proceeded to infer that Adlai's brilliant United Nations performance was stage-managed by others, and that he was a mere puppet. Presidential aide Arthur Schlesinger, Jr., was named as the author of Stevenson's "uncompromising" speech, and "tough-minded John McCloy," former commissioner to West Germany, was said to have been brought home hurriedly from a business meeting in Europe to consult with Stevenson. The implication was that a "weak-minded" Stevenson might well have written a "compromising" speech had he been left alone.

The article stirred up a fuss immediately—not only because of the accusation that Stevenson wanted to sell out national interests, but also because co-author Bartlett was known as a confidant of President Kennedy. Was the President using the *Post* to give Adlai a shove out of office? The tempest over the article made Stevenson the cover man on both *Time* and *Newsweek*. The *Time* treatment wasn't complimentary to Curtis. It called the Alsop-Bartlett piece a "panting account" of the Cuban crisis typical of the "hurry-up, behind-the-scenes exposés" of the new *Post;* and that some of the language seemed "to be left over from the magazine's serialization of *Fail-Safe.*"

Stevenson responded with fury and sarcasm to what he considered to be slights on his courage and common sense. "This must be some kind of record for irresponsible journalism," he said. "... the worst thing about the article [is] that the secrecy of one of the highest organs of the U. S. Government [the Security Council] has been seriously breached. Despite what has happened, I am convinced that most of the press in this country follows Joseph Pulitzer's very wise remark that accuracy is to a newspaper what virtue is to a lady. Of course, as someone pointed out, a newspaper can always print a retraction." In actuality, Stevenson said, he had supported the blockade but at the same time was "emphatically in favor of using the peace-keeping machinery" of the United Nations and of the Organization of American States. The *Post* stuck by the Alsop-Bartlett account, and Blair got the publicity he wanted: the story was on the front pages of newspapers for days. The issue of accuracy aside, the episode left a bad taste in many mouths. *Newsweek* concluded, after a four-page day-by-day recap, "The question is not whether one should admire Adlai Stevenson. The question is whether Adlai Stevenson—or any other member of the nation's highest councils of government—should not be permitted to speak his mind freely."

Blair later added a footnote to the entire incident by roundly roasting another journalist for the same type of advise-and-tell antics which gave Alsop and Bartlett material for their article. Emmet John Hughes, onetime aide and speech writer for President Eisenhower, wrote a no-rose-glasses insight into the White House in a sprightly book entitled *The Ordeal of Power*. The *Post* landed on him editorially with both feet as a "political renegade, a blabber of state secrets and a biased journalist." The editorial continued: "Suppose that you worked for the President of the United States. You drew your pay at the White House. The President trusted you and confided in you. You attended Cabinet meetings and were told the Administration's innermost secrets. What sort of loyalty would you owe the President in later life?" Adlai Stevenson conceivably might have liked to put the same question to the anonymous government official who leaked the "Munich" quote which the *Post* so eagerly printed.

Any resemblance to the *Post* of Hibbs vanished; Blair seemed to resent anything left over from the past and did his best to remove all traces of it. The week Sherrod resigned, Benjamin Franklin's silhouette disappeared from the *Post* title page.

("—— Franklin," he said.) The *Post* took on a new aura of sophistication. Hibbs had occasionally derided a person in print—gangster Mickey Cohen, for instance. But Blair jabbed indiscriminately. The *Post* poked fun at Grace Kelly and her husband, Prince Rainier of Monaco, for coming to Philadelphia to help Grace's brother Jack open a travel and vacation show. The whole point of two pages of sarcasm was that the Prince and Princess had no business inviting people to their country. Jarring notes appeared in unexpected places. A sparkling color layout carried Queen Elizabeth through a state visit to New Zealand. But the dignity was lessened by a shot of the queen with her dress at thigh level because of a gust of wind, the royal legs exposed to 6.5 million *Post* readers.

Blair's pages had heavy overtones of sexuality. The "Pete Martin Calls On . . ." pieces were replaced with spicy profiles of spicy Hollywood females—Melina Mercouri, Ann-Margret, Sandra Dee. Another star told candidly of her penchant for nude mixed bathing. (George Horace Lorimer, it might be said in passing, took a dim view of women who smoked cigarettes in *Post* fiction!) Blair reached the height of something or other with his issue of June 1, 1963, which devoted 28 pages and the cover (of a 74-page magazine) to Elizabeth Taylor, Richard Burton and the filming of *Cleopatra*. Readers were given a bed-by-bed account of the romance and the movie. A pixyish snapshot showed a piece of Elizabethan buttock peeking from beneath tight shorts; a cleavage shot dipped to within a fraction of an inch of the navel. "We got some letters about that issue," said a former office worker. "My, oh, my, did we get some letters. Yes, we got some letters."

The *Post* rang with a confident braggadocio which derided its past, lauded its present, and looked forward eagerly to its expected glorious future. An editorial March 2, 1963, said, "In years past, the purpose of *Post* fiction was simple: to provide easy escape and entertainment. Today the editors of the *Post* believe that if people want easy escape, they can get it from television. Fiction should serve a more noble purpose. It should enlighten the mind and provide new insight into our culture, our people and our problems, so that we can be better prepared to cope with the awesome age in which we live." A former *Post* editor said of this blurb, "Any man who calls William Faulkner—and we published quite a bit of his stuff—'easy escape entertainment' is either smarter than I and the English professors, or has access to some William Faulkner I've never come across, or is ignorant. I think the latter is the case." The editorial ticked off the short-story writers recruited by the *Post*—James Jones, William Saroyan, Graham Greene, Leon Uris, John Updike, Philip Wylie (the latter, incidentally, a *Post* contributor since the early 1940's). The *Post* made some other spectacular literary grabs: it published the Arthur Miller play, *After the Fall;* it introduced Kingsley Amis and Alberto Moravia to the mass American audience. But Stuart Rose, the former *Post* fiction editor, insists there is a vital difference. "In the old days the *Post* MADE writers; the *Post* today BUYS writers."

Blair shared Culligan's thin skin for personal criticism; *Time's* continual reference to its former reporter as "brash young Clay Blair" was particularly irritating. He was delighted when he had an opportunity to return the needling. An editorial went to great lengths to explain a Securities Exchange Commission report on a former *Time* business news editor who played the market on stocks of companies he featured in his section. This man, the SEC said, would buy a few days before publication, then sell when the stock rose on the basis of *Time's* laudatory story. He left the magazine before the report appeared, and *Time* wasn't nearly so detailed in its coverage as were other media. This tickled Blair; his editorial concluded: "It reminds us of an old story about the overworked *Time* editor. He got up from his desk, walked out into the hall, and shouted at the top of his lungs, 'I don't know.' According to the story, the whole building collapsed."

"The sons of bitches," William Emerson said recently of Time-Life's criticisms of Blair and the *Post.* "We got them back into enterprise reporting. *Life* and *Look* began going over the

Post carefully at their editorial conferences. We made *Life* reassess its own situation and start running more meaningful text. The professionals who were reading us saw a great advance. They were imitating us at any rate."

The *Post's* loudest bombshell of the "sophisticated muckraking" period exploded in the March 23, 1963, issue under the title, "The Story of a College Football Fix." But the bomb was as costly as it was noisy—both to the *Post's* pocketbook and the *Post's* reputation. An editor's note—now engraved in federal court appellate decisions—put the story and its implications into a nutshell:

> Not since the Chicago White Sox threw the 1919 World Series has there been a sports story as shocking as this one. This is the story of one fixed game of college football. Before the University of Georgia played the University of Alabama last September 22, Wally Butts, athletic director of Georgia, gave Paul (Bear) Bryant, head coach of Alabama, Georgia's plays, defensive patterns, all the significant secrets Georgia's football team possessed. The corrupt here were not professional ballplayers gone wrong, as in the 1919 Black Sox scandal. The corrupt were not disreputable gamblers, as in the scandals continuously afflicting college basketball. The corrupt were two men—Butts and Bryant—employed to educate and to guide young men.

The story that followed, under the byline of Frank Graham, Jr., a *Post* sportswriter, was damning to two of the most prominent—and popular—football coaches in the football-crazy Southeastern United States. Fellow Alabamans hold the same affection for the burly Bear Bryant as they do for their governor, George C. Wallace, simply because he turned out rough-and-tumble teams that won, and won handily and regularly. The name Butts was synonymous with football at Georgia, where he coached for 22 years and won membership in the Football Hall of Fame.

Succinctly, the *Post's* story was based on the word of one

man, George Burnett, an Atlanta insurance salesman. On September 13, 1962, Burnett testified later in federal court, he telephoned an Atlanta public relations office and suddenly heard a click on the line and an operator telling "Coach Butts" to wait while someone brought "Coach Bryant" from the practice field. Burnett, fascinated, listened for a quarter of an hour while the coaches talked. What he heard, he told Graham—and Graham told millions of *Post* readers—was a prattle-mouthed Butts reeling off offensive and defensive secrets of the Georgia team, and tip-offs on how to tell when the Georgia quarterback intended to pass. Burnett jotted notes as he listened. After the talk ended, he checked with the phone company and found a call had been made from Atlanta to the athletic department at the University of Alabama in Tuscaloosa. And he learned from the Atlanta public relations man, a friend and onetime business associate, that Butts had placed a long-distance call from a rear room of his office. Burnett concluded that an electronic quirk had cut his incoming call into the conversation between Butts and Bryant.

On September 22, nine days later, Alabama slaughtered Georgia 35–0, several touchdowns more than the predicted gambling spread. Through a mutual friend Burnett told his story to Johnny Griffiths, who had replaced Butts as head coach at Georgia the season before. Griffiths took the story to the Georgia regents; after an investigation, Butts was confronted with findings of a polygraph test on Burnett. He quit, effective immediately. But the regents were rough on Burnett and asked him embarrassing questions about a bad-check conviction on his record. Angered, Burnett got in touch with the Birmingham law firm of Beddow, Embry and Beddow, which was defending Curtis against a $500,000 suit filed by Bear Bryant the previous fall because of an article charging him with teaching players to be brutal. According to a Butts' brief that went uncontradicted, a member of the firm, Roderick Beddow, "initially sent [Curtis] this information about the alleged telephone conversation and was a principal in the initial work of the author Frank Graham."

The *Post* assembled the Butts-Bryant article on the dead run; so secretive was Blair's handling of it that he wouldn't let advance copies of the issue circulate even in the office before it was on the newsstands. Expense payments got the cloak-and-dagger treatment one would expect at the CIA. The article was undoubtedly the most sensational Blair printed while he ran the *Post*, yet he was so anxious to get it into print that it occupied the back of an issue and wasn't even mentioned on the cover, which had an earlier printing deadline.

On March 11, twelve days before the article was published, Butts' lawyer sent Curtis a telegram and letter, both protesting the "absolute falsity of the charges" contained in the story. The telegram and letter went unanswered, it was testified later in federal court. A long-distance telephone appeal by Butts' daughter also was unheeded.

The reaction was immediate, furious—and frightening to sober heads at the *Post*. Butts and Bryant made flat denials and filed suit for $10 million each. The Birmingham *News* proposed "*Saturday Evening Post* burning." The Alabama legislature, after a quicky investigation, gave its beloved Bear a clean bill of health. Georgia, however, found otherwise. Attorney General Eugene Cook said in a formal report, "The evidence, after a thorough investigation, indicates that vital and important information was given about the Georgia team, that it could have affected the outcome of the game and the margin of points scored."

Even as the libel suits headed for the courts, Blair couldn't resist a chortle over his scoop. A full-page editorial in the April 27 issue said that *Newsweek* begged to be let in on the story two weeks before publication and offered the *Post* credit if "you give us everything you have." Blair wasn't having any deals, however. "If *Newsweek* could beat us to the newsstands, we resolved to take it with a smile. That is what journalism is all about—the dissemination of truth, regardless of who prints it first." *Newsweek*'s leak on the story, the *Post* said, "was only hearsay which, in a story as powerful as this one, possesses no more validity than does hearsay in a court of law."

Curtis attorneys unsuccessfully tried to get the Butts trial out of Georgia on the theory it's best not to fight a hero on his home ground. The *Post* story lost some of its authenticity in a hurry. Sportswriter Graham admitted he hadn't seen Burnett's notes before writing the story. One of Burnett's associates said the notes produced in court weren't the same as had been shown him the day of the intercepted call. Players denied hearing Alabama defensive men shouting off Georgia plays in advance, as Graham had written. And then the jurors heard lawyers read a deposition in which Butts' attorneys cross-examined Blair about his "sophisticated muckraking."

A staff memorandum, written in January, 1963, read, "... you are putting out one hell of a fine magazine. The articles are timely, full of significance and exclusivity. The ... visual aspects have improved tremendously ... (fiction) could be one of the great breakthroughs in magazine publishing. The final yardstick: We have about six lawsuits pending, meaning we are hitting them where it hurts, with solid, meaningful journalism."

"You were not being facetious when you used the term 'sophisticated muckraking'?" Butts' lawyer asked.

"No," Blair replied.

"You meant it, then?"

"Yes."

"And you mean it now?"

"Yes."

Blair estimated that under the new editorial policy the magazine had traveled "25 percent along the way" toward the type of *Post* "I envision." And Butts' attorneys were careful to get into the record the fact that Curtis and the *Post* were losing money, and that the *Post*'s aggressiveness was motivated in part by economic necessity.

Blair also said in the deposition he had told *Newsweek* in an interview that one of his intentions, in addition to restoration of the "crusading spirit" in the *Post*, was to "provoke people, make them mad." Further, he admitted he had said: "But careers will be ruined, that is sure," and he did not quarrel with the fact that Butts' career was one of the careers to which reference was made in that statement.

Both coaches got on the stand and frankly said they had talked on the day in question. However, they said their discussion was a routine one on interpretations of new rules. Curtis attorneys were unable to prove from any players that information reached the teams. They were forced to attack Butts personally. University of Georgia officials testified his association with gamblers, his involvement with loan companies and his "night life" had tarnished the athletic director's image. Evidence was produced that he had been in contact with a known gambler. In final arguments Butts' lawyer, Allen Lockerman, shouted: "The *Post* has apparently gone into the business of buying libel suits. They have got untold millions of dollars in publicity. That's what they want!" A $10 million verdict for Butts, he said, "would be the greatest merchandising bargain the . . . *Post* ever bought."

The jury was out overnight, but much of the time was spent arguing whether it could give Butts more than the $5 million in punitive damages he asked. Its decision: $3 million punitive damages, $60,000 actual (based on $5,000 a year for 12 years, which the jury estimated as his remaining life span). A juror interviewed after the trial said that to the panel Butts symbolized "any person in the country that a magazine might have charged with 'fixing' or 'rigging' a game and 'being corrupt' without proving the charge."

In the closing days of the trial, suspense drew Blair to Atlanta; he was at the counsel table when the jury came in. He sat upright and listened to the price of the *Post's* scoop: roughly $1,000 a word. "We are disappointed and we shall appeal," he said. For one of the few recorded instances in his life Blair was totally lacking in bravado.

The trial judge later reduced the award to $460,000, saying

$3,060,000 was excessive. He told Butts either to accept the lower amount or go before a jury again. Both Butts and Curtis demurred, and the former coach started appeals for restoration of the full amount.

On July 16, 1965, the United States Third Circuit Court of Appeals in New Orleans, by a two-to-one decision, rejected Curtis' appeal, agreeing with the trial judge's opinion that "the guilt of the defendant was so clearly established by the evidence in the case so as to have left the jury no choice but to find the defendant liable." The dissenting judge, however, was favorably inclined toward an argument advanced by Curtis lawyers that Butts, as a "public official," could not be libeled. Curtis used as its arguing point *Sullivan vs. New York Times Co.*, a 1963 Supreme Court decision which held a public official can be criticized, even falsely, so long as the statements are not made with "actual malice." Curtis planned to advance the same argument to the Supreme Court, basing its "public official" definition of Butts on the fact that he was an employee of the University of Georgia, a state school.

Although Butts emerged as less than a sterling character, Curtis still was hit with the second highest libel verdict in United States history. The Curtis legal battery knew it could not tear down Bear Bryant's reputation; it couldn't get the trial shifted from Birmingham; it sensed an even worse licking. In early 1964, Curtis gave Bear Bryant a tax-free check for $300,000 to settle both the fix and the brutality cases.

The publicity generated by the Butts-Bryant affair was self-perpetuating; for months thereafter any libel suit brought against Curtis, no matter how trivial or unfounded, got a few lines in the daily press. The lay public, unused to reading the libel suit news that the daily press seldom prints about itself, got the idea lawyers were carrying away the Curtis Building brick by brick. However, Allison Page, of Pepper, Hamilton and Scheetz, the Curtis law firm, says this impression is unwarranted. A study of libel actions against Curtis, and the losses from them, showed no significant change in pattern over a 10-year period, Page says.

The tragedy of the Butts-Bryant article, from the *Post's* standpoint, is that it produced a welter of publicity when published, and even more exposure in court. To the layman—the average magazine buyer—the fact that a publication has been certified by a jury as unreliable is enough to dash his confidence in future controversial articles.

Excerpt from the 1963 Curtis annual report: "The new vitality of the *Post* was indicated by evidence from more than 40,000 news clippings and many excerpts from the *Congressional Record*. The *Post* was probably the most quoted magazine in America in 1963." (Commented a former Curtis public relations man: "Clay never understood the difference between publicity and notoriety. I saw little benefit in a bunch of clippings about Curtis being kicked around a courtroom.")

Concurrent with his supremacy at the *Saturday Evening Post,* Blair used his title of "editorial director" in an attempt to guide the other magazines. Repeatedly through 1962 and 1963 he skirted close to the provision in Joe Culligan's order that day-to-day operations of the magazines were the editor's responsibility. By doing so, he chipped at one of Curtis' most valuable assets, the editorial individuality of the publications. This asset doesn't appear as a dollar-and-cents item in the annual balance sheet—but whatever success Curtis had in past years was the product of the company's editors. Blair seemed surprised, almost resentful, that other Curtis publications recuperated and made money while the *Post* plunged deeper and deeper into red ink, and that his "sophisticated muckraking" didn't start a wildfire response among the reading public and advertising agencies.

Particularly surprising to the magazine industry was the phenomenal rebirth of the *Ladies' Home Journal*. As did the *Post*, the *Journal* skidded in the late 1950's. In 1961, for the first time in two decades, it lost money. When the Goulds retired as editors in 1962, they were replaced by a brilliant thirty-two-year-old Minnesotan, Curtiss Anderson, who had been managing editor. Anderson inherited the *Journal* in the spring of 1962, a few months before Blair became Curtis editorial director. The *Journal* went up; the *Post* continued its downward plunge. Blair was unhappy about this, and he also was unhappy about Anderson. For one thing, Anderson firmly believed that Cyrus H. K. Curtis' old dictum about "Find the right man and leave him alone" was still valid, and that was the basis upon which he took the *Journal* editorship. And he proved that a Curtis magazine could be made profitable without the intervention of Blair. Personal philosophies of editing also were involved. Blair wanted to stir up the animals. Anderson wanted to sit down with them and talk over their problems in a rational way.

Anderson had Edward W. Bok's knack of editorial innovation and Ben Hibbs' knack of editorial restraint; by a combination of the two the *Journal* performed what *The New York Times* called "one of the most amazing turnarounds in magazine history," both financially and editorially. From a deficit estimated at $2 to $3 million in 1962 (Curtis doesn't give figures on individual magazines for competitive reasons) Anderson pulled up the magazines by giant strides. His "World We Want" series represented vigorous journalism for women's magazines; the *Journal* explored the major problems of mankind, and proposed solutions for them—civil rights, welfare, peace, medical care for the aged, housing, birth control. Anderson gave publisher John J. Veronis a good product, and Veronis and Culligan sold it. In the first half of 1963 the *Journal* had only five issues rather than six, but total lineage increased 20 percent. The May, 1963, issue alone was up 37 percent, and June and July-August (the latter a combined issue) by 50 to 60 percent. The *Post,* meantime, under Blair was still losing an estimated $1 million per month and was down 20 percent in both newsstand sales and lineage.

Anderson began a cost-cutting program immediately upon

taking the editorship. The first step, in the early summer of 1962, was to move all the *Journal* editorial workers to New York. By so doing he consolidated two editorial staffs—food, decorating and fashion in New York, articles and fiction in Philadelphia—under a single roof. This Anderson did without adding office space in New York.

"The second act was the most difficult for me, but I realized it was essential to bringing the magazine back to a profitable level," Anderson says. "The staff I inherited numbered 170 people. We had cut back from 12 to 10 issues. But under no circumstances did I need so large a staff. I reduced its size from 170 to 80.

"I faced everyone I had to fire who was in Philadelphia— and at the end of the day I wept. If I'd had any idea what was to come in reference to the new regime, of course, I would never have accepted the responsibility."

In less than a year Anderson cut $1 million out of annual *Journal* production costs of $3 million. Additionally, he says, "We maintained the same high standards established so surely by the Goulds, while updating the graphics and becoming even more ambitious in elevating the quality of articles and fiction."

That Anderson righted the *Journal* at all was remarkable; that he righted the *Journal* in spite of the general financial chaos at Curtis puts his performance in the miracle category. By sheer will alone (plus a sense of humor) Anderson resisted attempts of Veronis to meddle in editorial matters with platoons of "consultants" and assistant publishers. Blair, however, continually pecked at Anderson. Blair thought the *Post* should be the "big name" magazine of the Curtis organization; the *Journal* (which, it will be remembered, he had recommended closing in 1962) was a prettied-up cookbook. When the *Journal* signed a new novel by Rumer Godden, a feminine favorite, Blair called the author's agent and directed that the work go to the *Post*. The baffled agent contacted the *Journal* and asked, "What goes on here?" The editor couldn't give a comprehensible answer for several minutes, then made it plain that

Miss Godden belonged to the *Journal.* The agent relayed the message to Blair: "I sold the novel to the *Journal,* and that's where it's going." (After Anderson's departure several months later, the *Post* took the Godden novel after all—sort of post-humously.) Again, Davis Thomas, an assistant managing editor of the *Post,* directed the *Journal* to buy a certain translation of *One Day in the Life of Ivan Denisovich.* Why? Well, the *Post* had purchased the "best" translation and feared a competitor would buy the other and publish it before the *Post* appeared. The *Journal* refused on principle, telling Thomas it was unethical to deceive an author and agent "with whom we had to work and give our word."

Although the *Post* was dipping to its lowest newsstand sales in modern history, Blair considered himself an authority on the selection of covers. He called the *Journal* each month with unhappy comments: Winter: "Why didn't you put Cary Grant on the main cover instead of the fold-out?" (Circulation research has proved men never sell on the covers of women's magazines.) March: "Why is the cover child off-center?" April: "Do you like that pink?" May: "Don't you think the pattern is too confusing?" (This from the man who okayed modern art illustrations for the *Post* and advocated "blur" photographs.) June: "Why red-white-and-blue in June?" The circulation company people added to the running commentary on covers: "Never run dark covers, light covers sell better. But never run two light covers in a row." Finally, in an attempt to test cover responses, the *Journal* scheduled two covers for different sections of the country for an issue. The idea was killed on the basis the magazine couldn't afford the cost. Thus unencumbered by positive intelligence, the critics could continue to carp at *Journal* covers at their pleasure.

In the late winter of 1962, Blair began pushing in earnest his plan of bringing the Curtis magazines closer together physically. He proposed moving the *Journal* staff from its offices at 1270 Sixth Avenue (where Anderson had consolidated them a few months earlier) to 666 Fifth Avenue, where the *Post* was established after its shift from Philadelphia. Under Blair's plan all editorial departments would be on one floor, with a mingling of certain staff members and a free interchange of ideas encouraged. The chief stated reason was economy. Once the move was carried out, Blair argued, the monetary saving would be considerable. Additionally, Blair would be in a better position to exert his authority as editorial director if the magazines were under one roof. Anderson resisted, and he was able to show there would be some immediate financial disadvantages. The *Journal's* lease on Sixth Avenue ran until 1964. The Goulds, 15 years earlier, spent $100,000 building a test kitchen there, which couldn't be moved. Anderson's strongest opposition, however, was the effect a consolidation would have upon his magazine. Any merger of editorial and art departments would "destroy the identity and individuality of the magazines. You can have the same switchboard, the same building, maybe the same photostat room, but nothing more. Hell, even newspapers with the same ownership don't share editorial facilities. That's the only way to preserve competition."

Anderson walked out of one merger conference in frustration; the next day he sent Blair a memo saying he was the "wrong editor at the wrong time" if the plan was carried out. Over lunch Blair was conciliatory; he told Anderson he didn't think much of the idea either (although he had advocated it in his 1962 memo for the executive committee). "I'm sorry to be stuck with these business assignments but we must do so to save money and the magazines," Blair told Anderson. (Translated loosely, that meant the floundering *Post* must be saved at all costs, even that of destroying the *Journal*.) Anderson went away still suspicious of Blair's sincerity, and his feelings were confirmed a few days later. One of Culligan's vice-presidents, at an editorial conference, mentioned that the *American Home* decorating editor, in her travels, found more material than she could use for her own magazine. "Some of it surely can slop over into the *Journal*," he told Anderson. "Your language is well-selected—it would be *slop-over*," Anderson replied. He tried to point out different approaches in decorating stories in the two magazines. Anderson tried to enlist the support of Hubbard Cobb, editor of the *American Home,* which also faced staff integration. "You can't fight City Hall," Cobb replied.

The consolidation talks dragged on through the spring of 1963; feeling the issue was dead, or at least indefinite, Anderson left for the Virgin Islands for his first vacation in two years. For a week he hoped to forget about Clay Blair and "Hungry John" Veronis and the consultants and the baby-care experts and the promotion department luncheon partners.

But no sooner had Anderson left town than Blair flung down the gauntlet. He ordered an article on birth control by Dr. Gregory Pincus, the discoverer of the first effective oral contraceptive, taken out of an issue. The import and the timing were clear. By challenging Anderson's independence in an undisguised frontal assault, Blair forced the *Journal* editor into the position of standing on his principles or yielding his independence forever. By acting while Anderson was out of the country, Blair indulged in a deft bit of psychological warfare. Would the editor be willing to leave the beach and come back and fight? *Journal* editors, loyal to Anderson and mindful of the struggle with Blair, summoned him home early. As it turned out, the issue was too far along for Blair to junk the entire article; as a gesture he rewrote the first few paragraphs. The confrontation when Anderson got back to New York was grim. "Are you going to be editor of the *Journal?*" Anderson asked Blair. "No, but neither are you," replied Blair. He said the article was too candid. Anderson sought to explain that the *Journal* was a highly intimate forum; that the "Tell Me, Doctor" column, in which the article appeared, was a no-holds-barred feature through which "the *Journal* managed to get closer to the woman than either her husband or her doctor."

But Blair wasn't having any of this. He had forced an issue and he now had a pretext for sacking Anderson. "After all," he said, "the *Journal* is not up to standards of Curtis Publishing Company." (This was one month before the *Post* devoted the cover and one-third of an issue to Elizabeth Taylor and Richard Burton.) Anderson bridled: "We'd have to go down to meet your personal standards," he told Blair. And with that Curtis Publishing Company lost the editor who had performed its most striking revival since Ben Hibbs saved the *Saturday Evening Post* in 1942.

There is evidence Culligan didn't know the seriousness of the Blair-Anderson clash until it was too late. Just before Anderson left for the Virgin Islands, Culligan offered him a generous stock option. He told Anderson he was on the "second level" of executives being let in on the plan—the "first level" apparently being Blair, Veronis, and newly recruited vice-presidents. Before Anderson could act on Culligan's offer, he was out of the company.

The assumption at the time, even among *Journal* staff members, was that Blair fired Anderson because of the birth-control article ruckus. "Birth control? MIRTH control," says Anderson. Of loyalty to Curtis he left without criticizing Blair publicly. But he did crystallize the dispute in a speech a few days later in which he said a true editor "cannot take his cues from some vaguely defined editorial director viewing his magazine from afar. And no one can edit more than one magazine at a time and maintain its individuality." Succinctly, Anderson wouldn't submit to the editorial director, whereupon the editorial director deliberately drove him out of the company.

Blair immediately dispatched a phalanx of *Saturday Evening Post* editors to take over the *Journal*. Anderson urged staff members not to resign in anger, pointing out they would lose severance benefits. Despite his personal treatment he didn't want to see the *Journal* blow up completely. Hubbard Cobb, editor of *American Home,* was put in as ostensible top man, but Blair and the *Post* crew arbitrarily junked and assigned articles without telling or consulting him. Cobb hung on gamely, pleading with staff members to remain with the magazine. The new editors, overnight, set out to remove any vestiges of Anderson's magazine. An Ursula Curtis book, *Child's Play* ("her best," said the man who bought it), was replaced by a James Michener novel on "nymphomaniacs in Asia." Year-old fashion pictures, taken by a female *Post* editor, were substituted for a feature already in type. Blair strode into the office and asked James Abel, the *Journal* art editor, if he liked *Journal* art. "Yes, of course, I designed it," said Abel—and was fired on the spot. Another man was discharged on the grounds that "you are too close to Anderson."

With Anderson out of the way, Blair and Veronis put through the merger plan he had opposed so vigorously. They set up a common fiction office to buy material for the magazines. They put the *American Home* and *Journal* offices under one roof. They established a common library, mail room and photographic and production staffs. The same group of editors was assigned to read, check and edit for style, copy for all the magazines. A common art editor was hired to select illustrations for both the *Post* and *Journal*. "We want to make the *Journal* a more contemporary and sophisticated magazine," said former space salesman Veronis.

These sweeping changes were announced in an unusual forum: in an interview Blair and Veronis gave Peter Bart of *The New York Times*. They also said "some 20 persons" would leave the *Journal* as a result of the merger. What they didn't tell Bart was that they had not informed the *Journal* staff of the shakeup. (Nor Joe Culligan, according to one report.) So editors got the news over their breakfast newspapers and went downtown to be fired. Seven heads rolled before noon. One woman marched into Cobb's office and asked point-blank: "Well, am I fired?"

"Who are you?" asked Cobb. "What do you do?"

"Poetry and fiction."

"Yes, yes, I guess so," murmured Cobb.

"Well, I lost my job through *The New York Times*," she announced when she came out.

Another editor handed Cobb a list of projects he had underway. "Have you read the *Times?*" Cobb asked.

"Yes."

"Obviously, these projects are no longer your concern."

The *Journal* offices were pandemonium the rest of the day. Editors who had quit or been fired wandered around, embracing and shouting, "I've been fired! I've been fired!" And some still on the payroll sat in grim little groups, complaining that they still had spots on the *Journal* masthead.

The dismissals forced upon him left Cobb broken and dispirited. "They made a liar out of me, they made a liar out of me," he said of Blair and Veronis time and again. The *Post* and the *Journal,* for the rest of the summer, were run by the same staff.

The revolving door at Curtis didn't turn—it spun, and so rapidly that the *Journal* masthead was outdated before issues got to the newsstand. In four issues the magazine had three editors—Anderson, Cobb (who was shipped back to *American Home* in two months) and Davis Thomas, the Blair crony from Time-Life who played a major part in designing the "new *Post"*—and four managing editors.

Blair's treatment of Anderson cost the *Journal* the man considered its most valued contributor, Dr. Benjamin Spock, the pediatrician who in ten years had developed an audience more devoted than that of any single department in the magazine. Previously, *Redbook* tried to hire away Spock at a higher price but he refused, saying his loyalty was with the Goulds and Anderson. Now he told Cobb he didn't like editorial policies of Blair and the *Post* and was leaving. ("Now the ship has deserted the sinking rats," said a *Journal* editor.)

Blair won, but his victory was Pyrrhic. By the end of the summer the *Journal* had so lost its individuality that wags in the trade called it "The Saturday Evening Journal."

Now happy elsewhere in publishing—as editor of Cowles' *Venture Magazine*—Anderson says he isn't bitter about any aspect of his Curtis career, "including its conclusion. I'm not sure that anyone could have been the editor of the *Journal* at that time—and serve with some degree of honor and integrity—without running head-on into Clay Blair. Perhaps no one would have touched the *Journal* had the *Post* been in a solid economic situation. While the *Journal* was losing money, it was insignificant next to the *Post*. The *Post*'s losses, as much as a million dollars a month, were always hovering, threatening every other product in the company.

"The *Post*'s drunk was our hangover—and anyone will grant that getting drunk *without* a hangover is an appealing slice of life, but having a hangover without getting drunk is the devil's own punishment."

The reasons Blair was able to ride roughshod over Curtiss Anderson cut to the heart of power politics. Curtis' lack of internal stability enabled Blair to do things that, had a firmer hand than that of Joe Culligan been at the controls, would have been whistled to a halt. Anderson had been editor of the *Journal* for less than a year when the struggle came to a climax; his support in the company simply wasn't as strong as that of Blair, and his magazine, despite a resurgence, had gone through financial agony. Another Curtis editor, however, proved that Blair wasn't omnipotent, and that good counterinsurgency tactics work as well in a corporation as they do in a jungle. This was Ted Patrick, creator of *Holiday*—editorial genius, bon vivant, jazz buff, gourmet, globe-trotter and a man capable of fighting like a love-hungry tomcat to protect his magazine. Patrick also had a pragmatic quality—mean streak might be a better description—sorely needed by anyone who gets into a rough-and-tumble brawl. Fight Blair though he did, Anderson was hurled bodily out of the *Journal*. Patrick, operating from a stronger position, frustrated by fair means and foul Blair's attempts to tamper with *Holiday,* and died in office.

As did Joe Culligan, Ted Patrick came to Curtis from Madison Avenue—same genus (advertising) but different species (creative, rather than sales). For almost two decades fellow admen recognized him as one of the best copywriters in the business. He dabbled in politics constantly, and inconsistently; Draper Daniels, of McCann-Erickson, wrote that Patrick "had the rare courage to change his mind publicly when he felt the facts warranted it." Patrick wrote pacifist ads during the 1930's (the most striking a skeleton with a steel helmet captioned "cornfed kid from the West"); he directed psychological warfare training when the war started. He helped Wendell Willkie win the Republican Presidential nomination in 1940—then turned around and wrote an ad that drew more Democratic contributions than any other of the campaign. Ted Patrick joined Curtis in 1946 on the "Magazine X" project, which was to have been the Curtis answer to *Life* Magazine. When Curtis abandoned this, Patrick switched to two-month-old *Holiday*, a puling, ad-thin infant, and molded it into something which defies a capsule definition. "Travel magazine" comes easiest to mind—because *Holiday* was about the world and the interesting things interesting people do in it. Patrick called it a magazine "with an international, intellectual point of view." It was also John McNulty writing on playing the piano in a silent movie theater, and E. B. White on New York; Cleveland Amory on society and James Jones on living in a trailer house.

As did Edward Bok, Patrick paid keen attention to what his readers said in letters. One conclusion was that people wanted to read about places to which they had traveled rather than about "the place they're going to. Everyone wants to pit his opinion of a place against what the writer has to say. Heaven help the writer if there is a difference of opinion." *Holiday's* idea was for editor and advertising director to yield some of their omnipotence so, as Clifton Fadiman put it, "to get the writer to produce the best he has in him, on the theory that you must give him his head before you can get him to use it." The text Patrick supported by the finest photography of his generation—Slim Aarons, Henri Cartier-Bresson, Burt Glinn.

Behind him Patrick had a four-man team unique in publishing history—Albert H. Farnsworth, executive editor; Harry Sions, editorial director; Louis Mercier, picture editor; and Frank Zachary, art director. But the slots they filled were irrelevant. "We didn't care about titles; we cared about Ted and the magazine," Al Farnsworth said last spring. "We worked our butts off, because we started from scratch." *Holiday* was always an island apart from Curtis Publishing Company; even in Philadelphia its offices were in a separate building from the other magazines. Sions was one of the few native Philadelphians ever hired by Curtis as an editor. He also knew of another barrier against him there. "You know," he told Patrick in 1946 when he was talking about his job, "I'd be the first Jew ever to work for Curtis at this level." This put Patrick into a rage. "Don't you ever mention that around me again," he said, and Sions didn't. (Sions adds he didn't think Curtis Publishing anti-Semitic—"only a-Semitic.")

Holiday was an artistic and intellectual success from the start; it reached the break-even point financially within five years and was the only Curtis magazine to gain steadily in circulation lineage and revenue through 1961. Here's a rundown, beginning in 1954:

Year	ABC Circulation	Revenue	Ad Pages
1954	846,302	$ 5,241,659	824.77
1955	849,937	5,833,825	888.76
1956	873,820	6,480,191	971.02
1957	918,273	8,328,486	1,133.84
1958	890,791	8,714,777	1,087.08
1959	930,702	9,472,537	1,139.15
1960	936,749	11,090,802	1,247.14
1961	922,633	10,339,381	1,062.48

As did other realists in the organization, *Holiday* staff members sensed the dry rot in Curtis long before the collapse. In the late 1950's, there was even a move to persuade Patrick to seek the *Post* editorship in an effort to produce a more modern product, on the assumption that Madison Avenue had to be met on its own grounds. Patrick squelched the movement. He was satisfied with *Holiday* and so were his editors. "Everything was clicking," Farnsworth says. "We had the right man as the advertising manager [Ralph Hench] and the right editor . . . we were beginning to hit." Per issue, *Holiday* was making more profit than the *New Yorker*.

Holiday watched with foreboding the advent of the Culligan regime. Ten days before Culligan was hired, Farnsworth reports, Patrick had a long talk with Walter D. Fuller, the Curtis board chairman. Fuller said, "The last person we need is a super salesman to be president of Curtis Publishing Company." But that is exactly what Curtis got. Within a month after Culligan's appointment *Holiday* for the first time had a publisher, Peter Schruth, former *Post* advertising salesman. Schruth promptly got into a fight with Ralph Hench, the advertising manager, and both men left the company. "Ted desperately wanted to keep Hench, but he couldn't do so," says Farnsworth. "Schruth and Hench had chewed themselves up." The fighting there and elsewhere in the company frightened the advertising department, and salesmen drifted away. By increasing rates, *Holiday* managed to correct the revenue plunge but continued to lose lineage through 1962 and 1963.

Patrick, meantime, had a problem of his own: Clay Blair, Jr., and the group of editors he hired for the *Saturday Evening Post*. "They roared in and out of the company like madmen," said Farnsworth. "They horrified Ted." Even more horrifying to Patrick was the idea of an outsider interfering with *Holiday*. Culligan was conciliatory. "Have lunch with Clay," he said. "He's a nice young man; you might get some ideas from him." "Lunch, hell," snapped Patrick. "I won't even talk with him on the telephone." Each time Blair attempted to exert influence in *Holiday*, Patrick figuratively kicked him out. A secretary called to say, "Clay wants to read the piece on Russia." "He can read it in the magazine," said Patrick.

In the early summer of 1963, two things happened that alarmed Patrick. First, he watched the manner in which Blair fired Anderson and then swept out the staff of the *Ladies' Home Journal*. Second, Blair made a direct threat to fire him. Patrick weighed several factors. Had it been he alone who was threatened, he would have walked out on Blair. But both his staff and his magazine were at stake. Patrick dipped his gloves in plaster of Paris and came out swinging.

Patrick's first move was a quiet contact with a public relations man, which gave him the mechanism through which to combat the "wild Indians." A tip was passed on to *Newsweek* that Patrick might be amenable to an interview. Sure enough, he was, and it was a salvo at Blair, published in *Newsweek*'s press section of July 1, 1963:

> It's taken a lot of hard work and seventeen years to build *Holiday* into the magazine it is today. This is a 24-hour-a-day job. No one can tell me that he [Blair] can edit the *Post* from 9 to 11, the *Ladies' Home Journal* from 12 to 2, and *Holiday* from 3 to 5 and still do any justice to any of them.
>
> This type of editing would be the kiss of death to *Holiday*. I realize the consequences of my speaking out. But we accept *Holiday* as it is today and we're quite happy living with it. We couldn't accept a *Holiday* that was emasculated. I'm glad that we won't have to. We've fought like hell to get where we are.

Patrick's outburst surprised Blair, who responded with a public vote of confidence: "*Holiday* is one of the best magazines in the country. I have done nothing about *Holiday* and don't intend to because it is a fine magazine. *Holiday* is sailing along beautifully and I read it with pleasure and pride." (Faint sounds of laughter could be heard from the *Holiday* offices.) Almost simultaneously, Culligan put out an edict: "No one in the Curtis Publishing Company or its subsidiaries is to grant an interview to any branch of the press. Any violation of this ruling will be regarded with extreme gravity by management." He ordered that complete details of any conversations with reporters—even at cocktail parties—be reported immediately to management.

The *Newsweek* piece effectively halted efforts of Blair to interfere with *Holiday*, but Patrick's troubles with an advertising-oriented management mounted. Some of these he confided in David Ogilvy, of Ogilvy, Benson & Mather, one of his closest personal and professional friends. Ogilvy is bitter in his memories of how he saw *Holiday* gradually tugged away from Patrick by "promoted space salesmen called publishers" who wanted the magazine "popularized" so it would appeal to a broader audience. Ogilvy contrasts the *Holiday* situation with that at the *New Yorker*, when it was edited by the late Harold Ross and owned by Raoul Fleischmann. "Ross paid no attention to advertisers at all; nor scarcely any to Fleischmann. He once wouldn't speak to Fleischmann for two years, and their only communication was through an intermediary. He thought Fleischmann to be some kind of a yahoo. 'All those advertisements,' Ross would say—'couldn't they be put on a single page?' If he didn't like an ad, he threw it out. The wife of the head of the J. Walter Thompson agency once asked Fleischmann for editorial support of the Girl Scouts, her charity. 'I'll talk to the editor,' he said. Fleischmann did, and Ross shouted four-letter words at his employer. What was the *New Yorker*? Ross. What was the *Post*? George Lorimer and Hibbs. What was Curtis Publishing Company? A promoter named Culligan who installs space salesmen to run the magazines and boot around editors."

All through 1963, Ogilvy watched his friend struggle to keep his head above Culligan. Then Curtis walked into a trap. The new *Holiday* publisher, James M. White, who replaced Schruth, thought an advertising tribute to Patrick would be a good promotional gesture and asked Ogilvy to write one under his signature to occupy a full page in *The New York Times*. To Ogilvy this was an unbelievable opportunity for good—and mischief. "I wrote the ad—good copy, if I say so myself—and got the eleven largest agencies in town to sign it." Addressed to Patrick "from twelve of *Holiday*'s 3,263,000 readers," * it read, in part:

DEAR TED:

Holiday is your baby. In 18 years as editor you have produced 210 glorious issues. They get more glorious every year.

---

* Holiday circulation at the time was more than 900,000; the 3,263,000 reference was to the actual number of readers, as reflected in surveys.

We applaud your belief that "an editor's only boss is the reader." We applaud your indifference to the pressures of advertisers and the heckling of publishers. Month after month, year after year, you entertain and you enthrall us. You have pursued excellence, and you have achieved it. You are a great editor.

To Ogilvy the ad was a means of "talking to those stupid, shallow jerks at Curtis in the language they can understand. It was a declaration that Patrick was not going to knuckle under to you; that if you fire him, we are not going to advertise with you. But you know, the people at Curtis were so damned dumb they didn't understand it!"

There is evidence that Culligan also wanted to move Patrick aside. Don Schanche, who was then managing editor of the *Post*, was called in before Culligan and Blair one day and asked in general terms if he would like to be editor of *Holiday*. "I was uneasy about the offer. It sounded like they wanted to unceremoniously kick Patrick upstairs. Anyway, nothing ever came of it."

In October, 1963, Patrick's wife died suddenly. This tragedy, coupled with his professional troubles, sapped the spirit from him; he spent long days alone at his beachfront home at Quogue, Long Island. Early the next year, Farnsworth noticed a yellow cast to Patrick's complexion and urged him to see a doctor. Patrick refused, retreated to Long Island—and on March 8 was taken to the hospital in an ambulance, gravely ill of hepatitis. He died the evening of March 11.

The *Holiday* office next day had the atmosphere of a funeral parlor. Secretaries and editors alike wept silently in their handkerchiefs as they tried to go about their work.

At 2:30 P.M.—19 hours after Patrick's death—Blair's secretary gave crisp telephone orders for Farnsworth, Zachary, Sions and Mercier to report singly to his office. Their grief-stunned minds found it hard to absorb the news: Schanche, of Blair's "sophisticated muckraking" staff at the *Post,* was the new editor of *Holiday.*

Schanche had been a Korean War correspondent for International News Service; he was one of the editors who created *Sports Illustrated* for Time-Life; as military editor of *Life* he obtained the exclusive contract for, and ghostwrote much of, the first-person stories of the original astronauts and their wives. He knew Blair casually in Washington when he joined the *Post* bureau there in 1960; when the *Post* began its new aggressive journalism in 1962, Schanche was one of its guiding forces and worked hand in hand with Blair. "When Blair and Culligan offered me the job when Patrick died," Schanche said recently, "I took it on the condition that Clay keep out of my hair. He never bothered me, either."

But to Patrick's editorial crew, Schanche's past association with Blair was enough to disqualify him, in their minds. They urged that Blair not make an immediate appointment. "This is more of your corporate politics," Farnsworth told Blair. "I had hoped you would have the vision to reach outside the magazine and bring in someone of stature." He suggested Theodore H. White or Theodore Sorensen, adviser to the late President Kennedy.

"You'll find Schanche quite a guy," Farnsworth said Blair replied. "Go meet him and talk with him." Blair's attitude to each man was, "Well, what are you going to do about it?"

Harry Sions asked Schanche bluntly why he got the editorship. "It was a reward for what I had done at the *Post,*" Sions says Schanche replied. Schanche also asked the four men to stay on. "I need you," he told Sions.

"I will continue as long as you do not corrupt the magazine that Ted Patrick created," Sions told him.

Later that afternoon the sobs of Patrick's secretary rent the office. A building superintendent had appeared and was impersonally throwing Patrick's effects into a wooden crate.

Almost immediately there began a clash of wills between the old and the new. In Schanche's opinion the four Patrick editors "thought they owned the magazine, that they had a proprietary interest in it." In Farnsworth's opinion Schanche had no desire to continue the magazine as Patrick had created it.

"It was soon obvious that Schanche brought to *Holiday* few, if any, qualifications for his position as editor of that particular magazine," Farnsworth maintains. "At no time during the months I served with him as editor was there any constructive give-and-take with him about his plans or what he thought of the magazine. In fact, for most of the early months he held the position, he either was away from the office entirely, or was receiving a constant succession of visitors from elsewhere in the company." According to an office log, Farnsworth says, Schanche was out of New York nine weeks between March and November. Not until later did the four sub-editors learn that some of this time was spent meeting with Blair and Marvin D. Kantor on plans to oust Joe Culligan from the presidency.

Farnsworth says that Schanche's criticisms of the magazines were legion—that the "special country" issues devoted to a single nation were "lousy." He also quotes Schanche as saying, "I have written a hell of a lot more than you," and thus should be a better editor.

"We tried desperately to teach him how to be an editor," Sions says. "After the first week or two he agreed that he would wait six months before making any changes. He had no experience with the essay form—which *Holiday* made famous—or in dealing with the type of writer we used." To Sions and Farnsworth, Schanche seemed to sense, and to resent, that he was dependent upon the editorial team left him by Patrick. Schanche summoned Sions into his office after a few months. "I don't like your title [editorial director]; it makes you more important than I am," he said. "Change it."

Sions balked.

"Go home and think about it," Schanche said.

"There's no point in it—I don't want to change."

The office became icy.

"Well, I guess I'll fire you," Sions said Schanche told him. "Why don't you?" Sions retorted.

"I don't want to."

Schanche didn't share the feelings of Farnsworth, Zachary, Sions and Mercier that *Holiday* was a near-perfect product which should be preserved. In a critique of *Holiday* which he later circulated among staff members he said he felt the magazine to be suffering from the same middle-aged tiredness which had caused so much trouble at the *Post* and the *Journal.* Schanche wrote, in part:

> Regrettably, *Holiday* has been moving away from rather than toward what I conceive to be its natural editorial domain and its ideal audience. I will not belabor the aging quality of its readership. I think you all sense it.
>
> To a degree, I believe this aging readership reflects unenlightened circulation policies and economies which have resulted in lackluster mailings to general Curtis lists almost guaranteed to bring in numerous undesirable subscribers. To a much greater degree, however, the deterioration of our audience reflects a certain passivity, aimlessness and ambiguity in the magazine itself.

Schanche said he was not condemning *Holiday* as it existed prior to his appointment, "because there was and is much in it that is superb" because of Patrick, Zachary, Sions, Farnsworth and Mercier.

> But there are flaws. Quite simply, *Holiday* has suffered and still suffers from essentially *passive* editing by men who have grown old with a favored and aging group of literary and photographic contributors. This is a natural process. But the fate of magazines which fail to grow with their times, which fail to find fresh contributors capable of offering valid, contemporary insights and, more important, which fail to guide their contributors toward vigorous, contemporaneous and editorially pertinent subjects is too well known, particularly here at Curtis, to require amplification. Passive editing, by which I mean the

tendency of the editors to permit old and favored contributors to determine by their own special interests the content of the magazine, has led *Holiday* to wobble all over the editorial front.

Schanche cited some specifics. By declaring it was not a travel magazine, he said, *Holiday* was "insulting not only its readers, but its most important advertisers as well." He criticized a profile of Charles de Gaulle—printed in 1960—as imitative of news magazines. He thought the magazine's appearance had atrophied.

Holiday's rigid approach to photography, best characterized by the static, highly stylized portrait with subject staring cata-tonically into camera, has become utterly predictable. By its consistent overuse of this device, I'm afraid the magazine has drifted into the unfortunate position of parodying itself. As a consequences, in an age best characterized by a peculiarly Amer-ican desire to get out and *do* things, too many *Holiday* photo-graphic subjects do nothing but stand stiffly, uninspiringly inert.

The *Holiday* "Shunpike Tour," a travel feature, was, Schanche said, "considered by most of my contemporaries to be the dullest regular magazine feature in American journalism."

Schanche mapped out a two-part change in editorial em-phasis. First, a clearer definition of *Holiday*'s editorial target, which he called the "world of actively rewarding leisure, encom-passing travel and the cultural pursuits of mind and body." Secondly, "we must move aggressively into an era of *active* edit-ing in which we seek out younger *American* writers . . . create subjects for them within the confines of *Holiday*'s own editorial domain . . . and encourage them to work with us in the revital-ization of a magazine which must become the bible of our new, actively rewarding world of leisure."

The changes, he stressed, "must be done subtly, without dis-turbing loyal readers and advertisers with sudden, jarring change. . . . We will not reduce our standards in any way. If anything, we will be less forgiving of inconsequential, aimless writing and weak photography than we have been in the past."

Farnsworth and Sions maintain that Schanche never suggested ideas nor called staff conferences to talk about changing the thrust of *Holiday*. Working with him, they said, was torture because he never proposed, only rejected, and in an out-of-hand manner that stifled discussion. To Sions he said, "The trouble with *Holiday* is that it's too well written." Jane Clapperton, a fashions editor, wrote a poem in caption style for the August, 1964, issue. *Holiday* people thought it charming. "That's a lousy poem—tear it out," exclaimed Schanche in front of the staff. He rejected covers with the same summary judgment, showing a liking for what Farnsworth called the "blatant art of the *Sports Illustrated* type—boats with garish red sails and that sort of thing." (Says Schanche today: "I like design covers, even some pretty cryptic ones. But I didn't like white backgrounds, and Farnsworth did. I'm also in the business of selling magazines, and it's well known that white covers don't sell.")

Why was he unable to establish a rapport with Patrick's old crew? "Well, Sions says we never conferred. The fact of the matter is that it's impossible to confer with Sions. He's a good editor, but he's opinionated and autocratic. You don't discuss with him, you listen." Schanche says now he probably would have been justified "in doing some sweeping" when he first became editor, but "I didn't want to disturb the character of the magazine, which is a pretty delicate thing."

So the impasse drifted, and many of the staff underlings sided with Farnsworth, Sions, Zachary and Mercier. A former naval intelligence officer, Farnsworth is convinced he was subjected to psychological warfare techniques. He says Schanche went through one phase when he drew the blinds in his window-ringed office until it was totally dark save for the light from the desk lamp. "There he sat for hours, almost totally incommunicado, emerging occasionally to snarl 'lousy' at something he didn't like," says Farnsworth. ("My God," said Schanche. "It's bright in here; there's such a thing as too much light, you know.") Farnsworth passed up his vacation that summer: "The staff was under a strain, and I didn't want to leave it. In the fall

I had to send two of the office girls away for a week's stay at a rest camp." Night after night he came home from the job he once had loved—bone-weary, mind-weary, and Schanche-weary.

So far as Blair was concerned, Schanche's appointment as *Holiday* editor rounded out his tacit control of the Curtis magazines. The *Saturday Evening Post* was his personal fiefdom. The reliable Davis Thomas had the *Ladies' Home Journal;* Don Schanche had *Holiday*. Hubbard Cobb, at the *American Home,* wasn't a Blair recruit, but Blair could count on him as a go-along-to-get-along follower. *Jack and Jill* was so small as to be insignificant.

Not even when the autocratic George Horace Lorimer was president of Curtis Publishing had he controlled directly more than one magazine. Now Clay D. Blair, Jr., a man who realized the mystique of power, had a power base unprecedented in company history. And he promptly put it to use.

Chapter Nine

In the spring of 1964, Don Schanche, the tough-talking new editor of *Holiday*, made arrangements for an office cocktail party honoring a staff member leaving for a one-year assignment abroad. Everyone showed up but the host, and, as the martinis flowed that evening, Schanche's absence was the subject of much speculation. Not that Schanche was particularly sociable; since he became boss many editors had heard him say only one word—"lousy!"—in rejecting story and picture ideas. Schanche spent a considerable amount of time, it seemed to them, huddled in his office with persons who didn't even work for the magazine. And he frequently disappeared for long conferences with Clay D. Blair, Jr., the Curtis editor-in-chief.

A few days afterwards, Al Farnsworth casually asked Schanche why he didn't come to his own party. "I had to go to a meeting out in Connecticut," he replied. "We had some trouble on the bridge." Farnsworth wrote off the comment as some of the insignificant, crisp nautical terminology that Schanche occasionally used around the office.

Had Farnsworth listened a bit closer, he might have heard the explanation for what it was—the beginnings of one of the most tumultuous executive suite messes in American corporate history. Appropriately, Schanche's words were right out of

Mutiny on the Bounty—with the locale shifted to Curtis Publishing Company.

Curtis Publishing Company entered 1964 with an outward appearance of recuperation. Matthew J. Culligan had performed an amazing 18-month turnaround on a dollars-and-cents measurement, cutting the 1962 losses of $18.9 million to $3.4 million. The Curtis magazines, in the last half of 1963, picked up advertising lineage and revenues; during the last quarter of 1963 and the first of 1964, Curtis accountants used black ink on the books for the first time since 1961. Serge Semenenko's bank syndicate had given Curtis breathing space by converting short-term loans into long-term obligations and supplying $4.5 million in operating capital. After the *Ladies' Home Journal* fiasco resulting in the firing of editor Curtiss Anderson and the mass resignations and ousting of other editors, Curtis seemed to have quieted down. If nothing else, Curtis was keeping its name out of the tabloid headlines and gossip columns. Culligan had predicted as early as August, 1962, that "1964 will be the black-ink year."

Yet behind the façade of cheer, Curtis Publishing Company was as wobbly as ever and the *Saturday Evening Post* still lagged. Cary W. Bok says flatly that Culligan seemed to lose interest in his job in early 1964. "He was a lot like John Kennedy," says Republican Bok. "He had the same Irish enthusiasm, the same wit, the easy flow and talk and banter. But he lacked stability. We needed a manager, a president who could settle down to the hard decade of rebuilding which our company needed. Culligan wasn't like that. After eighteen months he had done all he knew how to do. Then he walked out. He was in Mexico, fishing. He was out playing golf. He brought in the country club set, made them vice-presidents, and said, 'Any one of these men can step into my shoes right now.' Baloney. The long-range Curtis job was unglamorous, and Culligan wasn't interested in it." Bernard Gallagher, the consultant who put Culligan and Curtis together, had second thoughts. "Joe was Charlie Chaplin trying to play Hamlet," he says now. "Curtis needed someone who could stay home and mind the company while Joe was out flying with the angels."

In hindsight, Culligan's record during late 1963 and 1964 is splotched with errors. Chief among these was his downgrading of John McLean (Mac) Clifford as his chief administrative assistant. Clifford had done the cost-cutting and internal realignments that enabled Culligan to wipe red ink off Curtis' books. Clifford wasn't interested in titles or glory; as a businessman and as an administrator, Curtis came first. To Clifford a set of books that showed a profit was as beautiful a sight as an issue of the *Saturday Evening Post* was to Clay Blair, Jr., or as a four-year non-cancelable advertising contract was to Joe Culligan. In December, 1963, for reasons which he hasn't discussed publicly, Joe Culligan put his old NBC friend Mac Clifford on the second string, and proudly escorted a newcomer to the seat beside the throne—Marvin D. Kantor, a somewhat sallow-faced New Yorker who in ten years had come from Wall Street trainee to president of one of the street's newest houses, J. R. Williston & Beane, Inc.

The Williston firm, it will be remembered, was in the new-money group which cracked the Curtis board in the spring of 1962 by forcing President Robert A. MacNeal and the Curtis heirs to admit two outsiders, lawyer Milton Gould and broker R. McLean Stewart. As a general partner in Treves & Co. from February, 1959, through October, 1961, Kantor helped the outsiders accumulate the stock that springboarded Gould and Stewart into the company. J. R. Williston & Beane was organized in late 1961 and Kantor moved there, first as a general partner, then as president. He kept buying Curtis stock, working in tandem with the Treves firm. Kantor himself took a seat on the Curtis board in January, 1963, and four months later was put on the finance committee. He and Gould were close—professionally and personally—and old-line Curtis directors, rightly or wrongly, viewed the pair as "liquidation-minded." In the meantime, however, a situation developed in 1963 that gave

Kantor more things to think about than Curtis Publishing Company.

Over a two-year period a short, portly man named Anthony De Angelis with a record for shady speculations plunged heavily in the futures market on soybean and cottonseed oil. The Soviet Union was negotiating for the purchase of U.S. wheat; Tino De Angelis, as friends called him, thought the deal would expand to include vegetable oils, which are used in the manufacture of paints, plastics and foodstuffs. Through his own company, Allied Crude Oil Refining Corporation, of Bayonne, New Jersey, and cover firms, he bought 90 percent of the cottonseed oil contracts on the New York Produce Exchange and about 30 percent of the soybean contracts on the Chicago Board of Trade, the major market centers. Concurrently, he bought vegetable oils in bulk and supposedly put them in tanks his firm owned on the harbor front in Bayonne. American Express Warehousing, Ltd., a subsidiary of American Express Co., ran the tank farm and issued receipts purporting to show how many pounds of oils De Angelis had stored there. De Angelis used these receipts as collateral in speculating in the futures market, posting them with Kantor's firm, J. R. Williston & Beane, and another brokerage house, Ira Haupt & Co., which made the actual purchases. De Angelis' margin was paper thin—only 5 percent of the price of the oils. By October, 1963, De Angelis' holdings in futures contracts were so vast that for every cent per pound price drop he would have to post $9 million in new margin money. And that is exactly what happened. The USSR wheat talks broke off, the vegetable oils market collapsed, and Allied Crude and De Angelis filed bankruptcy petitions. Tino De Angelis' tank farm in Bayonne proved to contain water and air—not vegetable oils. The federal government charged later that he bribed warehousing employees to falsify the receipts which Haupt and Williston accepted as collateral. Haupt and Williston & Beane were faced with making good the margins which had been owed them by De Angelis. For Haupt this spelled disaster—a margin call of $15.5 million. Unable to meet its obligations, it was suspended from doing business at the New York Stock Exchange and folded. Williston & Beane faced the same problem, but on a smaller scale. It couldn't handle a $610,000 margin call, was suspended from trading for two days, reopened with loans from other brokerage houses, and shortly thereafter was absorbed by Walston & Co. In bankruptcy proceedings later the Williston firm listed its losses in the De Angelis debacle at $2.4 million. Marvin D. Kantor, as president, was the only major Williston & Beane officer not taken in by Walston & Co. Joe Culligan hired Kantor as his chief executive assistant, putting him in ahead of Blair, John Veronis and Mac Clifford. Previously Clifford was Number Two man. Now he was subordinate to Kantor.

(The *Post* ran a six-page article on De Angelis in its April 25, 1964, issue, after Kantor joined Curtis; the six pages contained nine lines about Williston & Beane, seven of them in sentences which also covered the Haupt firm's role.)

Why did Culligan do this? There is testimony to support several theories. Serge Semenenko, although involved in Curtis only a few months, had already realized that Culligan was something less than a managerial genius, and sounded out the hierarchy of the directors on finding him a top administrative assistant—someone with more authority than Clifford for operational matters. Too, Clifford's health was faltering under the strain of 18 months of 15-hour working days, and he spoke longingly of his home on the West Coast. Whatever the reason, Culligan seemed somewhat pleased over his new assistant, reports Cary Bok. "He bragged about 'winning Kantor over to our side and making a friend of him.' Kantor was always on the periphery with Gould, picking and shoving. Culligan went after him, cultivated him, finally put him in as head of the magazine division. Bad decision."

Blair, meanwhile, grew increasingly discontent with Culligan. Kantor guided him through the Curtis books and pointed out that things weren't quite as rosy as Culligan kept saying. Culligan said repeatedly he was selling more advertising; yet Blair could tell by the girth of the magazines that the *Post* was still in trouble. Weighing an issue in the palm of his hand one day, he said: "What kind of ―― has Joe been feeding me?" Figures belie Culligan's talk of an "upswing" for the *Post*. From January through June, 1963, the *Post* had advertising revenues of $37,368,299; the same period in 1964 produced only $30,897,723, a 17.3 percent drop.

The early rapport between Blair and Culligan faded once the editor's mind clouded with doubt. Culligan sat down on Blair hard for the Butts-Bryant libel losses and told him, in effect: "If the muck is that expensive, stop raking it. We can't afford to pay millions of dollars for a single story, no matter how much it enhances the reputation of a magazine." This rankled Blair because he thought the Butts loss to be unjustified, more a Southern jury happenstance than anything else.

Blair felt keenly the possibility of seeing the *Post* perish. By now he had invested three years of 18-hour days in the magazine; on his word, editors left substantial jobs elsewhere and joined the *Post*. He didn't want to have the *Post* floundering under Culligan, nor have to work as an editor under "some gray eminence of a banker," as he put it to a colleague. Also, colleagues began to sense in Blair a rebirth of his old desire for corporate power. "Something happened to Blair in the first six months of 1964," says Don Schanche. "He was thinking about more than the magazine."

In Kantor, Blair sensed a fellow activist, and a man experienced enough in high-level corporate politics to set forth a position and buttress it with enough argument to make it prevail. It was to Blair that Kantor turned for his orientation in the magazine division. Not everyone at Curtis was as impressed with Kantor as was Blair. "Kantor was smart in a glib sort of way," Cary Bok says. "He learned the patter in a hurry. He'd sit right there in that chair" (pointing across his apartment atop the Public Ledger Building in Philadelphia) "and reel off the right words. Oh, it sounded good. But he was shallow. He didn't realize what he was talking about."

Largely at Kantor's urging Blair was elevated to the Curtis board at the February 7, 1964, meeting. He replaced R. McLean Stewart, the Houston broker and oilman who had joined in the spring of 1962 along with Gould, and who now resigned to tend to other interests. The board seat gave Blair a more prestigious forum from which to voice some of the ideas he had first put forward in 1962 in his "Tomorrow Morning's Plan." Simply, his aim again was to orient Curtis around the *Post,* and to dispose of what he considered to be unneeded physical assets. Culligan, however, was set on a different tack, and he heeded a separate chorus of advisers. At a time when Blair and Kantor wanted to march in the other direction, Culligan got the board to allot some $5.5 million for additional printing facilities and expansion of New York & Pennsylvania Co., the Curtis papermaking subsidiary. Culligan hoped to boost outside sales of this company and relieve the magazines of the need to absorb such a high percentage of its production.

Even while Culligan was doing this, however, Kantor initiated talks with St. Regis Paper Co., with the aim of selling New York & Penn and contracting to buy better-grade magazine paper produced by St. Regis in the South. New York & Penn would be converted into a stationery-grade paper mill. Blair and Kantor argued with Culligan that a lighter paper—such as was being used by *Life, Look* and *Time*—would cut Curtis' postal bill by perhaps a million dollars annually. Culligan laughed at them. "As thin as the *Post* is," he said, "I'd be afraid it would blow off the newsstand if it was any lighter." He was prideful of Curtis' heavy cover stock. "Henry Luce doesn't have anything as good as this," he said. Blair and Kantor couldn't convince the other board members, either. Directors felt Blair and Kantor spoke with one voice. "They were the same way in meetings, always ratta-ta-tat ideas," says Bok. "They'd throw them out in a hurry—sell this, sell that, raise this much money. Selling a paper mill or a printing plant isn't that simple. It takes months of negotiations and signing of contracts—eighteen months, not overnight, even if somebody wants to buy it. We'd sit and listen, and they'd get upset because we didn't jump right into line."

The situation stalemated, but only briefly. Culligan thought the integrated Curtis empire could be made profitable, and that the best route to substantial profits was in the exploitation of the entire package. Too, the mills and printing plant had to be kept intact as a dowry offer to a merger partner. Blair couldn't see past the magazines. He was dubious of Culligan's abilities to oversee such a broad operation. "Joe can't even make money out of the magazines," he told one man. "How the hell does he expect to do anything with a paper mill? What's Joe going to do—sell billboard space on trees?

One stumbling block which Blair and Kantor removed in a hurry, once they formed an alliance, was John J. Veronis, whom Culligan had moved from within the ranks to the head of the magazine division. That Veronis and Blair eventually would meet in a fatal bloodletting was considered inevitable by those who watched them maneuver within the company. "They were 'I-guys,' who started every sentence in the first person singular," said a former Curtis editor. "With Blair and Veronis it was a week at the Kremlin—knives flashing—and then a week of honeymooning when they made up. Joe was caught first on the one side, then on the other." Kantor was the extra weight Blair needed to handle Veronis. As did Culligan, Veronis complained about Blair's editorial thrust and suggested a "more sensible sophistication." He also wanted to keep *Post* circulation close to the seven-million mark, even at the expense of cut-rate prices. The *Post* dropped its newsstand price to a dime to hold its circulation base. Veronis worked his brain overtime seeking ideas on how to bring more ads to the *Post*. Curtis offered a 50 percent discount to advertisers for "leftover" space in *Post* regional editions, to be run at the magazine's convenience. Even with the cut-rate, advertisers were guaranteed a maximum of 80 percent national coverage—to the distress of regular advertisers who would have had to pay the going price. Here there was a clash of wills. Veronis wanted to make the regional editions separate packages, with their own editorial sections. But Blair refused to supply the editorial material, and Veronis couldn't do anything about it. Even though elaborate promotional efforts had been made, the idea was dropped. All spring Veronis bucked Blair and Kantor. For weeks he pushed a plan to make the *Ladies' Home Journal* a biweekly. "This will revolutionize the women's service field," he said. Such a drastic change, however, was viewed by Blair and Kantor as unnecessarily risky at the moment. One week Veronis was a major company voice, loyal to Culligan and resentful of any designs on Culligan's power. The next week he was on the street outside the Curtis door, fired by Kantor, his meteoric career at Curtis at an end. Kantor took over as head of the magazine division.

For men more interested in editing magazines than indulging in corporate politics, the marshaling of forces by Blair and Kantor was puzzling. Al Farnsworth went to a White House press photographers' dinner in Washington and met Davis Thomas, who said, "I'm a Blair-Kantor man; how do you stand?" "I thought you were editor of the *Ladies' Home Journal*," Farnsworth told the man.

A complicating factor interjected early in the year was at once salvation and disaster for Culligan. In 1946, a thrice-removed Curtis subsidiary, T. S. Woollings Co., Ltd., owned by New York and Pennsylvania Co., bought about 38,000 acres of timberland near Timmins, Kidd Township, Canada, 540 miles north of Toronto. A year later it added 58,000 acres more by purchasing individual freehold claims which the Canadian government had granted Boer War veterans. Curtis' interest in the swampy, desolate land was the towering, 150-year-old black spruce trees which yielded dense, long-fibered paper, ideal for magazines. Woollings and Armstrong Forest Company, another New York & Penn subsidiary, began mineral explorations on their timberlands in 1949; Woollings actually made five test drillings near Kidd Township in 1954 but without success. Shortly after Culligan joined Curtis another paper company offered to buy its Canadian woodlands. Culligan said later that tests by the Canadian government had disclosed "interesting anomalies" on the Curtis lands. "We decided at that time not to sell our mineral rights even if we were successful in selling our timberlands."

Texas Gulf Sulphur Company and Canadian Nickel Company thrashed through the woods, taking core samples and using electronic devices. Texas Gulf Sulphur's man was Kenneth H. Darke, a young geologist assigned to make on-the-ground explorations and also to obtain contracts for prime land in the area. His first direct contact with Woollings was in 1959. On November 10 or 11, 1963, Darke's team found positive indications of a major lode of copper, zinc and silver. Drilling halted immediately, and Darke began a quiet program of land acquisition in the area. Texas Gulf Sulphur imposed secrecy for obvious reasons: Timmins is a mining town where the flimsiest of rumors about an ore find touches off wild speculations and claims staking. Enough information on the Texas Gulf Sulphur strike leaked to cause a flurry of promotions; one of the persons right in the middle of it, according to testimony later before a Canadian government inquiry, was geologist Darke. In less than a year he and two partners shared $900,000 cash profits, proceeds from claims they sold mining promoters, and estimated millions in Canadian stock market profits. However, an official of Texas Gulf Sulphur told the same inquiry that Darke acquired for the company all the land it wanted.

On February 4, 1964, T. S. Woollings Co., Ltd., signed a contract with Texas Gulf, giving the sulphur company the option to buy mineral rights under any 1,920 acres of its land within three years. During the period, Texas Gulf could explore 46,000 acres in exchange for a rental fee. If it did buy and exploit the 1,920 acres, 10 percent of the profits would go to Curtis— after amortization of rentals and drilling costs and depreciation of equipment and taxes.

Culligan says Curtis had competitive bids on the exploration contract from both Texas Gulf Sulphur and Canadian Nickel. Texas Gulf Sulphur, he told stockholders later, "accepted terms which Canadian Nickel had turned down because they were too severe and would set a bad precedent for exploration in Canada."

In April, 1964, Texas Gulf Sulphur confirmed rumors of the find and said the value ranged up to $2 billion. Soon more news leaked: The ore find was a mere 300 feet from the edge of the Curtis holdings. Curtis stock went wild. From $6 a share it soared, in a month of torrid trading, to $19.25. Some 30 percent of the outstanding shares changed hands—in 10,000 blocks— so rapidly that for several days the New York Stock Exchange had to suspend trading for hours to match buy-and-sell orders. In all of March only 71,200 shares of Curtis common were traded; the April volume was 578,000, with a threefold price increase.

This turn of events took Blair and Kantor by surprise because they, along with others on the board, had never heard of the T. S. Woollings development contract with Texas Gulf Sulphur. They made a quick check of minutes of previous meetings and learned, to their astonishment, that the contract had never been put before the Curtis board for a vote. The day after he heard of the proximity of the Curtis land to the Texas Gulf Sulphur strike area, Blair decided on a hurried inspection trip to Timmins to see what he could learn of the situation. Blair, Norman Ritter, a *Post* assistant managing editor and his chief administrative assistant, and a mining engineer clambered into the Curtis two-engine plane and flew northward through fog and snow to Timmins. They met Darke in a motel room and after only a few minutes Blair was both puzzled and nettled. Darke talked on the phone with several persons, and Blair said, "Something's going on here. This sounds like a stock deal." Darke wouldn't take the Curtis party to its drill site, saying the only available helicopter was broken. They returned to New York the next day.

Not until June did there come a firm announcement that the Curtis land indeed contained ore. Curtis released a letter from Charles Fogarty, Texas Gulf executive vice-president, which said two holes drilled on Texas Gulf property at a slant crossed underground into Curtis land. "Only one of these two holes have thus far reached the ore horizon," he said. "Visual estimates of cores from the hole indicate zinc and copper sulfide ore of good quality." No estimate of value was given then.

Prospecting fever hit Joe Culligan. Despite his public professions that "magazines are our basic business," in private he viewed the minerals as a windfall that could end, once and for all, Curtis' cash problems. A few months earlier he joked sardonically about having to become "one of America's foremost part-time libel experts" because of Clay Blair's muckraking troubles; now he talked like a graduate mining engineer. He called a press luncheon to discuss *Saturday Evening Post* business—and opened it by passing around a core of unrefined ore from Ontario. He peppered his talk with mining terms such as "only 30 feet of overburden," pelletizer, slurry, smelting and specific weight. The Securities Exchange Commission gently warned Culligan to stop talking about the Timmins holdings until firmer evidence was at hand. Culligan mentioned this in a talk at the Overseas Press Club and apologized for not being able to discuss the ore. Then he added: "If you see me walking down Madison Avenue with a piece of ore in my hand and an enigmatic smile on my face, you'll understand why." Culligan lined the walls of a room in the Curtis executive offices with geological maps and called it his "war room." To visitors he pointed out the drill holes and geological structure of the Timmins tract; he talked about "going public" in Canada with T.S. Woollings, Ltd., although nothing ever came of the idea.

Culligan took Clifford away from magazine business altogether and made him head of a "task force" to make lease deals for other acres belonging to Woollings. Clifford had the credentials for this job. Before joining NBC, he was land commissioner of the State of California, specializing in mineral work, and was instrumental in establishing the oil and gas division of the Securities Exchange Commission.

The new developments made Blair and Kantor fume all the more. It was a matter of Culligan's primary interest drifting farther and farther away from magazines, and of questioning whether the best deal possible had been made for exploitation of the minerals. In their view, Woollings should have explored the situation more before signing the contract which gave only 10 percent of profits from the tract. Assurances by Culligan that the contract was "standard" for Canadian mining ventures left them unimpressed. (Under questioning by a stockholder at the Curtis annual meeting in April, 1965, J.M. Clifford admitted the company didn't know the extent or the nature of the ore under its land. "If we knew we had those riches there," Clifford said, "we wouldn't have shared it with anyone. We had no knowledge of the ore being there.")

The Blair-Kantor position was bolstered in early May when preliminary estimates showed that Curtis faced a serious second-quarter deficit (which ultimately amounted to $3.7 million). If Culligan insisted on being a mineral man, they said, at least give them more authority on conduct of the magazines. At Blair's request several Curtis editors signed a letter to Culligan in May asking him to relinquish the job of chief executive officer to Kantor. "We did this pretty much on Blair's say-so," says Schanche now. "He was the one looking at the books then and telling us what was happening. And, as editors, we knew the magazines were in trouble." After a long weekend meeting at his home in Rye, New York, Culligan yielded partially and signed a letter of agreement which set up a three-man "executive committee" composed of himself, Blair and Kantor and gave them *carte blanche* to cut costs. But Blair and Kantor still weren't satisfied. They met M. Albert Linton and Moreau Brown, two powerful board members, at a Philadelphia hotel before a directors meeting and for the first time voiced Joe-must-go sentiments. The two elder statesmen weren't moved, and they thought the situation not quite as glum as indicated by Blair and Kantor. The failure left Blair despondent. Later that night, walking through Rittenhouse Square in Philadelphia, he said he had decided to quit Curtis; that the lack of support in his "struggle to save the company" made his efforts futile. Also, Blair and Kantor had trouble implementing the executive committee to which Culligan agreed. Phase one of their plan was a further consolidation of offices in Manhattan. Blair dispatched Ritter and a staff lawyer to Philadelphia to see what functions could be moved feasibly. Right away they met opposition. Maurice W. Poppei, who didn't think much of Blair and Kantor and their sharing of Culligan's executive authority, kept the two men cooling their heels outside his office for hours. The discussion, once they got inside, was brief and tumultuous, and ended in Poppei ordering Ritter and the lawyer to leave. Culligan dissolved the committee.

Blair's depression deepened. "He was in a real funk that summer," Schanche says. "We had another meeting out at his place, and I told him that it appeared hopeless that either he or Marvin could get the top job. I suggested that maybe a compromise man would be good—William Buckley [then a vice-president]. It was as if I had slapped him. He didn't want to even think about anyone else for the top other than himself or Kantor."

In the early summer, Culligan seemed away from New York more and more; Blair and Kantor practically forgot their personal lives and worried with Curtis nights and weekends. An aura of desperation also crept into their actions. Without consultations with Culligan they worked up a three-part plan—reversion of the *Post* to 51 issues annually, rather than 45; freezing the *Post* circulation base at 6.5 million, and concentrating on quality rather than quantity; and scrapping Culligan's old "Curtis Network" discount in return for one pegged on dollar volume only (5 percent for the first $500,000 and climbing 1 percent for each additional $100,000, up to 20 percent for contracts of $2 million or more). Their plan was aimed at placating the medium and small advertisers who didn't have resources to buy space in every magazine, as required in the "Curtis Network" and who were resentful at the higher discounts afforded large advertisers. Blair and Kantor put the plan before Culligan, and he approved it. "You haven't heard any questions in the last year of the survival of Curtis or in the last six months of the survival of any of its parts," he told the press luncheon where he announced the new ideas.

But Blair and Kantor knew Curtis was still in grave trouble. And, so it seemed, did other persons in the Curtis hierarchy.

Suddenly, that summer, Curtis officials found it hard to locate Culligan when they needed him. He had an office-suite in the Regency Hotel in New York. "This was for entertaining and making an impression and showing what a big man he was, I suppose," Cary Bok said. "Gram'pah [Cyrus Curtis] would never have taken a place like that. A situation would develop, and we'd start looking for Culligan. Someone would call his secretary, who would call someone else. Eventually, after four hours, or even the next morning, you'd hear from Culligan." Blair also took time off later in the summer; he and his family rented a house in Bermuda for ten weeks, and he shuttled between there and New York.

Despite their office worrying about Curtis' financial plight, Blair and Kantor did something that summer which upset some budget-conscious people at Curtis. The company got a chance to consolidate its offices at 641 Lexington Avenue in a new skyscraper building. By Curtis renting the second through fourth floors, and the 32d, the owners agreed to name it "The Saturday Evening Post Building." Blair was exuberant, and he and Kantor spent hours planning the décor of their offices. And, of all people in the company, they were the only ones to order new furniture. Culligan made do with the modernistic desk and chair he had used at 666 Madison Avenue; he took a corner office on the 32d floor, overlooking the East River and the United Nations. Kantor was at the opposite end of the floor, happy beneath the dark mahogany paneling he chose for his wall. Although he chose to be on the fourth floor, Blair topped them all—a private room for his secretary; an office with a built-in bar, refrigerator and color TV set; an Italian marble coffee table; a separate conference room with $200 armchairs lining the long handmade table. Blair also became the only person in the company with a private bathroom, which caused workmen to make structural changes costing additional thousands of dollars. The other Curtis editorial floors had functional metal doors; Blair, however, obtained mahogany at $500 for each doorway between his office and the fourth-floor elevator. Blair's plans hit only one snag. By the time the specially made furniture was delivered in the fall he had been dismissed.

By Labor Day, Curtis' 1964 losses were projected at $7 million, a devastating blow in view of Culligan's highly publicized "turnaround" statements earlier in the year. Blair returned from vacation one Monday morning and by noon had decided to move. "Are you with me?" he asked an associate at lunch. "We're going to have to shove Joe. It's really going to take some proselytizing of the board to convince them of the urgency."

There was one big uncertainty: Serge Semenenko. The banker was in Europe much of the summer, and his watchdog role was entrusted to two junior bank officers. Persons who worked closely with Blair and Kantor in this period are convinced that Semenenko was favorable to their efforts. The bankers seemed as worried as Blair and Kantor; as Blair put it later, they "started blowing their whistles. They asked what we were going to do."

The bankers, under the 1963 loan agreement, held life-and-death authority over Curtis. The agreement set aside $5.5 million which the bankers said could be made available to Curtis under proper conditions. But in September, granting of this additional money was by no means assured, and Blair and Kantor worried about having enough funds to keep the company in business. The agreement provided also that Curtis maintain working capital of $27.5 million (in cash and accounts receivable); were Curtis to slip under this level Blair feared the *Post* would be "just another magazine run by bankers." To understate, this he did not want. Curtis slipped perilously close to the limit in February, 1964, and was saved only by selling its interest in Bantam Books for $2,250,000, a deal arranged by Kantor.

The proposal Blair and Kantor gave the bankers contained 11 points, and parts of it were reminiscent of the old "Tomorrow Morning's Plan" which Blair first drafted back in 1962. Once again the Curtis Building was put on the expendable list, at a hoped-for price of $5 to $10 million (the price range perhaps indicative of their doubts of finding a buyer). Proceeds from the sale would be offset by $3 million expenses for moving 120 advertising, circulation and accounting workers to New York, and shifting mechanical and data-processing equipment and personnel to Sharon Hill. The plan called for "final resolution" of the paper company problem. If the facilities couldn't be leased to St. Regis Paper Co., as Kantor hoped, nor a federal loan of $15 million obtained under the depressed areas program, "padlock—get cash." Another point: "Resolution of Timmins—sell it for anything we can get." Blair and Kantor thought they could save $500,000 annually on both accounting and legal expenses by using only one firm in each category. (Curtis then had three law firms on retainers.) The company plane would have been grounded ($300,000 a year). The circulation company, manufacturing and magazine divisions would have been overhauled again (with a Blair-Kantor estimated saving of $2 million in the latter alone).

The proposal had another section entitled "Progress 1964," which told what Blair and Kantor had done to revamp the company through September. Twenty points were listed—covering everything from magazines ("Editorial stability. Improved products. No walk-out") to minerals ("Timmims perspective. Public disclosure.") The latter referred to a story given the New York *Herald Tribune* in the spring on terms of the Texas Gulf Sulphur contract, a move suggested by an SEC investigator.

Kantor was credited for widespread reform in the business and advertising sides of the company—for reduction of overhead in the magazine and manufacturing division; for consolidating and improving morale of ad and promotion departments; for selling Curtis' share in Bantam Books for $2,250,000, enabling Curtis to remain current on bank repayments and also clearing the way for its entry into book publishing on its own. According to this memorandum Kantor also got to the brink of a deal whereby Curtis magazines would have been printed by photo composition, a precedent for a major magazine publisher. The Blair-Kantor accomplishments, the memo said, boosted circulation of *Holiday* from 900,000 to one million, and the *Ladies' Home Journal* by 29 percent, permitting ad rate increases.

Another section of the memorandum, headed "Situation," started with the blunt statement, "firm feeling of ruin." By whom? Blair and Kantor, the board, the banks and "people." Because of the forecasted loss of $9 million in 1964 (a low guess, as events turned out), Blair and Kantor expressed "doubt of holding editorial personnel and quality in face of deception of management." The Curtis Circulation Company, they said in the memo, was "facing disaster because of competitive innovations of the *New Yorker*, Conde Nast publications, and a new school plan of Time-Life, Inc., and the *Reader's Digest*, all of which would siphon business away from Curtis. As another shortcoming they listed a booklet on the White House which Culligan prepared, gratis, as a presidential giveaway. Blair and Kantor also claimed the paper mills were a "continuing drain [and] cash loss," and that outside paper sales were declining— the latter point a repeated justification of the need to sell off these facilities.

But the dynamite in the proposal was a separate typed list of names and salaries, persons considered "excess baggage" by Blair and Kantor. The first name was Joe Culligan ($150,000); right under him was J.M. Clifford ($128,000). All in all, 20 names—8 vice-presidents; Bob Sherrod ($50,000), Blair's one-time idol at the Pentagon; Gloria Swett ($28,000), the svelte brunette who followed Clifford to Curtis from NBC as administrative assistant and corporate secretary; Johnny Miles ($50,-000), head of the Curtis Circulation Co. and Culligan's frequent golfing pal; Phil Ewald ($50,000), socialite ad salesman to whom no corporate door was closed; Robert Taplinger ($36,000 plus expenses), the outside public relations man whom Blair and Kantor considered a personal drumbeater for Culligan. On and on the list went: there was even room for Thomas J. Gibbons ($10,000), the onetime Philadelphia police commissioner who was now a sort of public relations man for Curtis.

In summary, Blair and Kantor proposed cleansing the Curtis corporate offices of the entire Culligan team—starting with Culligan himself. The recommended replacement as chief executive officer: Kantor.

All this the two executives did, as Blair said later, "without the coordination of the others"—i.e., Culligan. Blair also claimed that Semenenko reacted favorably. Then, and only then, did Culligan learn that Blair and Kantor—Culligan's right-hand man—were jockeying for his removal. Earlier in the year Culligan hadn't appeared to take seriously the churnings of Blair and Kantor; after their attempt in May to take part of his functions he even offered them a raise, to $100,000 annually each. Now, however, he was furious. He barged in unexpectedly on a meeting where Blair and Kantor were talking over strategy with a handful of key editorial aides. "I'm going to be running this place a long time," Culligan stormed, "and I don't believe in rebels." He called Blair and Kantor spoilers and backbiters and more; a dumping of assets, he said, would be an unmistakable sign of weakness which again would put Curtis on the toboggan slide of rumor. Too, he asked, did Blair and Kantor want the jobs of hundreds of paper-mill employees on their consciences if this asset were to be sold? Culligan was most contemptuous of Kantor, who after only eight months in the company wanted the top job. Culligan also went into a long explanation of the grievances which he knew Blair and Kantor had against him. "It was dramatic for a while," said an editor who was at this meeting. "But the longer he talked, the less effective he became." In the end Culligan agreed to appointment of another "executive committee" with which he would share management responsibility. But this time he would not put the agreement into writing and said Blair and Kantor must accept an oral binder.

Again, why didn't Culligan squelch Blair and Kantor by the expedient of firing them? Several reasons are advanced. Culligan knew that Semenenko was unhappy with the company's progress, and that renewed turmoil accompanying discharges could weaken his own position. Secondly, Blair and Kantor were both directors. What if they went over his head to the entire board, even after being fired, and won?

Go over Culligan's head they did, and with a direct attack. For the rest of September they sounded every faction on the board, even the Cyrus Curtis heirs; specific instances were cited in which they questioned the way Culligan was conducting the company. At one point Blair and Kantor thought they had enough votes to push through their plan and oust Culligan.

"What they didn't know is that they were doomed from the start, by the very nature of the Curtis board," a Curtis executive said months later. "Who do you have as members? Well, Walter Franklin, who was president of the Pennsylvania Railroad for twenty-five years. And Albert Linton, who's been running one of the nation's largest insurance companies (Provident Life) for decades. Blair and Kantor thought they could make men like these panic. If they had stopped for only one minute and made an objective evaluation of their chances, they would have realized they were out of their minds."

Blair and Kantor faced a crisis, and one in which they were arrayed alone against established authority. Blair moved swiftly. Already certain Curtis editors had asked him, "What goes on? Why aren't we making any money in view of what Culligan keeps saying?" Blair told them what he and Kantor were attempting.

To call the movement a "Blair-Kantor revolt" is an over-simplification. William Emerson said, "I was bound by a desire to save the magazine. I was more interested in this than in my own welfare. Something had to be done to protect the group of editors we had brought to the *Post*. I decided, by God, I'm going to be the last man on the ship if it goes down." Emerson says he did agree with Blair and Kantor that something had to be done about righting the company financially.

Blair was careful to carry out his next move in a manner which he later insisted made it legal under company law. He sent formal invitations to the editors and publishers of the Curtis magazines, inviting them to a joint session of the "editorial council" and the "publishers' council," two existing company committees; he set it for Sunday evening, September 27, at Manero's, a steakhouse in Greenwich, Connecticut, only a few miles from his home. After the plates were cleared away, Blair made his pitch. It was an acrimonious meeting, and not everyone agreed with him at the outset. But Blair stuck to one point: If Culligan continued at the helm, the magazines were doomed, and the editors and the publishers and their respective staffs would be out of jobs.

Blair went through the grievances. Didn't the directors know these things? one man asked. "Yes, but they're fuddy-duddy," Blair is said to have replied. "They have to be shown just how serious a matter this is." When Manero's closed at 11 o'clock, the group moved *en masse* to the home of Hank Walker, a *Post* assistant managing editor, and the meeting went on for perhaps three more hours. The decision, at the end, was unanimous; the editors and publishers stood behind Blair and Kantor.

The next morning, Monday, Kantor tried unsuccessfully to reach both Culligan and Linton. The first time he called Culligan, the company president was at the barbershop; the second time, he was at lunch with former New York Governor Thomas E. Dewey. Nor was Kantor able to get through to Linton in Philadelphia. "Blair got furious again," said Schanche. "He told me he was going to call the *Wall Street Journal* and leak the story. I told him to calm down while I asked around for advice." Schanche contacted a company lawyer, who listened to the grievances and said they should be put into writing. Schanche drafted a letter which couched the criticisms in general terms; it asked that Culligan be stripped of executive responsibility and be given another position in the company which would permit him to continue selling. Ritter carried it around the building and collected signatures; there were 15—Blair, Kantor, Schanche, Walker, Ritter, Emerson; Otto Friedrich, another *Post* assistant managing editor; Davis Thomas, editor of the *Ladies' Home Journal;* Caskett Stinnett, executive editor of the *Journal;* Jess Ballew, publisher of the *Post;* Jack Connors, ad director of the *Post;* Mike Hadley, *Ladies' Home Journal* publisher; and Garth Hite, advertising director of *Holiday.* Hubbard Cobb, the *American Home* editor, and John Collins, publisher, had not attended the Sunday meeting but added their signatures to the letter.

The night of Tuesday, September 29, Ritter took the letter to Linton's home in Moorestown, New Jersey. Linton, shocked, demanded more documentation. Blair and Kantor put Schanche to work on a crash project, writing a dossier that contained 32 basic complaints against Culligan which touched on virtually every phase of Curtis. Some charged errors of omission, such as not selling assets and contracting the printing (as Blair and Kantor had advised). Some charged errors of commission, chiefly his granting of what they felt to be overly generous discounts to advertisers who signed long-term contracts in the "Curtis Network" system. There was even a complaint about Culligan's spending—an assertion that the Regency Hotel apartment-office suite cost too much for the amount of company business conducted there and that some of Culligan's newly hired executives were outpriced and more at home on the golf course than in the office. On and on the document went—Culligan didn't exert enough control over the company; Culligan hadn't obtained a good contract on the Texas Gulf Sulphur Co. deal; and now he was devoting a disproportionate amount of his time to mining activities. Nothing was said to impute Culligan's honesty or personal conduct.

At the October 1 directors meeting Linton read the charges as Blair, Kantor and Culligan glared across the table. The charge that seemed to have the most effect on Linton was that about Culligan cutting prices indiscriminately for advertisers. "You mean there was no rate card?" asked Linton with an alarm reflecting his insurance background. "Yes, but Joe kept it in his pocket," replied Blair.

Only one supporter surfaced for Blair and Kantor—Milton Gould. If the charges were proven true, Gould announced, he "would demand Mr. Culligan's dismissal." Several times cooler heads had to hush Culligan and Blair as they snapped angrily at each other. But Linton didn't ruffle. He shut off the debate, saying, Let's don't do anything until we investigate. He appointed a special three-man committee to do so—himself as chairman, and as members, Moreau D. Brown and Gould, the latter to forestall any charges that the panel was stacked against Blair and Kantor. October 19 was set as the reporting date.

All directors were sworn to silence, and Culligan was told to continue his executive duties while the committee investigated. For several days the insurgents thought they scented victory. Banker Serge Semenenko was vacationing in Europe; one of his aides, after a transatlantic phone conference, told an editor: "We'll find you a new chief executive officer." But the secret lasted less than a week. In the October 7 issue of the "Gallagher Report," Bernard Gallagher gave a terse—and fairly accurate—outline of what was happening. Gallagher wrote:

> EXPLOSION AT CURTIS PUBLISHING. Due shortly. Tense October 1 meeting could have serious consequences. "Palace rebellion" reportedly headed by editor-in-chief Clay Blair. Ultimatum issued to oust chairman-president Joe Culligan. Magazine division chairman Marvin Kantor said to be disenchanted with Clay. Both Clay and Marvin would like to get Culligan's job ... Curtis directors would be wise to oust Blair and Kantor. Rehire [John] Veronis as president and chief executive officer. Keep Culligan as glad-hand chairman of the board.

After that it was a matter of time. Robert E. Bedingfield, a crack financial reporter for *The New York Times,* spent October 7 and 8 on the phone chasing the story. Two of his calls, at around 4:30 P.M., October 8, were to Blair and Kantor at the Curtis offices. Both men were in conference, and neither call was accepted. Later that evening, as Blair was leaving for Detroit for speaking engagements the next two days, he asked Ritter to inquire what Bedingfield wanted. Ritter couldn't reach Bedingfield but another *Times* reporter with whom he had worked at Time-Life read him the story. It was a shocker. Blair and Kantor, according to the *Times'* first article, were to be fired at the next directors meeting, and Culligan was to receive a full vote of confidence. Ritter didn't feel this to be a fair recitation of what was happening, and he tried futilely to reach Blair at the airport. Rather than see a story "weighed heavily in favor of Culligan" go into print, Ritter gave the Blair-Kantor side. The next morning, Friday, October 9, Bedingfield had himself a real live exclusive.

Bedingfield's story smacked into Curtis with bombshell impact—and Blair and Kantor lost the war in the first reverberation. Linton's reaction was prompt; he summoned the executive committee of the board of directors into an emergency session, talked with Culligan, and on the assumption the leak had come from Blair and Kantor, got approval of a decision placing them on "inactive status with temporary leaves of absence pending further action by the executive committee or the board of directors." Alarmed that Blair and Kantor were being harmed on the assumption that they were the source of the story, the *Times* informed Linton from whence it had obtained its information. But Linton was determined to force the issue to a head and resolve it once and for all. All that he believed about business and personal principle was being flaunted in his face; that such a thing as an executive revolt could develop in a company with which he was connected was unthinkable; that it be aired on the front pages of the nation's press was unforgivable, incomprehensible.

The day the story broke, Blair was in Detroit for his speeches. He sounded genuinely sorry that the news was in the open, saying it was "exceedingly unfortunate the management of Curtis has come to this crossroads," and that he had hoped his group "would make our views prevail within the established framework of the corporation." He also regretted that Curtis management "once again has become a subject of national concern." Being with Curtis, he added in one of those battlefield-shipboard analogies so beloved to his editors, "is like being pinned down at the Anzio beachhead year after year—you get to know your friends and your enemies." At the time, Blair was unaware that Culligan had already mustered enough support on the executive committee to put through the suspension. The only other public comment from the dissidents came from Jess Ballew, *Post* publisher. To inquirers he said the charges "in no way reflect on Culligan's ethics or morals." The charges, he said, were "predicated on cases we can document" and that the editors felt they could produce profitable magazines if the company were properly managed.

Then Curtis made a decision which company officers today concede to be a first-class goof. Public relations spokesmen were forbidden to give the press information on the affair, even background material which might have cast some of the events in a better light. One victim of this decision was Culligan himself. The dissident editors, with their press contacts, were able to put the substance of their story in friendly hands. Culligan, however, was bound by company policy and he kept his mouth shut about Blair and Kantor. Later he was to claim he was "pilloried" in the press and that he was at a disadvantage "because Mr. Blair is a reporter." Because of the Curtis policy the trade and daily press found news about Curtis as best it could. The only person authorized to speak for Curtis was Linton, and he was as guarded as a seventy-seven-year-old insurance executive could be expected to be.

On Saturday morning, Blair arrived at the University of Detroit a few minutes early for a speech to a student group. A faculty member called him to the telephone, and in cold, biting words, Blair heard Culligan say he was suspended. The news staggered Blair. He gamely gave his speech, then hustled back to New York to find Pinkerton guards stationed in strategic positions in the Saturday Evening Post Building. Blair and Kantor, their arms laden with brown file folders which contained documentation of their charges, got off an elevator in the lobby and headed for the street. There were heated words, threats, and the guards took the files back upstairs. Blair got out of the building with only one book, a diary in which he had kept a day-to-day account of his differences with Culligan.

Robert L. Sherrod, now an editor-at-large of the *Post,* was in Chicago with his wife for Chicago Opera social events. He crawled into bed at 5 o'clock Saturday morning only to be jarred out again by a call from Culligan. "Are they coming in for work Monday?" Culligan asked of the revolting editors. Sherrod, who had not been involved in the staff meetings, said he didn't know. At Culligan's request he called about 30 staff members ("It was funny, me out in Highland Park, Illinois, and phoning back east; the bill was $127") and gave them a message from Culligan: "Management expects you to come to work Monday and exercise your responsibility."

Blair and Kantor hoped that, with an airing of the dispute, middle-echelon executives throughout Curtis would flock to their side. This didn't happen. Linton put out a firm warning that he expected the publishers to stand behind Culligan (he apparently had no hope that Blair's editors would do likewise) and hinted that any other objectors who appeared would be thrown overboard. Only two more men joined the dissidents, Richard King and Joseph Welte, associate sales managers for the *Post.* The original dissident group made only one other joint effort: Feeling the firings were unfair, since Blair and Kantor didn't leak the *Times* story, they sent a telegram to Linton asking that the executives be reinstated. They insisted that Blair and Kantor be reinstated and that Culligan be suspended pending adjudication of the charges. Collins and Cobb, who had signed the protest letter against Culligan, were the only ones not on this message. (Blair and Kantor also abstained and advised against sending the telegram.)

There was a long meeting throughout Saturday at King's Manhattan apartment; the immediate future of the *Post* was one prime concern, since Blair was sidelined. Sherrod spent much of the day talking with two longtime contributors, Stewart Alsop and Harold H. Martin, about forming an interim editorial council to produce the magazine. But the idea was abandoned.

Semenenko, meantime, was in England with his wife and teen-age daughter, preparatory to the girl's entering college. A long-distance phone call jerked him aboard a New York jet and within twelve hours he was back at his office at the Hotel Pierre. This was one crisis, however, where Semenenko's presence really wasn't needed. The matter was so clear-cut that the Curtis board needed no prodding. Whatever the finding on the charges against Culligan, the *modus operandi* of Blair and Kantor had so damaged the company, internally and publicly, that the only path open was their firing. That the uprising had taken place confirmed Semenenko's judgment on another point, that Culligan was not a manager. The actions of the three principals, he felt, proved they could no longer work together as a team within the same organization; all must go, timing was the only question. Already Semenenko and the directors had been feeling around for a new executive officer. The banker speeded up the process by putting to work a major executive-hiring firm; as a backstop he personally lined up alternative prospects.

Semenenko abandoned a normal life for the weekend of the crisis. He worked in the Hotel Pierre until 2 o'clock in the morning, keeping a private switchboard busy as he groped for a way to extricate Curtis as gracefully as possible from its latest mess. During this period Semenenko talked with only one other client—Conrad Hilton, who wandered in to ask advice on building a new hotel in Paris.

Later that winter Semenenko said the mere fact that the battle broke out was proof positive that he was not guiding daily operations of Curtis. He said matter-of-factly, "If I had been running things, the rebellion would never have reached such proportions."

With a lid clamped on all participants ("The wisdom of the ages cries out for silence," said William Emerson), Linton's investigatory committee continued work. At the October 19 meeting, Culligan began easing out of the company. He volunteered his resignation as president, but remained as board chairman. Raymond DePue McGranahan, onetime West Coast publishing and oil executive and Semenenko's favorite for the presidency, was installed on the board and the executive committee to give him a chance to make a thorough study of Curtis management and financial problems. There were omens on the direction of the tide. After the meeting Culligan took ten other directors and his lawyer to lunch at the adjacent Downtown Club, a hangout for Curtis brass. He shared a luncheon table with Linton and Moreau Brown (also a member of the investigating committee) and to reporters said, "My lips are sealed. And that is a pretty hard position to put an Irishman in." Blair and Kantor left in a limousine without comment.

Thus was the stage set for the October 29 board meeting. Although behind closed doors on the 8th floor, it made itself felt throughout the building. In the second-floor executive suite, secretaries sat idle while their bosses paced the floor or glumly contemplated nameplates on their desks.

One by one Albert Linton went through the Blair-Kantor charges, rejecting them as unfounded or trivial. For almost an hour he talked. When he finished, his report had upheld "about two and one-half" of the 32 charges, according to a director at the meeting. These involved the special discount deals which Culligan had given certain advertisers. Linton said that while some of Culligan's decisions might have gone another way, there was nothing to indicate he was grossly negligent in his conduct of the company. Only one copy was made of the Linton committee report. Fearful of angering advertisers who had obtained less favorable rates under Culligan's discount plan, the directors ordered that this copy be locked in a safe and preserved for the company archives.

A motion was offered for dismissal of Blair and Kantor; it carried with a rapid show of hands, eight to three, with only Milton Gould joining with Kantor and Blair. (Gould said later his vote opposing the firings did not mean he supported them in "any action which led to this situation," but that he was "not satisfied with the grounds on which their discharge was based.") Culligan next stood and offered his resignation as chief executive officer, and the title was passed on to Clifford. Blair bounced and squirmed in his seat and then arose for a parting blast. His eyes snapped angrily, and his chest heaved with emotion as he pointed a finger across the room. "I thought the day would never come," he said, "when I would have to suffer the indignity of being in the room with this board of directors." With that he grabbed his briefcase and stalked out, followed closely by Kantor.

Outside there was chaos. In a condition best described as hopping mad, Blair and Kantor gathered reporters in a corner of the lobby. Secretaries and office workers clambered over iron grillwork for listening posts; just as Blair started talking, there was a loud crash as a glass showcase collapsed under the weight of reporters. Blair was particularly miffed because the directors had sent out word of the firings while the meeting was still in progress. This method, he said, "stunned" him, and Kantor called it a "personal affront." Blair and Kantor also denied that they led a "mutiny," or that the ultimatum signed by the editors and publishers at the September 27 meeting was a violation of company rules. Blair said, "It was not a revolt. It was a duly organized joint session of the long-standing editorial board and publishers' board of the Curtis Publishing Company. All fifteen signatories were duly constituted members of either board. They included all editors and all publishers of Curtis magazines." They said the move had been "fully and urgently necessitated and, in fact, mandated by the extraordinary events which led to Mr. Culligan's resignation." And, they maintained, their actions were "fully sustained and vindicated" by Culligan's leaving as chief executive officer.

Blair then waved his hand and asked that he be permitted to add a "personal note." The lobby hushed and some Curtis executives sidled to within eavesdropping range: "I devoted eight years of my life to the Curtis Publishing Company," Blair said. "The last four years I have given it everything I had, including my family, which is about the most any man can give a company. I want to say I think the action of this board is a disgrace not only to me personally but also to Marvin Kantor— who devoted three years of his life to the company—and the entire competitive system."

Curtis spent the bulk of the winter carrying casualties off the field. Claiming wrongful discharge, Blair and Kantor served notice of intention to sue for $500,000, which they claimed was owed under contracts which paid them $75,000 and $80,000 a year respectively. After sober second thoughts the other editors and publishers decided not to carry out their threat to quit unless Blair and Kantor were retained. During the suspension period Schanche had lunch with Blair and Davis Thomas at the Four Seasons, and Schanche quotes Blair as saying: "If Kantor can't be president or chief executive officer under me, he'll leave." This was the last straw for Schanche, who said he put his professional career in jeopardy to save the magazines—not to promote the fortunes of Clay Blair and Marvin Kantor. The men haven't been friendly since. Curtis fired outright Norman Ritter and Thomas Marvel, the *Post* production manager who had been close to Blair since his early days in Philadelphia. Hank Walker and Zen Yenkovig, a *Post* layout specialist (and non-signer), quit voluntarily, as did Davis Thomas several months after the revolt. Thus of the 17 men who put their names behind the Joe-Must-Go movement, a dozen remained at Curtis—Emerson as *Post* editor.

Blair threatened to write a tell-all book about Curtis; in banter with executives there he said it would be subtitled: "Who Put the Crack in the Liberty Bell?" On December 28, Curtis finally settled with Blair and Kantor for $75,000 each, $10,000 immediately and $65,000 in mid-1965. Under the settlement agreement, as announced by the company, they agreed "not to take voluntarily any action directly or indirectly injurious to the company for a period of two years." (Because of this agreement, Blair declined requests for interviews on the Curtis affair.) "I didn't do wrong, did I? I was right, wasn't I?" Blair is quoted as asking perhaps a dozen guests at a party after his firing.

The Culligan situation was a bit more complicated. His contract could not be terminated until January 16, 1966, and his $110,000 annual compensation was to continue for a year after that, then $22,000 a year in deferred compensation for ten more years. Culligan had set a high price for coming to Curtis, and Curtis would have had to pay dearly for him to leave. Culligan kept the title of chairman of the board but his responsibilities ended. After a long vacation he made soundings in Washington about a place in the Great Society—as public information officer in the State or Commerce Departments, or as a special consultant on fund-raising for child guidance and the underprivileged as part of the War on Poverty Program. But nothing developed. Culligan also talked with Bernard Gallagher and asked help in finding another management job.

"I wouldn't talk with him on that," says Gallagher. "I told him I would be happy to help him find a sales job, but that I couldn't recommend him to anybody as a manager."

Culligan spent quite a bit of time brooding about Blair and Kantor; privately he blamed them for sabotaging his career—perhaps even his entire life. Finally, on March 4, 1965, Culligan resigned as board chairman and director. His sole remaining role, according to the Curtis announcement, would be to "perform certain services ... on special projects, including development of broadcasting opportunities for the company and production of a history of Curtis." In his formal swan song Culligan said, "I am gratified to have been able to make a contribution to Curtis during some of its most difficult hours and I am reassured by the personal realization that all my efforts were directed toward the good of this historic institution. It is in the best interests of all who believe in strong, independent media of public information that Curtis now be given the time without harassment to continue to improve its magazines and market them more effectively to advertisers and the public. To all loyal employees—dedicated Curtis directors, the constructive bankers, advertisers and their agencies, and the fair and objective public, industry and trade press—I offer my sincere thanks." To the press, for the last time, he abounded with quotes. "I guess I should say that I long for the obscurity I undoubtedly deserve," he said. Culligan said someone had asked him earlier if he was prepared for the revolt. The answer was, "Was the captain of the *Titanic* prepared for hitting the iceberg?"

Culligan now steadfastly refuses to talk in detail about his months at Curtis. Nor, he says, will he tell "his side" of the dispute. The history he is planning, he says, will end with December, 1963, when he feels he had Curtis on the upswing. Arguing with Blair publicly, he said, "is not the constructive thing to do."

In the one interview he permitted for this book—which consisted of a 20-minute telephone conversation in which he said he would under no circumstances be interviewed—Culligan ticked off these areas of accomplishment which he said proved his success at Curtis:

—"We reduced the payroll sufficiently to generate savings.

—"We had a six-month profit as a result of this and other changes, the fourth quarter of 1963 and the first of 1964.

—"Advertising revenues were turning up—for the *Saturday Evening Post* and all the magazines.

—"We improved the distribution and printing operation.

"Then," Culligan said, with more than a little bitterness in his voice, "something happened which turned it into a nightmare. I'm not a whiner or a bleeder, but there were definitely improvements in certain areas. I saved the company; there's no question about that."

What about the charges of "mismanagement and unmanagement?" "I made a complete change in the image of Curtis Publishing Company to that of a vital, going business instead of a shambles." He rejected any suggestion that he faced a hopeless situation. "We proved that it was do-able," he said.

Culligan seemed rankled that his selection of personnel was criticized. Blair, he said, was at Curtis long before he became president; "Kantor was in the picture eighteen months ago." And there was no problem with either for months, he added.

"Look who's running the company now—I brought them in. I made very few mistakes on people—I made two."

After an agonizing president-hunt Curtis finally turned to J. M. Clifford. Directors felt the situation was so serious there was no time for presidential on-the-job training. Clifford had slipped into the executive vacuum in October and kept the company going during the Blair-Kantor-Culligan inquest. His humorless, no-nonsense demeanor appealed to directors who were tired of the Culligan era. So on November 12 he was named president and chief executive officer.

Son of a wealthy Idaho rancher, Clifford studied law at the University of California and Southwestern University, Georgetown, Texas. After graduation in 1930 he had a brief law practice in Long Beach, California, and then joined the Bank of America, Los Angeles, as a trust counsel. He became a specialist in mineral and oil problems and eventually went to Washington to establish, and then direct the oil and gas division of the Securities Exchange Commission. He joined the Radio Corporation of America as assistant general counsel in 1945 and moved up to become executive vice-president of NBC, responsible for all staff operations except programming. It was in this role that he got the reputation of being the "manager behind Joe Culligan." Culligan brought him to Curtis as executive vice-president for finance and operations in 1962.

Clifford wears his stark-white hair in a bristling crew cut which contrasts sharply with jet-black glasses and suits. He can easily be overlooked in a crowd. Any affection he feels for Culligan he keeps carefully hidden, if it is existent. Culligan says, magnanimously, that one reason he got out of Curtis altogether is because the "new guy . . . deserves a clean field of action."

The backlash of the Blair-Kantor affair, meanwhile, was felt at *Holiday*. Don Schanche remained as editor despite his involvement in the moves against Culligan. Management was aware that Farnsworth, Harry Sions, Louis Mercier and Frank Zachary, Ted Patrick's old team, didn't like working under Schanche. A few days after Clifford became president, Farnsworth says he received a telephone call from Maurice W. Poppei, who was working as Clifford's chief assistant. According to Farnsworth, Poppei said he was "aware of the situation at *Holiday*" and continued: "I consider it an outrage. It will be taken care of." Poppei asked Farnsworth to maintain staff stability as best he could.

Farnsworth found on his desk one morning a memo from Schanche stating he "would be out of the office for several days devoting his full attention to the future of the magazine." If any decisions had to be made, he added, he could be reached through his secretary. Farnsworth called Poppei's assistant, Michael Hueston, and asked an explanation. After all, Farnsworth said, he and the other three had to "think in issues months in advance," and Schanche "has almost totally defected from his job." Poppei and Hueston came to New York, and according to Farnsworth, said "the last thing Curtis could stand was more unfavorable publicity, that if another public fracas developed, bankers and advertising agencies would withdraw their support." "It's impossible but it's the best I can do," Poppei is quoted as saying. Again Poppei said he was "aware of the situation" and asked Farnsworth to continue holding the staff together. Poppei said Schanche was off writing a memo on *Holiday*'s future for A. Edward Miller, whom Curtis had hired as a consultant. It would be a good idea, Poppei added, for The Four to write a similar memo. Farnsworth considered this unfair; "The magazines we produce speak for themselves," he said, "and we're too busy editing a magazine to write memos."

The impasse deepened. By mid-November Schanche wasn't speaking with Farnsworth and Sions; any communication they had was through formal memoranda. The Four lost patience with Poppei's pleas for patience, and on November 19 sent a letter to Clifford:

> We, the signatories to this letter, are the senior members of the editorial staff of *Holiday* Magazine. Under the leadership of the late Ted Patrick, we took command of a faltering publication and, through almost two decades of work and devotion, helped to make it one of the finest magazines in the English language.
>
> On March 11 of this year Ted Patrick died. Within twenty-four hours Clay Blair appointed Don Schanche, of the *Saturday Evening Post,* editor of *Holiday.* Out of loyalty to the magazine and to the company, we have made every effort compatible with our consciences, and our conception of quality, to work harmoniously with Mr. Schanche. We have now reached a point where our standards of excellence and Mr. Schanche's view of the magazine's function diverge so widely that, in our belief, further cooperation is not possible. We feel that Mr. Schanche is not qualified to be the editor of *Holiday.* He lacks the experience, the scope, the taste and, above all, the imagination to guide the progress of this magazine.
>
> We can only hope to hear from you, at your earliest convenience, in order to discuss this urgent problem.

It was signed by Farnsworth, Sions, Zachary and Mercier.

"They really thought they had me on the ropes then," Schanche says, "because I had been mixed up in the things with

Culligan. They were surprised that I'd lasted as long as I did. One of them told me after six months, 'You know, we'd have gotten [rid of] Jesus Christ by now.' " Schanche declines now to hash over the day-to-day minutiae which followed. Succinctly, as editor, he felt he made an honest effort to work with Patrick's old staff, not all of whom wanted to recognize him as boss, and that *Holiday,* as does any other group undertaking, must have someone ultimately responsible. That position had been given him; he was capable of filling it, and he intended to continue doing so. He further thinks that bitterness warped the outlook of his opponents, particularly Farnsworth and Sions.

Clifford met The Four in his New York office a few days later. Farnsworth quotes him: "I am new at this job and I know nothing of this business. I'm getting things unraveled." As did Poppei, Clifford said Curtis couldn't afford another public brawl over firings or mass resignations.

The Four stressed to Clifford that they did not seek the editor's post for any one of them. (Sions, for instance, said he preferred his job as editorial director.)

Clifford broke off the meeting saying he intended realigning many people right after the first of the year, and for The Four to bear up until then. "He repeated his request to keep cool and do nothing that would lead to unfavorable press attention," Farnsworth said.

Three weeks later Schanche called in Zachary and Mercier singly and told them everything had been resolved. "The company has given me a vote of confidence," he told them. "You'll have to make up your mind whether to give me loyal and complete support." He also said he had a "mandate" to revamp the magazine and that editors not loyal to him and his concept could get out. Schanche gave Zachary and Mercier a nine-page prospectus for the "new *Holiday,*" but neither was interested. They told Schanche, in effect, that the *Holiday* they had created with Ted Patrick was the only type of magazine they cared to work for. Schanche didn't approach Farnsworth or Sions; "It

was hopeless to try to do anything with them at this late stage,"
Schanche says.

Clifford had asked that if any further problems arose, they
be aired with Poppei. Poppei met The Four in his office, but
refused to see them as a group. Zachary, an emotional man
even under normal circumstances, became highly agitated. He
charged that the Clifford-Poppei agreement had been broken
and ended by declaring he could no longer tolerate "immorality,
venality and pusilanimity." The Four left in a body—Farnsworth, Sions and Mercier having remained silent. It was late
in the day, and Zachary was still excited. To quiet him down,
they adjourned to P. J. Clarke's for a drink, and then home.

Immediately after the meeting with Poppei broke up,
Schanche called the *Holiday* staff together and announced The
Four had resigned. He telephoned Robert Sherrod, who had
been put in as chief Curtis editor after Blair's firing, and gave
him the same message, adding The Four "were on the way to
the papers."

That evening a siege of telephone calls began—from the press,
writers and friends—wanting to know why The Four had
"resigned." "This was the first we knew of our 'resignation,' "
said Sions. "It was impossible, and it just wasn't true."

News of the new internal conflict infuriated Semenenko. He
directed Robert Taplinger, his public relations man, to find a
broker who could talk with both sides. Taplinger recruited
Slim Aarons, *Holiday* photographer whose friendship with
Sions dated to their wartime service on *Yank* Magazine. Aarons
rounded up The Four via telephone, and Semenenko scheduled
a meeting for them in Philadelphia with Clifford. The next
morning, December 3, into a rented Cadillac limousine they
piled, Aarons, Taplinger, The Four, for the ride south.

"You fellows broke your word; you said you wouldn't go to
the press," Clifford greeted them. Told this wasn't true, Clifford
continued: "Well, that's what Poppei tells me. Furthermore, I
don't like to negotiate with the four of you at one time. It
reminds me of the time I was dealing with labor unions."

Farnsworth says, "We told him what exactly had happened to bring this about, that we had precipitated nothing but that a lot seemed to have been precipitated by Mr. Poppei and Mr. Schanche. I asked Mr. Clifford what he wanted us to do, that it was obviously impossible to return to work under the conditions that were developing and had developed, in that Mr. Schanche had announced to the staff that we had resigned." Clifford said the situation would have to be settled earlier than January 1, and he told The Four to stay away from the *Holiday* office and say nothing until Tuesday, December 8. "Say nothing to anybody, particularly the press," he said.

The next morning *The New York Times* carried a story stating Farnsworth, Zachary, Sions and Mercier had resigned. The article gave the impression they had sought the editorship for themselves. To the public, not knowing the details, Curtis Publishing Company had itself another editorial ruckus. Management was now in a box; if it backed The Four, and fired Schanche, the action would be interpreted as a sign of continuing executive weakness. If it backed Schanche, and fired The Four, some very angry editors would be set loose in New York. Schanche had powerful factors on his side. He had aided in obtaining the appointment of Garth Hite as *Holiday* publisher, and Hite was popular among Curtis advertising men. His prospectus on the "future of *Holiday*" was persuasive with Miller, the new magazine consultant. Schanche convinced Miller, Poppei and Clifford that the time to tinker with a magazine's content and thrust is when it is still successful; that the renovation is doubly hard when a magazine is slipping, as witness the *Saturday Evening Post* and *Ladies' Home Journal* in 1961 and 1962. Until this weekend The Four felt Semenenko was on their side, based on the statements given them by Taplinger. Now Semenenko also was in a difficult position. Even if he sided with The Four, he couldn't risk vetoing Clifford at a time when the new president was still feeling his way. In the end the decision was left with Clifford. And, as in the case of Blair and Kantor, it was foreordained: Subordinates don't get away with criticizing the boss in a corporation, even when they think him to be wrong. On Saturday each of The Four got two telegrams from Schanche, which indicated Clifford had reached a decision in advance of his Tuesday deadline: The first said, "Maurice Poppei has informed me that you will receive normal severance benefits in connection with your separation from the company. I thought you ought to know."

In the second, Schanche offered an explanation for some of the things he had done:

As you know, I regret very much what has transpired in the past few days. Your negotiations throughout this affair have been conducted entirely with the Curtis Publishing Company management and not, at any time, with me. I understand that there is a dispute at present over the question of whether you did or did not resign in your meeting with the company management on Wednesday. I was informed by the management that all four of you did resign. All actions that I have taken since that time, including my statement in response to press queries, have been with the full knowledge of the company management. I understand that you are to meet with Mr. Clifford on Tuesday to discuss the situation. In view of what has transpired, I am sure you will understand that your presence in the editorial offices of *Holiday* at any time prior to your meeting with Mr. Clifford will not be desirable. I therefore must insist that you remain away from the editorial offices until that time. After your dispute with the management has been resolved, you are perfectly welcome to come in. Again, I am sorry this happened as it did.

On December 8, The Four saw Clifford singly in New York. Clifford's face was red-mottled with anger, and he lectured them at length on responsibility. "You and the others are guilty of the same thing as Blair and Kantor," he told Farnsworth. ("This I resented because at no time had I or the others filed mismanagement charges nor asked for Mr. Schanche's removal; we had simply stated it was not possible to work with him," says Farnsworth.) Clifford said that one man must be boss in any organization, and that in the case of *Holiday* the man was Don Schanche. "Make your peace under whatever terms are satisfactory to Mr. Schanche," he told Sions. "And what do you intend to do?" "I intend to search my conscience," Sions replied. Clifford reasoned with him. "Think very carefully what you are doing before you sacrifice eighteen years of your career at Curtis over what you call principles," he said. "What else is there?" answered Sions. He didn't even bother to go back to the *Holiday* office.

"Naturally, I refused to make my peace with a man who was determined to get rid of me," said Sions. "We all agreed that the magazine now being programmed would not be the *Holiday* we knew and loved, that it would in time become cheapened, vulgarized, and corrupted. I called Schanche and told him that I could not work for his kind of *Holiday* and he fired me—the official term is 'involuntary separation.'"

Farnsworth did go back to the office. He sent Schanche a note saying he was at his desk "at the request of Mr. Clifford." Schanche called him in, expressing regrets over what had happened. But, Farnsworth quotes him, "everything must be one hundred percent my way." "I replied that I was told we were to work things out, that with such a statement he had committed the magazine to disaster and that my position was untenable." Farnsworth paused a moment and said, "I have not resigned nor have I been fired." Schanche then spread out prepared severance forms on the desk and told Farnsworth it would "look better on the record if he resigned rather than was fired. . . ." Promised full severance, Farnsworth signed the forms, "obviously a forced resignation. There was no way out despite Mr. Clifford's statements and other assurances." By day's end the other three also were off the payroll. Five more editors walked out with them, and girls in the office wept as desks were cleaned.

Meanwhile, as news of the trouble faced by The Four circulated, friends of the editors groped for a way to lend them support. Peter Lyon, who wrote frequently for *Holiday*, conceived a full-page-ad tribute, patterned after what David Ogilvy had written for Ted Patrick, to show Curtis management that contributors to the magazines sided with The Four. He deputized writers throughout the world as "regional chairmen" to round up signatures. William Manchester took the Washington area; Clifton Fadiman the West Coast; V. S. Pritchett, England; others handled Ireland and Italy. Lyon wrote the copy; the ad appeared in *The New York Times* on December 10, two days late for any practical value, but still it was felt in the communications world.* The headline, in two-inch-high letters, said, FOUR SPECIAL MEN. The text read:

> Frank Zachary, Harry Sions, Al Farnsworth and Lou Mercier are editors with various responsibilities, but we know them as the men who, with the late Ted Patrick, created *Holiday* and made it into a magazine of the highest editorial standards and integrity.
>
> The magazine they have led is both an artistic and a financial success—with the promise of an assured future.
>
> We—writers, artists, photographers—are proud to have had our work appear in its pages. We have worked well with these four editors.
>
> But contributors only contribute: editors guide and manage and shape and, when they are good editors, also inspire.
>
> We believe these four are good editors.
>
> Gentlemen, we salute you.

* Signatories were Slim Aarons, Cleveland Amory, Bill Ballantine, Peter S. Beagle, Alfred Bester, Stephen Birmingham, Elizabeth Bowen, Faubion Bowers, Eugene Burdick, Arthur C. Clarke, Tristram Coffin, James Dugan, Maurice Edelman, Elliott Erwitt, Clifton Fadiman, Jules Feiffer, André François, William Golding, A. B. Guthrie, Jr., Jacob Hay, Tom Hollyman, Hammond Innes, Alfred Kazin, John Knowles, Harry Kurnitz, Kenneth Lamott, Jack Ludwig, Peter Lyon, William Manchester, Wolf Mankiewicz, Fred J. Maroon, Joe McCarthy, Aubrey Menen, Arthur Miller, Frederic Morton, Arnold Newman, George Nelson, Sean O'Faolain, Helen Papashvily, Robert Phillips, Merrill Pollock, V. S. Pritchett, Santha Rama Rau, Norman Rosten, Arnold Roth, William Sansom, Budd Schulberg, Ronald Searle, Carroll Seghers II, John Lewis Stage, John Steinbeck, Kenneth Tynan, Laurens van der Post, John D. Weaver, Jerome Weidman and John Williams.

Months after his departure Farnsworth was still puzzled and embittered—puzzled because he and the others were unable to get their story across to Clifford; embittered at loss of a position to which he had devoted eighteen years of his life. In the spring of 1965 he suggested to Linton that management reconsider its actions. Linton's reply, in part, said, "In my position over many years of responsibility I have found it difficult to draw a firm conclusion from a maze of conflicting stories. And in this matter of *Holiday* there are many conflicting stories. I must trust the present management, so recently installed, to handle Curtis' future." Linton said he noted an improved morale at Curtis, and concluded: "Some personal injustices may have been involved and these we greatly regret. However, in the best interest of the company, it would not seem wise to make any changes unless the present improved situation should not be maintained."

"A corporation out of control," says Farnsworth, "like a society out of control, is a frightful thing to witness. But society usually has set up adequate controls whether they operate at the moment or at a later date. And this decidedly has not been the case with the *Holiday* people although we went to the most extraordinary efforts to operate in the best interests of the company . . . And then to have it all turned around as though we had planned a revolt against authority when what we were really asking for was a decent climate in which to work!"

Chapter Ten

W HAT will happen to Curtis?" That question has been asked countless thousands of times since 1961—by employees, ad people, readers of the company's magazines, shareholders, investors, even by Curtis management itself. The answer has always been an unpredictable one and, based on the company's constantly changing fortunes the last three years, is likely to continue so. In the March quarter of 1965, the first full three-month reporting period in which Clifford was president, Curtis had a modest operating profit of $36,000, a sharp turnaround from the $7.6 million loss of the final three months of 1964. The 1965 stockholders meeting on April 21, at which these figures were announced, was significant in several respects. Clifford didn't brag about Curtis, nor make promises. What he did say, and with the ring of sincerity, was that "the Curtis Publishing Company has sound basic business strength. . . . We believe we have improved our operations—and we know we cannot relax. Our firm objective is to return your company to a sound basis of continuing profitable operations." Under brisk cross-examination by stockholders, Clifford wouldn't go further; unlike Culligan, he would not predict a profit this year, nor the next, nor the next; what he did say was that Curtis hoped to make "substantial" improvements.

The magazine editors, per Curtis tradition, made talks on their plans. But ore samples from Curtis' Canadian lands, chunks of red-tinted rock spread on a table, attracted more stockholder attention than news that the *Ladies' Home Journal* intended to publish the new Kinsey Report. There was only one question from the floor on the magazines ("Why do you get into so many libel suits? I recommend that a lawyer read all the stories first!"), but a spate about the mineral holdings and the liquidation value of the timberlands. Maurice Poppei's attempt to present findings of the new Politz magazine readership survey, which showed the *Post* reached more readers per $1 of advertising expenditure than *Life* or *Look,* was hooted down. "If it's such a good magazine, why aren't people advertising in it? Baloney. Sit down. We aren't going to buy any advertising."

Almost incredibly, no stockholder evinced the slightest interest in the Blair-Kantor tussle with Culligan; indeed, even the only mention of this was Clifford's remark in his opening statement: "As we said in the annual report, we do not gloss over the fact that 1964 was a bad year. Curtis lost almost $14 million —and internal personnel conflict was a major reason. However, we have resolved that problem. Our purpose here today is not to rehash what is over and done with—but to bring you up-to-date on what we have been doing to right the company and to set it firmly on the path to recovery."

A chief aim of the new management (echoes of Clay Blair) was to whittle off some of Curtis' appendages considered unnecessary to the publishing business. High on the list of disposable assets were the printing plant at Sharon Hill and the paper mills. The biweekly frequency of the *Post,* which became effective in January, lessened its importance as a captive customer to these facilities and made them less essential to the company. The same held true for the Curtis Building itself; by attrition and dispersal the company gradually reduced its space requirements until it was occupying only a fraction of the usable 900,000 square feet. The Semenenko banking group pressured management to dispose of any or all of these facilities to increase its working capital, and to reduce its indebtedness without having to unload any magazines.

The first major asset sold was the Lock Haven, Pa., paper mill, which was purchased in May by Hammermill Paper Company. Curtis didn't list the price; part of the money went toward repaying the Semenenko syndicate loan. The new Clifford management, in the second quarter, continued to cleave away at losses; red ink totaled $2,605,000, compared with $3,974,000 for the corresponding period in 1964. The new biweekly frequency of the *Post* took a heavy toll of ad revenue. For 12 issues in the first half of 1965 (compared with 25 in 1964) the *Post* had $17.3 million, down from $30.9 million (before discounts and ad agency commissions). This was a 44 percent decrease; pages were down 37 percent, from 755.7 to 478.4.

But Curtis had another "asset" almost as valuable as the book price of the paper mills—the $40 million-plus deficit, which under the federal corporate tax structure is useful as a carry-forward. This is a rather complicated procedure, but, in general, provides that a corporation may carry back a loss to three prior years and carry forward a loss for five subsequent years. The $18.9 million loss of 1962, for example, could be applied dollar-for-dollar to any Curtis profits through 1967; the $13.9 million loss of 1965 through 1970.

Not even Clifford expects Curtis to earn $40 million in the next five years. But the tax carry-forward was also available for use by Curtis in acquiring or merging with a profitable enterprise. So managament's chore was to find a firm big enough to put the carry-forward to use, and one whose business was "substantially" the same as that of Curtis, as is required by the tax laws. (Early in the research for this book I began compiling a list of companies whose merger with Curtis was "imminent" or "likely." I stopped when it reached 17.)

The imponderable in the Curtis situation is the Canadian ore holdings. Based on test drillings the Curtis land holds 6.5 million tons of ore, assayed at silver, 1.6 ounces per ton; copper,

3 percent per ton, and zinc, 14.6 percent per ton. In informing Curtis of these findings, Texas Gulf Sulphur wrote:

> ... Value is much more difficult to determine than tonnage or grade. Metal prices vary so drastically, percent of recovery of metals from the ore is not fully known at this time, and mining, milling and smelting costs are so indefinite that any realistic dollar value is difficult to achieve. However, using present metal prices of $1.29/oz. for silver, $.034/lb. for copper and $0.135/lb. for zinc, the gross value of metals contained in a ton of average ore is $61.86.
>
> ... The number is substantially greater than the value of metals that will be recovered, and there is no deduction for costs of any kind, which makes the figure difficult to evaluate. As you know, the ore body will be refined over a considerable period of years, which makes it hazardous to assign a total present value to it, at least until mining rate and recovery are known.

Six and one half million tons at gross average value of $61.86 comes to $402,090,000, of which Curtis would receive 10 percent of the net profits after mining expenses. "That arithmetic would add to $40 million as the Curtis share," J. M. Clifford says; "of course, as the report pointed out, you have to get the ore out in order to sell it, and there is no deduction in these figures for costs of any kind."

The Texas Gulf Sulphur ore find is a subject of continuing controversy. On April 19, 1965, the Securities Exchange Commission sued TGS and 13 of its officers, directors and employees, charging they bought stock in the company, or advised others to do so, before the discovery was announced. The suit asked reimbursement by the insiders—and possibly by the company itself—of persons who unknowingly sold their stock to insiders or insiders' friends. By Wall Street definition, an insider is an officer, director or major stockholders in a company.

The SEC cited three dates and events in its federal court suit: That TGS made the initial find November 12, 1963, and "certain" company officials became aware of it and bought stock at low prices; that on April 12, 1964, TGS put out a "false and misleading" press release, downplaying the importance of the discovery; and that on April 16, TGS finally said the discovery was major—but that insiders had already done brisk trading since April 12. The Securities Exchange Act of 1964 makes it illegal for a person to make a false statement concerning material facts or to omit disclosure of material facts in connection with the purchase of any security. TGS and the officials named denied these charges in a formal answer filed on July 8. TGS said the November, 1963, drillings produced only "limited data" and that there were no "reliable indications" as to the value of the strike until the following April. It conceded geologist Darke concealed the November drill site with brush in a "customary" ruse to give time to acquire rights to adjacent land.

A month later, on May 25, a Curtis stockholder challenged the lease agreement with TGS, charging management made "a bad deal," and asking that it be voided. Dr. Ray M. Chaitin, a Brooklyn physician owning about 100 shares, lodged the suit against TGS and Curtis directors.

The Curtis editors, taken collectively, have the sound of men who wish they could forget business worries and get on with the editing of the magazines. As *Post* editor William Emerson put it at the 1965 stockholders meeting:

"For years we've heard nothing but the snap of the jackals and seen nothing but buzzards overhead. Now it's time to get a crop in."

Epilogue

"Yesterday ended last night."—*Favorite saying of Cyrus H. K. Curtis, as quoted by Edward W. Bok*

Tucked away in a corner of the white marble lobby of the Curtis Building on Independence Square is a glass showcase with issues of the *Saturday Evening Post* and *Ladies' Home Journal* dating to their founding. Beneath the magazines are neatly typed white cards with names of editors over the years. The last line on the *Post* card reads, BEN HIBBS. 1942—. On the *Journal* card is BRUCE AND BEATRICE GOULD. 1935—. Perhaps it's indicative of the latter-day turbulence at Curtis, but somehow no one ever got around to changing the cards. (Four names could be added to each list of editors.) Farther along, goldfish splash in a lobby pond beneath the mosaic mural, "The Grove of Academe," presided over by Plato, which Louis C. Tiffany executed with more than one million bits of glass from sketches by Maxfield Parrish. To the left, at the approach to the wood-paneled old elevators, is a gleaming white bust of Benjamin Franklin, the same as the *Post* formerly published on its anniversary covers.

Persons weak and strong have strode through this lobby; whatever Curtis Publishing Company was yesterday, and whatever it is today, and will be tomorrow, is their responsibility—Cyrus Curtis himself, trim and erect, not a hair of his beard

ruffled as he received the doorman's half-salute each night;
Edward W. Bok, a solid-looking Dutchman, eyes quizzically
pondering the world and the people around him; George
Horace Lorimer, massive and heavy-footed, the best fiction of
the nation in the briefcase hanging rocklike from his hand;
Mrs. Mary Curtis Bok Zimbalist, dogs straining at the leash
as she came in for a chat with Walter D. Fuller or Ben Hibbs;
Robert A. MacNeal, who likely as not would find something
to inspect before boarding the elevator; Matthew J. Culligan,
a man of arm-swinging gusto, often with a vice-president at
either elbow and both fore and aft, pausing to joke with the
pretty receptionist. Maxfield Parrish's glass Plato saw all these
figures, looking down from the Grove of Academe; he also
watched the winter day in 1964 when Clay Blair used the lobby
as a forum for his bitter farewell speech, and when J. M. Clifford
and Maurice Poppei arrived at dawn daily for weeks afterward
to make sense of the corporate shambles they inherited.

Today there is another Curtis lobby, at 641 Lexington
Avenue, New York. To the lay eye it is indistinguishable from
scores of its cousins in the immediate vicinity; there is no lobby
pond for goldfish, nor a Louis Tiffany mural—only artificial
potted palms. But 641 Lexington Avenue is functional; it
houses, in addition to Curtis, the Zambian delegation to the
United Nations, stock brokerage offices, an architect or two,
ad agencies.

And, somehow, it just doesn't seem the kind of place one
would expect to find Ben Franklin.

BIBLIOGRAPHY AND
ACKNOWLEDGMENTS

Bibliography and Acknowledgments

In the four years since 1961, The Curtis Publishing Company commanded as much attention in the press as it did in the four preceding decades. The day-to-day framework upon which *The Curtis Caper* is built came from that coverage—in the Philadelphia *Inquirer*, Philadelphia *Bulletin*, *New York Times*, *Wall Street Journal*, New York *Herald Tribune*, *Time*, *Newsweek*, *Advertising Age*, *Printers Ink* and *Business Week*. Behind-the-scenes peeks were taken regularly by the "Gallagher Report," and I am grateful to Bernard Gallagher for permission to reprint his item of October 7, 1964 (copyright 1964, The Gallagher Report) which was the first public inkling of what is popularly termed The Editors' Revolt.

Reporters are professional brainpickers. This book is a distillation of the ideas, knowledge and opinions of dozens of persons both within and without Curtis. Many of them, now with other publishers and advertising agencies, granted interviews on the pledge of anonymity. For information and insight on a complicated subject I am indebted to:

Ben Hibbs, Stuart Rose, David Ogilvy, Curtiss Anderson, Don A. Schanche, William A. Emerson, Robert K. Farrand, C. Richard Ficks, Albert H. Farnsworth, Harry Sions and Cary W. Bok. I also give thanks to those sources who spoke freely and candidly about Curtis in the interest of journalistic history, but for professional reasons asked not to be named.

The Curtis Caper is an amplification of a six-part series which was published in the Philadelphia *Inquirer* in January, 1965. Valuable editorial advice at that stage came from E. Z. Dimitman, assistant to the publisher; John S. Gillen, managing editor; Morris Litman, executive city editor, and Philip B. Schaeffer, city editor. Mr. Litman's encyclopedic knowledge of Philadelphia was invaluable in directing me to persons who contributed key sections of this book. The library staff of the *Inquirer* was infinitely patient in unearthing file material on Curtis. The recitation and interpretation of fact herein, however, are my own, and not necessarily that of the *Inquirer*.

Financial data in *The Curtis Caper* was gleaned from Curtis annual reports and files of the Securities Exchange Commission. Circulation and advertising figures came from Curtis, the Audit Bureau of Circulation and the Publishers Information Bureau, Inc.

A publishing company writes its own history weekly and monthly through its printed products. The character of Curtis is readily discernible in its magazines over the years: The *Saturday Evening Post, Ladies' Home Journal, Holiday, Country Gentleman, American Home, Jack & Jill* and *New Home Journal*. I delved liberally into files of Curtis magazines at the Free Library of Philadelphia as a foundation for *The Curtis Caper*. Other primary printed sources are as follows:

BOOKS

Bok, Edward W., *The Americanization of Edward Bok*. Charles Scribner's Sons, New York, 1923.

———, *A Man from Maine*. Charles Scribner's Sons, New York, 1923.

Mayer, Martin, *Madison Avenue, USA*. Harper & Row, New York, 1958.

Mott, Frank Luther, *History of American Magazines* (Volume Four). Harvard University Press, Cambridge, 1957.

Peterson, Theodore, *Magazines in the Twentieth Century*. University of Illinois Press, Urbana, 1956.

Rockwell, Norman, *My Adventures as an Illustrator*. Doubleday & Co., Inc., Garden City, 1960.

Stern, J. David, *Memoirs of a Maverick Publisher*. Simon & Schuster, New York, 1962.

TEBBEL, John, *George Horace Lorimer and the Saturday Evening Post.* Doubleday & Co., Inc., Garden City, 1948.

Ladies' Home Journal Treasury. Simon & Schuster, New York, 1956.

Ten Years of Holiday. Simon & Schuster, New York, 1946.

ARTICLES AND PERIODICALS

Business Week: Unsigned, "Hibbs and the Satevepost: A Happy 10-Year Marriage," March 15, 1952.

Esquire: Martin, Pete, "I Call on Joe Culligan," March, 1963.

Journalism Quarterly: Hibbs, Ben, "You Can't Edit a Magazine by Arithmetic," Fall, 1950.

New York Times: Lawn, Victor H., Serge Semenenko interview, April 5, 1964.

————: Rossant, M. J., Serge Semenenko interview, October 22, 1964.

Printers' Ink: Unsigned, profile of Robert A. MacNeal, October, 1958.

Saturday Review: Amory, Cleveland, "First of the Month," January 6, 1962.

Show Magazine: Lawrenson, Helen, "Go, Joe, Go: Life of a Salesman," July, 1963.

Sigma Phi Epsilon Journal: Robson, John, "Philadelphia Success Story: Ben Hibbs," November, 1952.

MISCELLANEOUS

HALSEY, Ashley, Jr., *A Short History of the Saturday Evening Post.* Curtis Publishing Company, Philadelphia, 1949.

HIBBS, Ben, "Some Thoughts on Magazine Editing." Tenth annual William Allen White Memorial Lecture, William Allen White School of Journalism and Public Information, University of Kansas, February 10, 1962.

HIBBS, Ben, "Some Random Thoughts on Editing," address for *Saturday Evening Post* sales meeting, January 19, 1960 (unpublished).

(Unsigned) *The Editors*. Profiles of Robert Lee Sherrod and Clay D. Blair, Jr., Curtis Publishing Company, Philadelphia, May, 1962.

United States House of Representatives, Select Committee on Small Business, Subcommittee Chairman's Report to Subcommittee Number One, "Tax-exempt Foundations and Charitable Trusts, Their Impact on Our Economy," Government Printing Office, Washington, October 16, 1963.

Wallace Butts versus Curtis Publishing Company, opinions in United States District Court for the Northern District of Georgia, and in the United States Court of Appeals for the Fifth Circuit.